European Business Cycle Convergence

Hohenheimer Volkswirtschaftliche Schriften

Band 69

PL ACADEMIC RESEARCH

Jennifer Schneider

European Business Cycle Convergence

Portfolio Similarity and a Declining Home Bias of Private Investors

PL ACADEMIC RESEARCH

Bibliographic Information published by the Deutsche Nationalbibliothek
The Deutsche Nationalbibliothek lists this publication in the Deutsche Nationalbibliografie; detailed bibliographic data is available in the internet at http://dnb.d-nb.de.

Zugl.: Hohenheim, Univ., Diss., 2011

D 100
ISSN 0721-3085
ISBN 978-3-631-63974-0

PL Academic Research is an Imprint of Peter Lang GmbH

www.peterlang.de

Preface

Die vorliegende Dissertation entstand im Zeitraum von 2006 bis 2010, während ich als externe Doktorandin am Institut für VWL, Lehrstuhl für Außenwirtschaft an der Universität Hohenheim tätig war.

Ich möchte mich bei den Menschen bedanken, die zum Fortschreiten der Arbeit beigetragen haben. Mein besonderer Dank gilt meinem Doktorvater, Herrn Prof. Dr. Ansgar Belke (Universität Duisburg-Essen, Lehrstuhl für Volkswirtschaftslehre, insb. Makroökonomik) für die wissenschaftliche Betreuung der Arbeit und seine wertvollen Diskussionsbeiträge. Darüber hinaus schätze ich die Möglichkeiten, die er mir zum Austausch mit anderen Wissenschaftlern eingeräumt hat, sehr. Herzlichen Dank an Herrn Prof. Dr. Hans-Peter Burghof, der freundlicherweise das Zweitgutachten übernommen hat und Herrn Prof. Dr. Harald Hagemann als Vorsitzenden beim Kolloquium.

Ohne den Rückhalt meines Mannes und meines privaten Umfelds wäre die Dissertation nicht zustande gekommen. Für die Motivation und Flexibilität vielen Dank!

Content

Tables

Graphs

Abbreviations

2SLS	Two-stage Least-squares
AUT	Austria
BEL	Belgium
BUL	Bulgaria
CAPM	Capital Asset Pricing Model
CPIS	Coordinated Portfolio Investment Survey
DEN	Denmark
DS	Datastream
EMU	European Monetary Union
ESP	Spain
EST	Estonia
FAAR	Foreign Asset Acceptance Ratio
FGLS	Feasible Generalized Least Squares estimation
FIN	Finland
FRA	France
GER	Germany
GRE	Greece
HUN	Hungary
IAPM	International Capital Asset Pricing Model
IMF	International Monetary Fund
ITA	Italy
n.a.	not available
NET	The Netherlands
NOR	Norway
POR	Portugal
ROM	Romania
SLO	Slovak Republic
SWE	Sweden

Variables

CPT	consumption correlation
SPEC	specialisation index
RELFW	relative financial wealth
RELINC	relative income
GDP	GDP correlation

A. Introduction

1. Motivation

One issue for currency areas such as the European Monetary Union (EMU) is that not necessarily one size fits all, i.e. the interest rate setting of the central bank cannot consider different states of the economy in different member countries. A country in recession would prefer low interest rates to stimulate the economy; whereas, for a country in boom, low interest rates might cause inflation.

As Mundell (1961) – in his fundamental work – puts it, an optimal currency area is an economic unit that is independent from national borders. Only if all countries taking part in the monetary union behave as an economic unit and react similar to asymmetric shocks can a common monetary policy react. Otherwise, contradictory signals for the interest setting might be a consequence and might raise costs for being a member of a monetary union. Most economists agree that, so far, the countries participating in the EMU do not have synchronised business cycles (see e.g. Artis, 2003; Gros and Hefeker, 2004). To reduce the costs of giving away power over monetary policy, a business cycle convergence of the participating countries would lead to less ambiguous indicators for monetary policy decisions.

But which factors contribute to business cycle convergence? Besides well known factors such as trade integration or factor mobility, one factor could be the synchronized consumption of private households in EMU member countries. Synchronized consumption can in turn be influenced by similar private (financial) investment strategies, leading to similar returns and consumption out of financial wealth. Financial wealth of private households has grown substantially in recent years. In Western Europe, financial wealth amounts for over 150 % of GDP, and the estimation of the annual growth rate of financial wealth is 4.2 % (2002-2006) (Uni Credit Group, 2007). Further growth is expected.

The growing importance of financial wealth implies that investment decisions have a growing influence on income, the standard of living – and therefore also on consumption. Investment strategies are usually assumed to be rational,[1]

1 For a start I will assume rationality of investment decisions although it is known that investors do not necessarily behave rational.

meaning investors would reach similar investment decisions. A plausible "common" investment strategy could be the International Asset Pricing Model (IAPM), which is based on the Capital Asset Pricing Model (CAPM) by Sharpe (1964). According to this model, a portfolio should reflect the relative world market weights of all countries to achieve the best risk-return-ratio (De Santis and Gérard, 1997, p. 1881 et seqq.). This model has recently gained much attention in popular finance media which addressed the widely observed phenomenon of home bias. Basically, home bias means investing mainly in one's home country instead of benefitting from international diversification, e.g. in Germany, about 83 % of the Germans invest in German companies although financial literature has been recommending diversification over different countries, asset categories, etc. for years (Zydra, 2008). Interestingly at the same time, the Germans became more risk-averse and were selling their bonds and shares in the aftermath of the financial crisis (Schroers, 2008) – a contradiction to the ideas of the mentioned financial investment literature of diversification. This development can only lead to the conclusion that investment behaviour is not necessarily rational. Opposed to these trends, on a European basis, a declining home bias can be observed in recent years even after the crisis.

Home bias is a phenomenon not only discussed in the financial literature but also on a macroeconomic level, as well under the label of international risk sharing. International risk sharing means that individuals hold claims on the output of other countries to diversify their risks and achieve consumption smoothing. Consumption or income smoothing can either be achieved *ex ante* (by holding claims on the output of other countries over financial markets) or *ex post* (through either credit channels or a federal transfer system). Whereas, in the management literature, dealing with the International Asset Pricing Model (IAPM) and home bias, the personal advantage of individuals is stressed; the macroeconomic literature of international risk sharing concentrates on consumption smoothing. The link between these two directions is business cycle convergence: similar investments lead to similar consumption and therefore to a convergence of cycles. This link has only been simultaneously addressed in the literature in the sense of keeping the two topics apart (Sørensen, B.E., Wu, and Zhu, 2007; Lewis, 1999).

However, the positive link of the investor position and macroeconomic dimension of business cycle convergence has not been discussed in the literature yet. It is one of the tasks of the dissertation to highlight the theoretical link from personal advantages derived by rational investment strategies to business cycle convergence. The most important part is to investigate empirically if the theoretical link holds for the EMU countries. One may note that the rationality of investment decisions is not the important factor of business cycle convergence itself. This factor is the similarity of portfolios which result in similar income effects – whether portfolio strategies follow the IAPM or not. Following the IAPM is the second step that does not only contribute to synchronisation of the cycles but also contributes to smaller amplitudes, i.e. consumption smoothing. Why is the IAPM still examined, if it is not the driving factor for similar income effects? The thought is that if all investors follow the same strategy, necessarily, the portfolios must reflect the similarity of investment and create similar income effects.

Summarizing the basic ideas analysed and investigated in the dissertation, it is as follows: The main task is to investigate the linkage between business cycle convergence and the impact of a declining home bias. The focus is on private investors due to the rising importance of private financial wealth. The main hypothesis is that similar portfolios contribute via a convergence of consumption cycles to a convergence of business cycles.

The pre-conditions for a positive judgement of the main hypothesis are numbered below in a chain of hypotheses. This chain needs to be analysed and proved empirically in the course of the dissertation until it finally leads to the conclusion that the main hypothesis can indeed be empirically verified.

1. The linkage between financial wealth and income effects exists, – or put in other words – "wealth influences consumption". Otherwise, investment strategies would have no influence, and the investigation would not be appropriate.
2. The IAPM is a plausible investment strategy. It is likely that investors behave according to it; therefore, the optimal portfolio weights derived by the IAPM can act as a benchmark to measure home bias.
3. Portfolios in the sample became more similar.
4. A lower home bias is an influencing parameter for a higher similarity of portfolios. Otherwise, the similarity of the investment strategy, the IAPM, would not be important for the portfolio structure.
5. A higher similarity of portfolios results in more similar returns out of this investment. This linkage is necessary because I argue that the transmission channel runs via consumption and the most important influencing factor for consumption is income.
6. Similar investment contributes to consumption cycle convergence.
7. A convergence of consumption cycles contributes to business cycle convergence.

The following graph illustrates the transmission channel of the theses chain: It runs from similar portfolios over similar financial returns and over similar consumption to converged cycles.

Graph 1: Transmission Channels from Similar Portfolios to Business Cycle Convergence

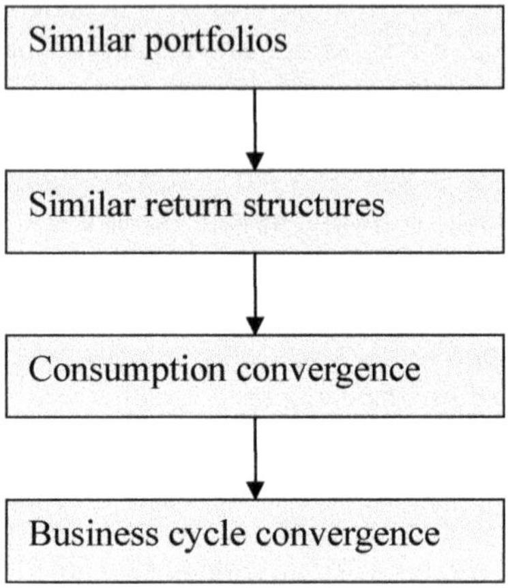

The investigation includes several steps:

The theoretical links are highlighted. This includes important preconditions, such as influences on business cycle convergence or the consumption-wealth linkage. The main theoretical part is built by an account of portfolio theory, especially the IAPM (Part B). The major investigation is led in the empirical part. It consists of an analysis of the status quo of home bias in the EMU with a special focus on the similarity of private portfolios. The core part comprises the empirical investigation of the linkage between the similarity of private portfolios and consumption/business cycle convergence of EMU countries (Part C). The last part summarizes; gives an overview on possible political actions and concludes (Part D).

The main contributions of this dissertation, which are new to the research area, are:

- It sets the investigations on home bias on the basis of a longer, more recent time series as previous studies.
- It is the first time that a similarity index is applied on portfolios.
- The similarity of portfolios is brought in the context of consideration that the financial world has an impact on business cycles and contributes to business cycle convergence via consumption.

B. Theoretical and Empirical Background

As argued in the introduction, international diversification (a small home bias) and similar portfolios could have an impact on business cycle convergence. The proceeding in the next sections can be described as follows:

Firstly, it is shown why converged business cycles are important for a monetary union such as the EMU. A special focus is laid upon financial integration because of its major role on investment possibilities and business cycle convergence.

The second question is: Can financial wealth alone have an influence on business cycle convergence? The answer is probably "no" if investment strategies do not converge and lead to similar income effects. Consider e.g. an investor who puts money on current accounts as compared to an investor who buys bonds. Probably, the income effect is different. A plausible transmission channel would run from financial wealth to consumption, which has an impact on portfolios and the business cycle. This first linkage is described in the second step: the consumption-wealth-linkage. If portfolios are similar, the consumption should be also similar, at least out of financial wealth

The third and major part of Section B provides the theoretical foundation of modern portfolio-theory as a basis for similar portfolios, discussing the IAPM and the home bias phenomenon. Whether or not the IAPM is a plausible starting point is investigated in this part as well.

2. Business Cycle Convergence and Consumption

2.1 Optimal Currency Area Criteria

As mentioned above, synchronised business cycles are important for monetary unions because the degree of synchronisation defines the costs of giving up the power of interest rate setting induced by joining a monetary union. However, which factors contribute to business cycle convergence?

The concept of the optimal currency area criteria, founded by the works of Mundell (1961), McKinnon (1963), and Kenen (1969), provide a framework for the analysis. Basically, theory says that joining a monetary union is advantageous for a country if the benefits of being a member (lower transaction costs due to exchange rate certainty) outweigh the costs (losing the exchange rate and monetary policy as a stabilizer). Both the amount of benefit and cost are dependent on the degree of economic integration between a single country and the other members of the monetary union, e.g. a country that trades much with the other member countries gains more from the cessation of exchange rate uncertainty. Costs arise if an asymmetric shock hits a member country. In this case, neither monetary policy nor the exchange rate can cushion the effect. In well-integrated countries, the adjustment process after a negative asymmetric shock will be less costly because price reductions will attract more demand from other countries and factor mobility can act as compensation.

The closer the business cycles of member countries are, the more they benefit and the less costly adjustments are to asymmetric shocks because monetary policy can react. The optimal currency area literature therefore concentrates on discussing the effects of shocks and the functioning of adjustment channels in the case of asymmetric shocks. A common reaction to shocks and the ability to absorb asymmetric shocks are key factors for a synchronisation of business cycles.

The optimal currency area theory examines the following factors:

Economic integration of countries is supported by the degree of openness – a country that trades much has closer links to the other countries and should therefore be influenced by the state of the economy of other countries. One may note that Frankel and Rose (1998) argue, that trade links can lead to converged cycles, meaning that converged cycles are not necessarily a precondition for joining a monetary union but endogenous. They argue that the positive linkages of trade overweigh the negative implications of trade-induced specialisation

An adjustment channel is factor mobility, for example migration. Workers who migrate keep their income stable and do not suffer from the shock (Mundell, 1961). Another adjustment channel is fiscal transfers. In a monetary union they act as an ex post adjustment to dampen the impacts of a shock (Kenen, 1969).

In newer literature the willingness of politics to implement necessary reforms to achieve adaptations to economic situations is named as an adjustment instrument to optimize monetary unions (Heinemann, 1998). This argument is a very prominent one in the current 2010 euro area crisis induced by the possible breakdown of the member state Greece.

An important aspect of the optimal currency area is the reaction towards shocks. Asymmetric shocks are less probable the more similar economic structures are. For example, if industrial sectors are similar in two countries, it is probable that an idiosyncratic shock in one country infects the other country via trade linkages. However, this is dependent on the kind of trade linkages. If intra-industry trade prevails, an infection and for this reason a similar shock reaction would occur. A dominating inter-industry trade would cause the opposite effect (Imbs, 2004).

Different financial structures in countries might oppose the idea of a common monetary policy because they lead to different effects of a common interest rate (Belke, Eppendorfer, and Heine, 2002). E.g. the UK with its mostly variable mortgage rates should react in its consumption a good deal more sensitive to interest rate changes than Germany with its mostly fixed rate financing system. As a consequence business cycles might de-synchronised through different structures. As fiscal policy does not seem to compensate these differences, market solutions such as country risk premiums are discussed, leading in fact to different interest rates in different member countries (Hughes Hallet and Piscitelli, 2002). Therefore a similarity of financial structures can be a condition for joining countries.

Another channel for cushioning shocks is financial market integration, having in turn influence on industry specialisation. Due to its importance for the dissertation, the next section pays special attention to this topic.

2.2 Financial Market Integration and Business Cycle Convergence

Complete financial market integration has the result that the same asset has the same return in two countries. The instruments for measuring integration mentioned in the literature range from cross-border capital mobility and international capital flows to shareholder rights (for an overview see Imbs, 2004). International portfolio diversification, as suggested by portfolio theory, preconditions the possibility of free cross-border capital flows. This precondition is given within the EMU and for most industrialized countries in the world, though the remark should be included here that financial markets in EMU are not completely, but highly and growingly, integrated according to several empirical studies (e.g. Fratzscher, 2002, for stock markets). In a monetary union market, channels such as trade in assets or credit channels have an important function to absorb shocks. Among different market channels, the channel of diversified property holding proved to be one of the most important contributions to risk sharing (i.e. shock absorption) in the EU (Mélitz and Zumer, 2000).

Financial market integration and its effect on business cycle integration are discussed ambiguously in the literature. One line of arguments deals with the affects of financial market integration on business cycles via specialisation, while the other line discusses a direct impact of financial market integration on the real economy. The basic chain of arguments runs as follows:

First, financial integration enables countries to specialize because resources are allocated according to the best possible utilisation. If countries specialise, they are encountered by different economic influences, and asymmetric shocks may hit these countries. Business cycles tend to diverge.

Second, financial markets do have a direct impact on business cycles. The influencing factors are investment strategies of companies that amplify cycles via shock transmissions, e.g. through herding effects. Market integration leads to synchronisation of cycles because of the similar impact of finance on it.

These two main lines have been discussed in the literature so far. The main line of argument followed in this dissertation runs as follows:

Third, financial integration leads to more similar portfolios because it is plausible to diversify risks internationally. Consumption converges because of the harmonisation of financial income. As consumption is the major part of GDP, consumption correlation leads to business cycle correlation.

This third line contravenes the first line of arguments. In the first line, the negative role of specialisation with concern to asymmetric shocks dominates; whereas, the third line stresses the positive effects of income similarity on consumption. The consumption argument will be adopted throughout the dissertation.

To start with, a literature review of the first two arguments is provided:

The properties of financial markets influence industrial specialisation, and specialisation does have an impact on business cycles. A result of specialisation is that sector-specific shocks have a similar impact on countries with similar industry structures, e.g. Ricardian models would suggest that countries produce whatever their comparative advantage is. With financial market integration, this specialisation is easier because specialisation does not necessarily need to be fulfilled by trade, but could be compensated by assets (capital allocation function). Specialisation leads to different reactions in the case of asymmetric shocks, leading to a dispersion of cycles.

The background for this first line of arguments is laid by empirical investigations of the question as to whether or not financial integration leads to industry specialisation, e.g. Svaleryd and Vlachos (2005) concluded for OECD-countries that a well-developed financial sector contributes to growth and facilitates specialisation although the authors assume financial markets to be quite immobile to national borders. Their main argument is that only a factor that is fixed within national borders can induce a comparative advantage according to the Hecksher-Ohlin model. Still, this is no counter-argument to apply the main line of arguments that a well functioning financial market can induce specialisation. This is indeed a main argument of the international risk sharing literature: Kalemli-Ozcan, Sørensen, and Yosha (2005) find out empirically that risk sharing has increased in the decade of the 1990s within the EU. Risk sharing means that portfolios are diversified in a way, that national income is held constant. The authors attribute this observation to higher financial integration, as expressed by higher international asset holdings. Although the same time specialisation in industries rose, GDP did not vary as much as expected because the nature of shocks was not asymmetric in the time range of the analysis.

The linkage from specialisation to business cycle correlation is conducted by Belke and Heine (2006, 2007). They examine the influence regional industrial specialisation has on the respective regional business cycle measured by employment cycles. The results indicate that cycle synchronisation is indeed influenced, but the direction depends on the kind of industry pattern. Countries that specialised in the same industries will show closer cycles; on the other hand, inter-industry specialisation induces a decreased convergence.

The second line of argument deals with a more direct impact of financial markets on GDP. Authors advocating a (direct) negative impact of international asset trade on business cycle convergence are Heathcote and Perri (2004). They argue that in times of a positive country shock, a domestic firm would be willing to invest (at home) with the consequence of fewer dividends for their domestic shareholders. A domestic firm calculates that the domestic demand is not cut by this step because income out of foreign dividends has to some extend a compensating effect if diversified portfolio holdings are assumed. Therefore, in times of high productivity, companies are willing to invest – strengthening the positive trend in the domestic country; and in times of less productivity, companies will not invest – strengthening the negative trend. All in all, this leads to the conclusion that more financial integration leads to less business cycle integration. The authors depart from the precondition that shocks became more and more country-specific since the 1970s, making international diversification more attractive. Therefore a country, particularly its investors, receives money whichever state its economy is, making its business cycle more idiosyncratic.

In a two-country model, Pierdzioch (2004) provides an ambiguous picture and investigates how asymmetric shocks in a monetary union are propagated with the background of increasing financial market integration. The model compares the transmission of shocks in the case of a market exclusively for risk free bonds against the case of a complete market of state-contingent claims. State-contingent claims mean that the payout depends on the state of a certain economy. In theory, this leads to perfect international risk sharing with equal marginal utility of households and also therefore to equal consumptions in two countries. The intuition behind this is that households can hold perfectly diversified portfolios, and therefore consumption does not change if shocks are negatively correlated in the member countries of the monetary union. The author concludes that how output reacts depends on the kind of asymmetric shock. In case of a productivity shock, business cycle volatility is increased because consumption is assumed to remain on the same level with state-contingent bonds. In this case, households need to adjust labour supply and terms of trade to adjust to good market equilibrium. A permanent government spending shock does not affect output since the terms of trade are not changed. Shock absorption through financial market integration and international asset trade has therefore two sides according to Pierdzioch (2004).

The negative view is doubted by the majority of authors. Highly integrated markets include the possibility to withdraw capital quickly, e.g. Calvo and Mendoza (2000) show that financial market integration leads to more herding and contagion effects defined as "portfolio allocations" that are not necessarily justified by changes in fundamentals, but are more or less due to rumours and arbitrary market moves. The basic assumption of the model is that information costs decrease with a growing globalization. Portfolios become more sensitive for changes in returns, and as information becomes less costly, it becomes more likely that following the herd is a good decision for optimizing the portfolio. It is expected that the (acting) market participants are well informed and a country specific premium incurs less worth. Another factor in theory is that if marginal information costs exceed the gain, it is reasonable for portfolio managers to imitate market portfolios. If contagion becomes more probable with a growing market, money is likely to be withdrawn simultaneously from several countries, leaving these countries with a lack of capital and a possible recession as a consequence. Several authors investigated in this topic, see Decamps and Lovo (2006) among others, Hey and Morone (2004), and the initial work of Baneerje (2004). The same time other countries profit from herding because of the capital inflows withdrawn from other countries. Consequently herding might lead to a de-synchronizing of cycles. However, the desynchronizing will only take place between the winning country group and the losing country group. Within these, group cycles are rather synchronized.

Put together, theory provides arguments in favour and against a positive impact on financial integration on business cycle convergence. Negative implications are expected from its effects on specialisation; the direct links are ambiguous.

Imbs (2004) puts the arguments above together and estimates their different effects in a set of simultaneous equations, using data sets of 24 countries. He came to the conclusion that although financially integrated countries tend to be more specialised, having a negative effect on synchronisation, the direct effects of integration far outweigh the negative effects. All in all, this leads to a better synchronization of financially well-integrated countries.

The same conclusion was derived in another empirical study. This study covers the European countries and indicates positive effects of financial market integration on GDP correlation (Schiavo, 2008). The arguments brought forward are the efficient allocation of resources, risk sharing, and the business cycle correlation induced by closer trade linkages in a monetary union. In a system of simultaneous equations measuring output correlation, the determinants of synchronisation are financial integration, trade, and industrial specialisation. The hypothesis of a positive correlation between financial integration and business cycle correlation is confirmed in this study.

What is the linkage to private portfolios in Europe? As concluded above, financial market integration is advantageous for business cycle convergence. So far the scientific world has not discussed that international portfolio diversification – or to be more precise similar financial income structures – might have a positive and direct impact on business cycle convergence. The dissertation investigates a channel for the important optimal currency area criterion of business cycle convergence that is new to the literature so far.

2.3 Consumption

2.3.1 Consumption Function

Consumption makes up a large part of GDP, is influenced by several factors, and explained by different theory lines. Generally speaking, consumption is the value of all goods and services used in a certain period (Eurostat, 2009). Consumption can be allocated either to government or to private households. Throughout the dissertation, the term is used for private consumption.

The basic model of consumption goes back to Keynes. According to the Keynesian model of consumption (see macroeconomic textbooks, e.g. Sørensen, P.B. and Whitta-Jacobsen, 2005, p. 466 et seqq. or Felderer and Homburg, 2005, p. 104 et seqq.), consumption is mainly dependent on disposable income although the propensity to consume declines with an increasing income. Put in other words: a greater part of income is saved instead of consumed if income rises. Two counter-arguments to this position are usually brought up: first, it is questionable if only current income influences current consumption; second, empirical studies show that over a longer time range the proportion of consumption to income stays quite stable in countries which became richer, e.g. the US. It was expected that with rising income, consumption becomes smaller. The first objection is encountered by the hypothesis that a consumer usually tries to maximize life-time utility, which is constrained by her or his budget. It is assumed that consumption in an earlier period is valued higher as consumption in a later period, but different weights are preferred if different consumers are considered (Neokeynesian model). The idea that households take income expectations into account is confirmed for the US in a recent study by Pounder (2009). She uses survey data to estimate expected future income and finds out that higher expected future income results in higher consumption today under the preconditions that future income is certain, or that the households are not risk averse. This is important for the dissertation with regard to the focus on equity and bonds since these instruments are often used in pension plans. However, although they might not bring current income, these instruments bring future income which again should bring stable returns in order to have an impact on current consumption.

The second objection, the stable proportion of consumption and income, is analysed in the following section dealing with the consumption-wealth linkage.

In another theory line explaining consumption – the neoclassical theory – the allocation of income to consumption and savings is determined by the budget constraint and by the interest rate, with the thought that an interest rate increase would be an incentive to save more. Consumption is therefore only dependent on the level of interest rate – a thought that cannot be empirically confirmed.

Keynes himself mentions around 24 factors that possibly affect the consumption function (Felderer and Homburg, 2005, p. 104) although without doubt a major faction of consumption is disposable income – both earned income and income out of financial wealth.

The topic of consumption should be understood in the context of this dissertation. In summary, first of all, consumption influences GDP, and via GDP consumption influences business cycles. Business cycle convergence would mean that the inflation targeting is easier for the ECB because monetary policy would have more similar impacts if it is conducted in similar business cycle stadiums of different countries.

Some empirical research investigated the direct relationship between consumption and the transmission of monetary policy. Barrell, Byrne, and Dury (2003) had a closer look at the euro area and choose a model which regards the euro countries as homogenous. This is conducted in the sense of an experiment to see which monetary rule the ECB should choose in a certain situation. Depending on the goals of policy makers (inflation target, output stability and price stability), different policy rules make sense. The two-pillar strategy combines inflation targeting with a nominal target (setting interest rates according to deviations from a chosen nominal aggregate like the GDP). The combinations of goals with inflation targeting as the set goal of the ECB would always lead to a preference of the nominal target compared to the two-pillar strategy, which would probably make monetary policy simpler.

2.3.2 Consumption-wealth-linkage

The aim of the dissertation is it to show that portfolios have an influence on business cycles via consumption. Therefore, the next issue that needs to be considered is the question, "Whether or not and how much the consumption out of financial wealth contributes to the overall consumption, the so-called consumption-wealth linkage." The consumption wealth linkage is defined as the marginal influence of a change in wealth on consumption.

Intuitionally, wealth should clearly have an influence on consumption. The basic idea is that higher returns out of wealth stimulate private consumption because disposable income is increased. However, if in a very extreme case nobody would ever touch financial resources, portfolios could be identical but would have no effect on consumption and synchronisation. The income source out of financial wealth is closely related to investment and wealth. The term investment is used in this dissertation in the sense of financial portfolio investment, not in the sense of manufacturing equipment or other investment for production purposes.

Wealth is part of the consumption function according to the life cycle hypothesis (Ando and Modigliani, 1963). This hypothesis assumes that planned consumption is a function of wealth; whereas, wealth consists of human wealth, financial wealth, and tangible wealth. In general, compared to other components, a higher impact of financial wealth on consumption is expected due to its more liquid characteristic. Yet in recent years, housing wealth has attached a growing attention in this context due to better possibilities to borrow against housing wealth.

Ludwig and Sløk (2002, p. 6) list the driving forces of the theoretical motivation for the connection between financial (stock market) wealth and consumption:

- Realised and unrealised wealth effects (realised in the sense of selling assets at a higher price, unrealised in the sense of having gains just "in the books"; the latter one leads to higher income expectations);
- liquidity constraints effect (it is easier to borrow against a higher value of the portfolio) and
- value-effects for the holders of stock options.

A more general relationship, i.e. relative income differences (out of total income) do affect business cycle synchronisation, has been approved in the literature (Imbs, 1999) though the explanation for this result comes from the conclusion that similar income levels (industrial countries vs. emerging markets) usually have the same industrial structures as a background, leading back to the topic of inter- and intra-industry trade that has been discussed above.

Numerous studies concerning this topic exist (for an overview see Poterba (2000) or Barrell and Davis (2004)). Following Poterba (2000), there are several issues concerning the transmission from financial wealth to consumption that have to be considered:

- Composition of household wealth: proportion of financial wealth to total wealth. The bigger the financial wealth proportion is the higher should be its effect on consumption.
- Distribution of financial wealth: how is financial wealth concentrated in the population? The more concentrated wealth is, the more a smaller fraction of the population (in this case the wealthy households) would have to change its consumption behaviour. This usually means that in the concentrated case, wealth grows on higher levels than consumption does.
- Timing: time lags of consumption vary from an immediate response to wealth changes to long lags, e.g. bequeathing heirs. Other timing examples are that retirement funds are usually not touched as easily as other funds, or that taxing influences inheritance and consumption decisions.

These factors are in turn influenced by the financial system. In EMU countries, bank-based financial systems seem to prevail (Ludwig and Sløk, 2002, p. 8 et seqq.). Bank-based systems often have smaller stock markets, and payment in stock options is less prevalent. This proceeding leads to a smaller proportion of financial wealth in the total wealth portfolio. One may note, however, that the importance of shares and financial wealth grew in recent years for EMU countries as well, motivated among other aspects by a growing income (wealthier people tend to invest a higher amount in stocks compared to less wealthy people) (Slacalek, 2006, p. 6).

Other than the already mentioned, empirical literature also shows that wealth indeed has a substantial effect on consumption, though this effect seems to apply rather in the long run than in the short run. The long run effect is underlined by a line of research that concentrates on the consumption-wealth linkage in the event of shocks. The influence of shocks and other changes in wealth on consumption seems to be rather small in the short run. For example, monetary policy shocks have minor or almost no impact – depending on the chosen model – on consumption (Ludvigson, Steindel, and Lettau, 2002). A closer look at the nature of shocks reveals that transitory shocks usually have impact on wealth itself, and that only permanent shocks (more often affecting housing wealth than financial wealth) have impact on consumption (Lettau and Ludvigson, 2004; Kishor, 2007).

These results are opposed by Slacalek (2006). His results suggest that the housing wealth effect is bigger than the one out of financial wealth only in the UK and in the US; for EMU countries, a slightly larger effect of financial wealth could be found. His results are confirmed by Sousa (2009) who finds out that housing wealth has almost no influence in the euro area and does not turn out to be significant.

The conclusion that stock market wealth clearly was a more and more important force for consumption in recent years (for bank-based systems in Europe) is reached by Ludwig and Sløk (2002) as well. It is important to see that their results imply that elasticity of consumption (especially the long term elasticity) out of stock market wealth is estimated to be much higher – almost twice as large in market based financial systems compared to bank based systems. A much higher sensitivity towards stock market prices with regard to consumption is expected in these countries. All of the core European countries like Belgium, Germany, France, Italy, and Spain are considered as banking-based systems with the exception of the Netherlands (Ludwig and Sløk, 2002, p. 9). For Germany, Hamburg, Hoffmann, and Keller (2008) still find a small impact of changes in asset prices on consumption for the years 1980 to 2003. They ascribe their findings to the reluctant attitude of Germans towards stock ownership.

However, most authors find positive long-term marginal propensities of private consumption out of financial wealth. Examples for a positive relationship in single countries are Italy (Bassanetti and Zollino, 2008) or Portugal (De Castro, 2007). For a more detailed overview on single countries, see a European Central Bank publication (Eurosystem Household Finance and Consumption Network, 2009). Very recently Sousa (2009) analysed the marginal propensity to consume in the whole euro area. His contribution uses data from 1980 till the end of 2007 for the aggregate euro area. In contrast to other studies, the author uses complete consumption and does not distinguish between consumption in non-durables and durables. The reasons are convincing (Dreger and Reimers, 2006, p. 10): total consumption should be considered when the reaction of consumption towards wealth changes is considered because households may switch expenditure between these two groups, and changes in wealth might lead to postponing durable investment. Still, an effect on GDP can be observed no matter how consumption is divided. The development of shares and mutual shares in portfolios stresses the expressed statement above, that stock market assets become more and more important. Their proportion in the total financial wealth portfolio rose from 15.8 % in the early 1980s to 29.7 % in the period from 2005 till 2007.

Another reason for the (in some cases) smaller financial wealth effect compared to housing effect given in the literature, is its higher volatility (Bostic, Gabriel, and Painter, 2009). This result, however, is opposed by the trend towards international diversification and the IAPM with its high degree of risk diversification leading to smoother returns.

Put together, a growingly higher influence of financial wealth on consumption can be expected, especially when considering the still growing amount of private financial wealth. There is no doubt, however, that poorer and richer households (and probably in its aggregate: poorer and richer countries) show different behaviour: richer households usually have a greater participation in stock market wealth and drive aggregate measurements (Eurosystem Household Finance and Consumption Network, 2009, p. 16).

What are the dimensions of the consumption-wealth effect? Empirical studies propose a propensity to consume out of wealth at ranges from three to four percent when wealth rises by one unit, while consumption out of wealth seems to be a little bit lower in Europe (Slacalek, 2006, p. 3 et seqq.). Positive shocks to housing wealth in the UK are examined by Disney, Henley, and Jevons (2003). They find a marginal propensity to consume for surprising shocks ranging from nine to 14 %. Ludwig and Slok (2002, p. 14) report marginal propensities to consume out of stock market wealth of two till five per cent which is confirmed by Dreger and Reimers (2006). Somewhat smaller is the effect for the whole euro area (Sousa, 2009) with 1.4 % propensity to consume out of a net financial wealth increase.

In the light of these results, it is considered that the precondition, financial wealth does influence consumption, is fulfilled. This is the foundation in considering hypothesis number one to be true.

Hypothesis 1:	*The consumption-wealth linkage exists. This means that wealth influences consumption.*

A note on one of the implicit preconditions on consumption is in order: in the quantitative part of the dissertation, it is assumed that the propensity to consume is roughly the same in all countries of the sample and is not modelled explicitly. The empirical studies presented above, unfortunately, either report only aggregated results and not results for single countries; or, studies concentrate on countries outside the sample of the dissertation; or, studies come to very different conclusions. Take for example Kishor (2007) who concludes for the US that financial wealth hardly has an impact on consumption, as opposed to Slacalek (2006) who finds out very different reactions in different countries towards changes in financial wealth. As the latter study includes, many countries that are in my sample, as well a graph of Slacalek (2006, p. 1), is presented. It shows the growth rates of consumption opposed to a re-scaled growth rate of wealth for the years 1994 till 2002 (re-scaling is necessary because the slope "can be interpreted as the marginal propensity to consume" (Slacalek, 2006, p. 1). One may note that the wealth definition of his paper includes housing wealth.

Graph 2: Marginal Propensity to Consume Out of Wealth in Different Countries

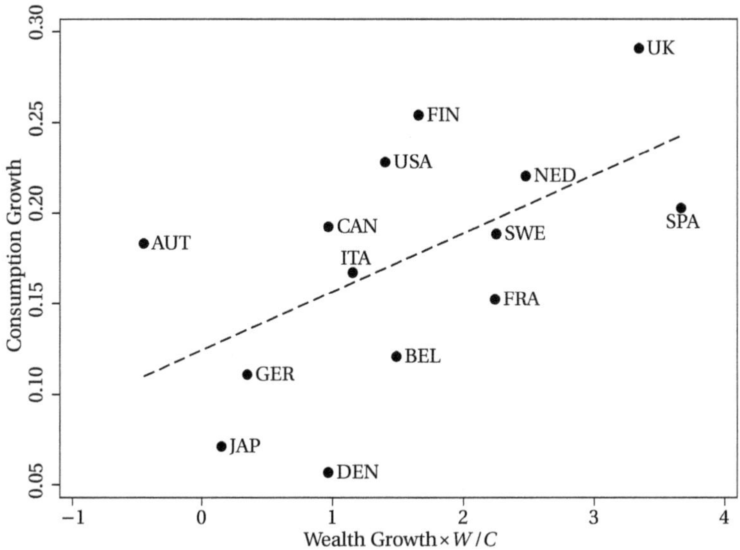

Note: Consumption growth and rescaled wealth growth between 1994Q4 and 2002Q4; wealth growth is rescaled by multiplying with the wealth–consumption ratio of 1994Q4. Slope of the regression line, MPC_{w}^{LR}= 0.032, t-stat: 2.36, p-value: 0.018.

Source: Slacalek, 2007, p. 1

Further interpretation is that first, consumption out of financial wealth is positive; and second, that the marginal propensity to consume is different in the countries of the sample dependent on the financial system. Another consideration comes from the different levels of wealth; probably the propensity to consume is higher in poorer countries. The countries above the regression line are those that consume more out of wealth and often correspond to market-based systems. For the dissertation, this means that although empirical studies bring very different results with regard to the propensity to consume, the financial system at least needs to be considered in the qualitative analysis of the results.

2.3.3 A Side Note on Financial Systems and Monetary Policy Transmission

Several times, the financial systems of countries and the respective role of financial wealth were mentioned. In the section before, focus was put on the effect of stock market wealth on consumption. There are more aspects of this topic worth mentioning. If the financial structure has an influence on consumption, how is it defined? Do different financial structures mean a different impact of monetary policy? Both questions are discussed ambiguously in the literature.

Basically, in a bank-based system, banks have the role of an intermediate institution for companies to obtain loans; in market-based systems, companies directly get money from the capital market. An advantage of the first system is the cheaper control of companies (only one intermediary controls a company instead of several stock holders); advocates of the latter system stress the role of transparency (seen from the lender's side) in the market.[2] There are several definitions to judge whether a financial system can be described as a bank-based or a market-based system. Attributes that are often used to classify economies are the size of the stock market, dispersion of stock market wealth over the population, issue of stock options for employees, a comparison of stock market activity versus bank activity, and the efficiency of the system measured by liquidity and cost (Levine, 2002; Ludwig and Sløk, 2002). The different criteria are used with different weights and different ways of measurement. Yet, the results are that most of the major euro area countries are banking based economies with the exception of the Netherlands. Sweden and Denmark are considered as market based systems as well. For the Eastern European countries, a classification is harder to get because for this world region, there are often only studies on single countries. An exception is the one of Elbourne and de Haan (2006) who lists all accession countries to the EMU although the authors do not definitely categorize them into the two categories. Still, the characteristics of these countries are marked. In the context of the dissertation, the activity of banks and the accession to stock markets are especially important factors. If these two criteria are taken into account, Hungary and Estonia rather turn out to be market-based economies; Bulgaria, Romania and the Slovak Republic are bank based economies.

Why should different financial systems respond diversely on monetary policy? In a bank based system, a change in interest rates leads to changed costs for banks to refinance themselves. These costs are passed trough to their customers. Higher interest rates lead – other things equal – to higher costs, less economic activity, less inflation, and the other way round. In a market based system, investors are less dependent on banks, and the interest rate channel is weaker. The

2 An analysis of the two opposing systems can be found in Rajan and Zingales (2001).

transmission of interest rate setting on shares runs as follows: shares are valued by their discounted cash-flow. If the interest rate rises, the discount on the cash-flow is higher, and the stock price decreases. If the market capitalization of a company decreases (a company is worth less), finance over capital markets becomes more difficult. In both cases higher interest rates lead to less economic activity though the effect is expected to be lower in market-based economies.

The transmission effect is usually not stable because it depends on several factors (Belke et al., 2002):

- Maturity of loans: The longer the maturity is, the longer it takes for a transmission process to come into effect.
- Competition: If companies have a choice to finance over banks or over stock markets, banks have fewer possibilities to pass through interest rate changes.
- Timing of interest rate changes at the capital markets: Interest rates of the ECB affect short-term interest rates (money market). The changes in interest rates are passed on to the longer-term interest rates (capital markets). In the situation of higher interest rates, private households need to pay more for their long-term loan and adjust consumption; companies calculate with new cash-flows. The faster the long-term interest rates react, the deeper the effect of monetary policy is.
- Structure of financial wealth: In countries in which fixed income strategies prevail in the portfolios of investors, interest rate changes come into effect only if the maturity is short. With a strategy based on variable rates of interests or on shares, a more immediate impact might follow.
- Size of companies (Elbourne and de Haan, 2006): The smaller a company, the more it is dependent on bank finance. Economies with many small companies will tend to follow the banking transmission channel.

Empirical results on the effect of monetary policy in different financial systems are ambiguous. Two studies using data just before the start of the EMU (Mojon, 2000; Arnold and De Vries, 1999) come to the conclusion that before the EMU was established, different reactions towards monetary policy shocks can be found. The authors of both studies expect these differences to diminish once the common monetary policy and single currency comes into effect. The latter study finds its result by the insight that capital market structures are highly dependent on inflation experiences of the past. With common policy, inflation will be the same for all member countries.[3] The higher the uncertainty on inflation is, the

---

3 Looking from a later point of time the expectations concerning inflation similarity could not be fulfilled completely. Inflation rates are still different in the different countries of the Eurozone (Erber and Hagemann, 2010).

lower the maturity in capital markets in the case of non-hedged inflation risks is, and the shorter maturity the higher the effect of monetary policy is. Mojon (2000) deduces common reaction to policy in the future because of the common currency and the assimilation of importance of debt markets for all EMU countries. Unfortunately, there seems to be no current study on the Eurozone that distinguishes between the transmissions of the common monetary policy in the different financial systems. At least for the EMU as a whole, the general effectiveness even in the recent financial crisis is confirmed (Čihák, Harjes, and Stavrev, 2009).

For the Eastern European countries, the different indicators for a financial system (e.g. stock market capitalization, number of banks per capita, etc.) were opposed to the reaction functions of the economy (output and inflation) after a change of monetary policy by Elbourne and de Haan (2006). Although some indicators emerged to be significant (e.g. stock market capitalisation), it could not be excluded that the results were the same if the data was randomly drawn. The authors state that it cannot be concluded that the financial system influences policy transmission.

2.3 The Context of Consumption and Business Cycles

This subsection closes the circle to business cycles: only if private consumption is an important part of business cycles, a contribution to convergence can be expected.

Business cycles are usually measured by GDP. Introductory textbooks about economics describe the usual measurement of the GDP as the sum of consumption, gross investment, government expenditure and net exports in the form of an expenditure equation. In the Eurozone, the private consumption part had a share of well above 55 % in the last years according to Eurostat-data, and is therefore the most important factor for GDP.

Although consumption is usually smoother as output (GDP), it should be a good indicator for output unless the other factors building the GDP, like government expenditures, are not counteractive.

At a first glance empirical data reveals a contradictory picture. It suggests that output in different countries is even more correlated as consumption (Backus, Kehoe, and Kydland, 1992; Pakko, 1998) although theory predicts the opposite. This could lead to the impression that consumption is not a plausible channel for business cycle convergence. However, this finding does not contradict the proposition that an increasing consumption correlation is favourable for an increasing output correlation.

To sum up, the second chapter identifies optimal currency area criteria as the main reason why converged business cycles are an object worth studying in the environment of the EMU. Among the criteria, the importance of financial market integration is stressed because of its relationship with portfolio investment. Further, the main results of the literature concerning the consumption-wealth linkage are embraced with the result that, in theory and according to empirical studies, financial wealth has an influence on consumption. These findings are emphasized by the development of growingly integrated financial markets in the EMU and rising private financial wealth. Combining the insights, this leads to the conclusion that portfolio decisions of private households impact consumption and probably influence business cycles via consumption as well.

3. Portfolio Theory

3.1 Motivation

So far, the advantages of following the insights of portfolio theory have not been questioned. The third chapter builds the fundament for the explanation of private portfolio composition by outlining the basics of modern portfolio theory within the concept of the IAPM and the home bias phenomenon. This issue of similar portfolio is theoretically founded in the next sections. It starts with the basics of portfolio theory and the CAPM, followed by its enhancement, the IAPM. The goal of these sections is to provide the necessary basics on portfolio theory and to justify the plausibility of the IAPM as a starting point for the empirical work of the dissertation. Empirics are conducted in Chapter C, which analyses the transmission and link between similar portfolios over return and consumption to business cycle convergence. Chapter three starts with an assertion as to why portfolio theory and the phenomenon of home bias play a significant role in explaining the importance of private investment for business cycle convergence.

The last chapter concludes that financial investment has an implication on consumption and with that on business cycles. Which impact could portfolios have on business cycle convergence? As discussed above, the important features are factor mobility and a common reaction to shocks with the result that consumption, as a major proportion of a business cycle, reacts similarly. If consumption structures in the Eurozone are similar, it is likely that business cycles have a similar development as well. This intuitively leads to the conclusion that the same should be true if the factors leading to consumption similarity are converging. Thus, a similar development of financial returns should lead – other things equal – to more similar business cycles. However, the question as to whether or not the similarity of portfolio returns contributes to consumption convergence deserves a second look. Preconditions for a consumption convergence via returns are:

First, in the past differences in returns in different investments and different country indices could be observed. If the same returns prevailed already in the past, no effect out of return convergences can have influence in the future.

Second, home bias is pronounced and resulted in the past in portfolio strategies that again resulted in different returns out of financial investment. Otherwise, home bias and portfolio strategies would not be an interesting subject to study.

Put these two points together, it is assumed that investors composed portfolios in a way that returns were different, and that these returns led to different consumption. A reason for this observation could be that income out of financial wealth was an income source only available for a certain part of countries. These differences diminish because the return structures become more similar.

One may note that for a convergence, it is not necessary that poorer countries become richer; convergence only says that consumption develops in the same direction and does not say anything about the consumption gap or level. Of course, other sources of consumption – especially earned income – should not move in opposite direction and offset the effect of financial income. These aspects will be considered in the empirical part of the paper.

This leads to the question: when are financial returns similar? Indeed, this should be a consequence if private investment is similar in the sense of return-structures. In a financial context, return can never be considered without risk since both things are closely related to each other. Especially in short investment horizons, risk is not mirrored in the expected return, and instead rather reduces expected return. As the certainty of returns should affect investment as well as consumption decisions, risk should be considered. Put together, similar risk-return-structures of portfolios support similar financial returns. Financial returns again become more similar if the portfolios themselves are similar.

However, how probable is it that portfolios are similar? To answer this question, portfolio theory provides an answer with the International Capital Asset Pricing Model by Solnik (1974a), which is based on the Capital Asset Pricing Model developed independently from each other by Sharpe (1964), Lintner (1965) and Mossin (1966). The concept of IAPM suggests that the best risk-return-ratio can be achieved by investing internationally, depending on relative weights of countries; hence, it would be rational for investors to follow the IAPM as will be shown below. If all investors would follow the model, the portfolios in the EMU should look the same with regard to country distribution in portfolios and, for this reason, probably risk-return structures. The deviation from the IAPM is discussed as the home bias phenomenon in the literature.

Similar portfolios of private investors indeed have at least one positive implication for business cycle convergence: if investors hold similar portfolios, at least consumption out of these portfolios should be similar (assumed that the consumption-wealth linkage holds) with the convergence of cycles as a consequence.

One might argue that there could be a second positive transmission channel of the IAPM. The second implication is that amplitudes of consumption cycles might become smaller when portfolios are diversified internationally (Sørensen et al., 2007) and therefore could lead to more similar cycles (Duval, Elmeskov, and Vogel, 2007). However, it depends on the definition of convergence if smaller amplitudes automatically lead to better synchronisation of business cycles and would need further research. Holding claims on output on other countries (e.g. through portfolios) is discussed in the literature under the name of international risk sharing. The basic idea behind risk sharing is that the risk of changes in (national) outputs are diversified internationally by holding claims on outputs on other countries as well. The IAPM follows similar ideas as international risk sharing and could be interpreted as a special form of international risk sharing. However, while risk sharing is mainly motivated by income and consumption smoothing, the IAPM has portfolio-optimization in mind. Both concepts lead into the same direction, but have different goals. As the impact of smaller amplitudes on cycles needs more research to be identified clearly; the dissertation will concentrate on the transmission channel of similar portfolios, keeping in mind that a cycle convergence might be caused partly by smaller cycles as well.

Put together, similar portfolios which follow the IAPM are a rational scenario for private investors. Investment, according to this, would lead to a convergence of European business cycles.

3.2 Basics of Modern Portfolio Theory

3.2.1 Core Elements of Portfolio Theory

Each investor is opposed to a great number of investment opportunities for a portfolio. A rational investor is interested in the return of the chosen assets and how safe return is. Therefore, return and risk are the input factors for optimizing a portfolio.[4]

Return is the sum of price changes, and payments for interest or dividends on stocks and bonds. As return is often not fixed in advance, the expected value of return for an asset is used as an input factor for portfolio decisions. The expected

4 Sections 3.2 to 3.2.3, if not otherwise noted, are derived by Elton, Gruber, Brown, and Goetzmann (2007), but could have been derived by other textbooks such as Spremann (2006) as well.

value is the average outcome, calculated by the sum of the products of the return in different situations and the probability of incidence in a certain situation.

$$\overline{R_i} = \sum_{j=1}^{M} P_{ij} R_{ij} \qquad \textbf{F 1}$$

with $\overline{R_i}$ *as the expected return of the* i_{th} *asset (expected values are denoted with a bar)*
M as the total number of situations j
P_{ij} *as the probability of the* j_{th} *return on asset i.*

As expected return is an average, the dispersion of the different outcomes might be large. An investor might be confronted with very different outcomes and might want to know the real outcome variation from the expected value. This is measured by the variance of an asset, denoted by σ^2.

The variance of an asset is calculated by squaring the difference between the return in a certain situation *j* and the expected return (to avoid cancelling out positive and negative deviations to 0) multiplied by P_{ij}. This quotient is taken for each situation *j* and is summed up.

$$\sigma_i^2 = \sum_{j=1}^{M} \left[P_{ij} (R_{ij} - \overline{R_i})^2 \right] \qquad \textbf{F 2}$$

The root of the variance is the standard deviation, the dispersion around the expected return and the risk measurement for each asset *i*.

An investor is not only interested in the characteristics of single assets, but also in the combination of assets that are parts of the portfolio.

Return of a portfolio in situation *j* is the weighed return:

$$R_{Pj} = \sum_{i=1}^{N} (X_i R_{ij}) \qquad \textbf{F 3}$$

with *N as the number of assets in a portfolio*
X_i as the proportion of asset i in the portfolio (proportions add to 1)

Analogously, the average portfolio return $\overline{R_P}$ is the weighted average of mean returns of the assets.

$$\overline{R}_P = \sum_{i=1}^{N} (X_i \overline{R}_i) \qquad \textbf{F 4}$$

Portfolio risk can vary distinctly from the average risk of its components, the single assets. The reason for this observation is that different assets might react differently in different market situations, i.e. their correlation is not 1. The correlation coefficient takes values from -1 to 1. A correlation of 1 means that assets co-move perfectly, whereas a coefficient of -1 means that assets move in exactly the different direction. In reality, the correlation coefficient normally takes an intermediate value above 0.

A portfolio that exists of two assets with equal proportions and perfectly opposing correlation coefficients ensures that positive outcomes above the expected return and losses cancel out. The risk of such a portfolio would be 0. Portfolio risk therefore depends on the correlation between assets – how much they move together in the market. Although the example is an extreme situation, it shows that variance can be reduced by combining assets.

How is the variance of a portfolio calculated? As mentioned, the co-movements of assets play an important role. As demonstrated in the single asset case, the difference between the return of a portfolio and the average return are taken and squared.

$$\sigma_P^2 = E(R_p - \overline{R}_P)^2 \qquad \textbf{F 5}$$

with E indicating expected values

Utilizing the formulas for R_p (F3) and $\overline{R}_P$ (F4) in the portfolio, variance formula (F5) and rearranging yields:

$$\sigma_P^2 = \sum_{j=1}^{N} X_j^2 \sigma_j^2 + \sum_{j=1}^{N} \sum_{\substack{k=1 \\ k \neq ju}}^{N} (X_j X_k \sigma_{jk}) \qquad \textbf{F 6}$$

with k denoting security k

σ_{jk} is the covariance of securities j and k; or: $(R_{ij} - \overline{R}_i)(R_{kj} - \overline{R}_k)$ (product of the deviations of the return from security i from its mean and the deviation from security k from its mean)

The correlation of two assets explain why efficient portfolios usually have a lower risk than single assets (the only exception is that all assets in the portfolio have a correlation of 1). The first scholar who gained that insight is the founder of the portfolio theory, Harry M. Markowitz (1959, based on his initial work from 1952). The basic idea is that in a well-diversified portfolio, the correlation between assets can be chosen in a way that risk is minimized by using the correlation characteristics of assets. In a very well-diversified portfolio, the individual risk of an asset, the so-called unsystematic risk, can be completely eliminated. On the other hand, the risk that lies behind all portfolios – the market risk – cannot be diversified away as this is the common factor that accounts for all assets in the market. It is the so called systematic risk (Spremann, 2006, p. 314 et seqq.). This consideration is used in the assumptions of the single index model (Section 3.2.3) as well.

3.2.2 The Efficient Frontier

Usually, an investor prefers more return to less, and in the literature, it is usually assumed that investors are risk averse. If there would be no risk aversion, investors would put all their money into the single asset that offers the highest return. Portfolios that lay on the so-called efficient frontier are those that are preferred according to their characteristics of risk and return. The shape of this line demonstrates why an investor would only choose a portfolio on the frontier.

Graph 3: The Efficient Frontier

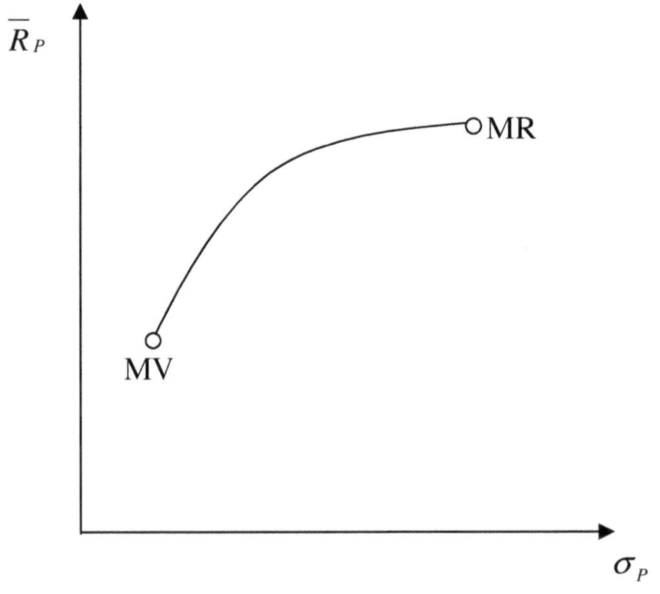

Source: Elton et al., 2007, p. 81

The higher the return an investor wants to achieve, the more risk she or he needs to take. All portfolios that are under the curve are characterized by more risk for the same return, or less return for the same risk. Therefore, a risk adverse investor would always prefer a portfolio on the efficient frontier. The more risk adverse, the closer to the origin the chosen portfolio is.

The portfolio with least risk is called the minimum variance portfolio (MV); the portfolio with the biggest achievable return is called the maximum return portfolio (MR). The efficient frontier is a connection of these two points that necessarily needs to be concave (concave includes a straight line). This approach is appropriate because the combination of assets can never be more risky than the sum of the risk of the assets in the portfolio (Elton et al., 2007, p. 81; Steiner and Bruns, 2007, p. 11).

From the previous sections to this section, the assumption that only risky assets are part of the portfolio was made. Tobin (1958) added the possibility of riskless lending and borrowing as components of the portfolio. In reality, completely riskless assets – this means assets with a variance of 0 – do not exist. Though government bonds in EMU-countries are considered safe and exhibit low variances, these bonds may still vary in their return.

Riskless borrowing would mean that investors can short-sell[5] a riskless asset at the riskless rate R_F; riskless lending means buying assets at the riskless rate.

The investor chooses to invest a certain proportion X in combination with an efficient portfolio A and invests *(1-X)* into the riskless asset.

The expected return of this portfolio-combination is

$$\overline{R}_C = (1-X)R_F + X\overline{R}_A \qquad \textbf{F 7}$$

Considering that $\sigma_{AB} = \rho_{AB}\sigma_A\sigma_B$ with ρ_{AB} being the correlation coefficient and applying the two-asset case to equation F6 brings

$$\sigma_P^2 = \sum_{j=1}^{N} X_j^2\sigma_j^2 + \sum_{j=1}^{N}\sum_{\substack{k=1 \\ k\neq ju}}^{N}(X_jX_k\sigma_{jk})$$

$$\sigma_C^2 = (1-X)^2\sigma_F^2 + X^2\sigma_A^2 + 2X(1-X)\sigma_A\sigma_F\rho_{FA} \qquad \textbf{F 8}$$

The riskless rate has no variance, that means $\sigma_F = 0$. Considering this and taking the root, the equation reduces to

5 Short-selling means that the seller does not own the asset the moment she or he sells.

$$\sigma_C = X\sigma_A$$ **F 9**

This means that the proportion X that is invested in portfolio A should be

$$X = \frac{\sigma_C}{\sigma_A}$$ **F 10**

Replacing this expression for X in the equation for the expected return (F7), the portfolio return can be expressed by a line which represents the efficient frontier:

$$\overline{R}_C = R_F + \left(\frac{\overline{R}_A - R_F}{\sigma_A}\right)\sigma_C$$ **F 11**

Graph 4: The Efficient Frontier – No Borrowing Allowed

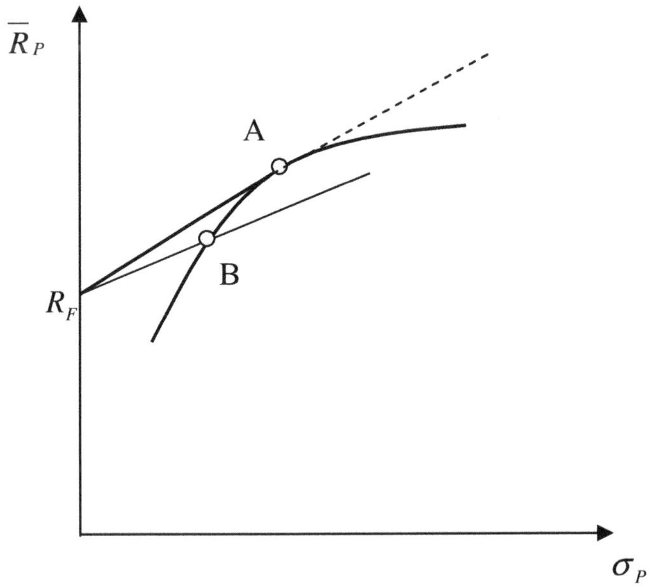

Source: Elton et al., 2007, p. 88

All portfolios to the left of A mean lending (buying) at the riskless rate; all portfolios to the right mean borrowing (short-selling) at the riskless rate.

An investor could theoretically choose portfolio B on the efficient frontier with a combination of the riskless asset. As all combinations on the line $R_F A$ offer either more return for given risk or less risk for a given return, the line must be the efficient frontier and A must be the optimal portfolio. No other combinations of portfolios with the riskless asset can provide a more favourable risk-return ratio.

As riskless borrowing is usually not possible for private investors, the efficient frontier needs to be adapted. The part to the right of portfolio A is therefore still the original efficient frontier.

3.2.3 The Single Index Model

Calculating efficient portfolios demands several inputs. Especially the number of correlations between each possible aspirant, investment for a portfolio needs to be calculated. If for example only 100 assets are on a short-list for possible investments, 4,950 correlations need to be calculated. In addition to this issue, the expected return for each asset and the variance need to be computed, followed by the optimisation procedure for the portfolio (calculating the efficient portfolio).

Return and variance of an asset are usually factors that are more easily available for investors. Correlations between the enormous number of available titles in the world, or even on country level need, to be separately calculated and are probably hardly tangible for investors.

To simplify the calculation and to forecast correlation structures, the insight is used that there is a common factor to all traded assets that affects their development. Usually, if the market goes up, most share prices go up as well, and the other way round. Often, changes in the market are considered in the single index model as the shared factor. If, for example, a country is considered as the market, economic policy could affect all listed titles, or if a monetary union is considered as the market, monetary policy could influence the performance of all assets. If all assets have a common reaction to market changes, this may lead to the conclusion that the correlation of each asset to the market as a whole might be sufficient to represent correlation structures.

For a single asset *i,* this relation can be expressed as

$$R_i = a_i + \beta_i R_m \qquad \textbf{F 12}$$

with a_i *being a random variable, representing the part of the return that is not dependent on the market*

R_m *being a random variable, representing the return on the market index*

β_i *indicates the relation between the return on the market and the return on asset i*

A 1 % increase (decrease) in the market is reflected by a β_i % increase (decrease) of the asset. Thus, the closer β_i is to 1, the closer is the co-movement of market and asset.

There are different techniques for estimating β_i. One example is using the least-square deviation in a regression analysis of historical data (for an overview of estimation techniques see Elton et al., 2007, p. 139 et seqq.).

The term a_i needs to be divided into the expected value α_i and an uncertain part, the random variable e_i : $a_i = \alpha_i + e_i$

Considering this, the expected return of an asset *i* needs to be rewritten to

$$R_i = \alpha_i + \beta_i R_m + e_i \qquad \textbf{F 13}$$

The random variable e_i has an expected value of 0 and is considered to be uncorrelated with R_m. Formally, this means that the covariance of these variables is 0. If the two variables are not correlated, then equation F12 shows that market return is not dependent on the return of asset *i*.

The most important assumption of the single-index model is that the random variable of asset *i*, e_i , is independent from all other random variables e_j from asset *j*. In other words, the change on the market is the only factor why assets co-move.

For a portfolio of assets, the asset-market-relationship is implemented by combining equations F4 and F12, which is the return of the portfolio.

For portfolio risk equation, F8 builds the basis and represents the single-index case if the two following equations, F14 and F15, substitute the according expressions.

The variance of a security is adapted by using equation F13, and considering that e_i has an expected value of 0:

$$\sigma_i^2 = \beta_i^2 \sigma_m^2 + \sigma_{ei}^2 \qquad \textbf{F 14}$$

The covariance between two securities with regard to the single index model by using the definition of R_i above, and the assumption that e_{i} is zero:

$$\sigma_{ij} = \beta_i \beta_j \sigma_m^2 \qquad \textbf{F 15}$$

These two equations demonstrate that the whole portfolio is dependent on the correlations between assets and markets. One may note that the single-market model is a model that functions due to the made assumptions. The single index model is the fundament for the Capital Asset Pricing Model.

3.3 Capital Asset Pricing Model

3.3.2 The Standard Model

Three authors – Sharpe (1964), Lintner (1965) and Mossin (1966) – derived the standard Capital Asset Pricing Model (CAPM) autonomously from each other. Even as its age seems to be antiquated compared to the rapid developments on financial markets, the model is still widely used and constantly adapted.

The CAPM is an equilibrium model. The basic idea of equilibrium models is that if the single investor behaves "optimal" (behaves as predicted by models), then it should be possible to describe how all investors behave and what impact this behaviour has on the market.

The assumptions of the CAPM are quite restrictive. However, as can be seen later, even under these assumptions, the CAPM describes stock market reality quite well.

- There are no transaction costs and no taxes that distort portfolio choice of an investor.
- All assets of an investor are marketable and are divisible.
- Perfect competition prevails, that is, no investor influences prices by his or her actions on the market.
- The choice of portfolio composition follows the procedures described above, that is, on the risk-return-characteristics of a portfolio.
- All investors have homogenous expectations on portfolio return, variance and correlation between assets, and they consider the same time-period.
- Short sales and riskless borrowing and lending are allowed.

The starting point for the CAPM is the efficient frontier and the fact that all portfolios on it are efficient. In Section 3.1.2, it was shown that all investors hold combinations of a riskless asset, and that the portfolio is farthest out on the efficient frontier. The conclusion is drawn because no other portfolio offers more return for given risk or less risk for a given return. The combination with the riskless asset allows for all degrees of risk aversion of an investor because the more risk averse an investor is, the more investment into the riskless asset is conducted (see e.g. Lapp, 2001, p. 18 or Tesar and Werner, 1995, p. 475).

Now, if all investors have homogenous expectations as assumed in the CAPM, all investors hold the optimal portfolio (denoted by M in Graph 5). In market equilibrium, all assets are sold and bought, the consequence is that necessarily all investors hold the market portfolio. The market portfolio is the portfolio that contains all risky assets of the market. The proportion of an asset in an individual portfolio corresponds to the proportion of a respective asset of the total market value.

Graph 5: The Market Portfolio

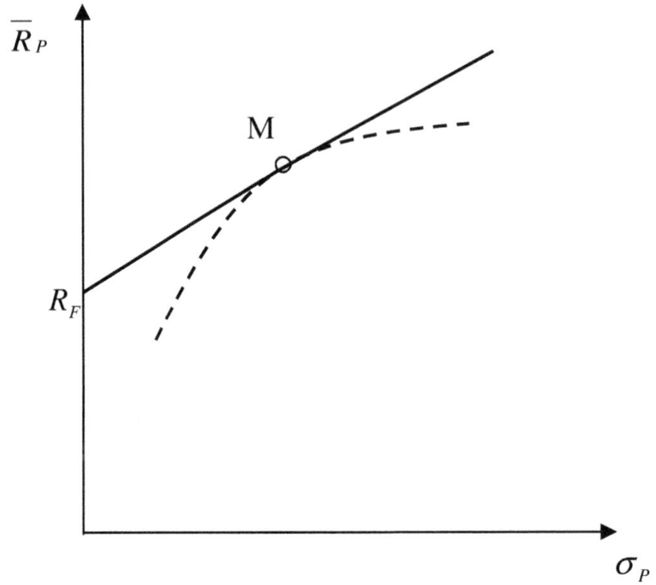

Source: Elton et al., 2007, p. 287

The line starting in R_F and going through M is called the capital market line, and it represents the efficient frontier. It can be described by equation F11, while the A is replaced by an M to indicate that it is the market portfolio. σ measures the risk of the whole portfolio.

$$\overline{R} = R_F + \left(\frac{\overline{R}_M - R_F}{\sigma_M} \right) \sigma \qquad \textbf{F 16}$$

The equation breaks down the determinants of portfolio return into a price of liquidity (the riskless rate) plus the price for taking over market risk (the term in brackets is the reward-to-risk ratio of the market portfolio) multiplied by the amount of risk in the whole portfolio. Thus, there is a proportional relation between the risk of a single title and the market risk, which is the main conclusion of the CAPM (Spremann, 2006, p. 302).

This equation only applies to efficient portfolios, but does not explain return on any other portfolio. To find out about portfolio risk on a more general basis, the considerations of the single index model are included.

As argued above, for a very well-diversified portfolio, the market risk as the systematic risk is the only risk for a portfolio. This risk is represented by β. The market portfolio that is held by assumption by all investors fulfils the requirement of a well-diversified portfolio. Therefore, only the expected return of a portfolio $\overline{R}$ and its risk β play a role in the investment decision. In equilibrium, all portfolios must lie on one line of the expected return-beta-space; otherwise, riskless arbitrage opportunities would exist.

Graph 6: CAPM – The Security Market Line

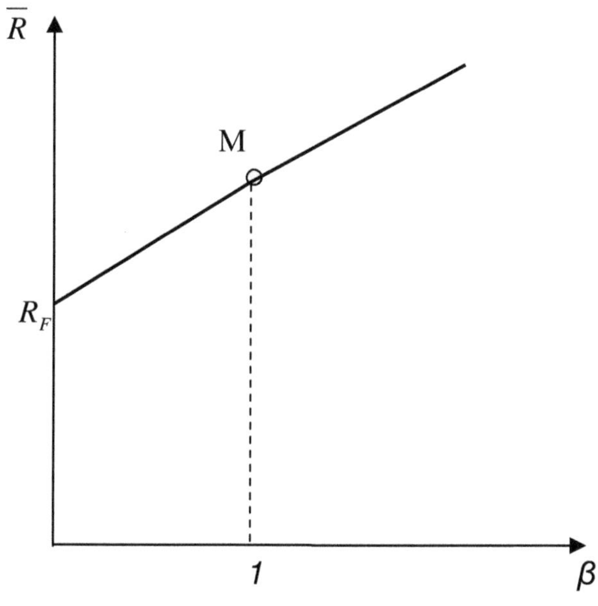

Source: Elton et al., 2007, p. 290

As the market portfolio has the same development as the market as a whole, its risk must be completely correlated. As a consequence, β must be 1, and the return of the market portfolio is $\overline{R}_M$ (the weighted average of the expected return of each asset in the market).

The equation for the efficient frontier in the CAPM subsequently is

$$\overline{R}_i = R_F + \beta_i(\overline{R}_M - R_F) \qquad \textbf{F 17}$$

The equation shows that β is the only reason why returns on securities differ, as R_F and R_M are independent from individual securities. It shows as well that taking over unsystematic risk (that is, the risk of a single security that could be diversified away) brings no extra-return as it does not even appear in the equation. If unsystematic risk can be eliminated totally, there is no reason to pay a risk premium on it. This relation underlines that holding the portfolio that is diversified on the highest level available is a rational consequence for an investor, and this means holding the market portfolio.

It is important to stress that the market portfolio is an efficient portfolio, and that it is rational for investors to hold it because there is no other portfolio with a better risk-return-ratio.

3.3.3 Shortcomings of the Standard CAPM

The CAPM is an intuitively attractive model though it suffers from some shortcomings. Critiques of the standard CAPM basically follow two lines:

The first line pursues the argument that the assumptions are too strict with regard to real investment decisions. The assumptions do not reflect investment reality. The second line states that the results of the CAPM do not reflect reality either.

This section provides a short overview on the arguments against the CAPM; the next sections deals shortly with empirical findings. What are the arguments behind the first line, that the assumptions are too strict and do not reflect investment reality?

The CAPM as an equilibrium model can describe macro returns, but cannot explain individual behaviour (very few investors hold a market portfolio in reality; see Section 3.4.3 on home bias). An explanation might be derived by some of its assumptions.

The most controversial assumptions with regard to private investors are that short sales are allowed, that riskless borrowing is possible, that homogenous expectations prevail, that all assets are tradable, and that there are no transaction costs or personal taxes that affect the investment decision.

All of these assumptions have been dissolved one at a time and led to modified models. It could be shown that basically the main aspects of the model still hold although the enhanced models describe reality better (e.g. investors hold different portfolios due to personal taxes or the slope of the security market line changes if riskless borrowing is not allowed; see Elton et al. (2007, p. 305 et seqq.) or Steiner and Bruns (2007, p. 28).

The modifications just mentioned would lead to more complex models that hardly resemble the original model if all assumptions were relaxed the same time. Therefore, some of the critique on the model is valid.

The second argumentation, that the results of the model do not reflect reality, can be divided in several aspects. The model leads to some results that need further examination.

One implicit assumption in the intuitive approach chosen in Section 3.2.1 is that beta is the real risk measure, but this is not necessarily true. But even when the optimal portfolio[6] is calculated, a CAPM with the same results (beta is the relevant risk measure) can be derived (Elton et al., 2007, p. 293 et seq.). If the market portfolio is correctly calculated, there is no other possibility but that the CAPM needs to hold (Spremann, 2006, p. 309; Roll, 1977, p. 130).

Another argument is that the market portfolio is not necessarily efficient and measured correctly. Efficiency in this case means that expected returns are linearly related to the market and that market betas fully describe the cross-sections of expected returns. The argument against the efficiency of measurement of the market portfolio can be further divided:

First, not all assets are tradable or can be evaluated, e.g. human labour or pension claims. For this reason, the market portfolio cannot contain all assets and empirical testing is not possible (Fama and French, 2004, p. 25; and Roll's fundamental critique (1977, p. 130).

Second, if the chosen market portfolio is not the "real" one, it is probably not diversified perfectly and therefore contains unsystematic risk. The relation between beta and the market would not be the real risk measure anymore (Roll, 1977, p. 130).

Third, there is no capital market equilibrium in reality.

All of these arguments cannot be offset completely; however, the model should be judged upon how well it fulfils its predictions, or in this case, how well it describes the real happening on capital markets. The standard CAPM is an influential model that has been dominating the financial literature for a longer time, and that is the origin of many adoptions and enhancements to describe capital markets.

3.3.4 Empirical Findings

The CAPM has been tested extensively. Because the CAPM needs to hold if the market portfolio is calculated correctly, the empirical investigations rather test if investors really follow the recommendations of the CAPM. The market portfolio itself is usually not calculated, but instead approximated by market indexes (Spremann, 2006, p. 331).

---

6 The optimal portfolio is the one that is optimized in its risk-return characteristics without the idea of a common factor, represented here by the market beta.

The main results are listed shortly for reasons of completeness, although the international form of the CAPM is the more relevant for this paper.[7]

Tests that confirmed the CAPM:

In an early study, Sharpe and Cooper (1972) approved in a simple setting that for a period from 1931 to 1967 on the New York stock exchange, higher betas meant a higher return.

Black, Jensen and Scholes (1972) confirmed in their empirical tests that higher betas are closely correlated to higher returns. The further results are consistent with another form of the CAPM, a two-factor-form of the CAPM. This means that beta is not the only factor that defines risk.

Fama and MacBeth (1973) use a different methodology to test the CAPM in their influential study. They test as to whether the CAPM is really an equilibrium model; that means that deviations from it are only random. Indeed, they found out that the residual e_i has no influence on return. Additionally, they conclude that the expected relation between beta and return is applicable.

The following studies rejected the CAPM, especially the prediction that risk premiums are only paid for market risks:

Bühler (1995) showed that risk premiums vary under different macroeconomic circumstances. This means that investors expect a risk payment if, for example, times are more unsecure (conditional CAPM). If in these situations the unconditioned CAPM is used, systematic risk seems to be rewarded.

In other studies, the relation between beta and risk premiums did not fulfil expectations either. The so-called size-effect says that assets with small capitalisation often have better returns then expected. This can partly be explained by the issue that the market index does not represent all assets. The same applies to assets with a low growth potential (value-effect) and temporary effects like the known January-effect contradict the return assumptions of the CAPM as well (Fama, 1991; Fama and French, 1992).

Broadly, only the results in the early studies mentioned above confirm the ideas of the CAPM. However altogether, the empirical results are ambiguous. There seems to be evidence that investors do not follow the CAPM no matter how rational the model seems to be. Reasons could either be that investors are not rational, or that the CAPM just does not include all factors for investment decision (Fama and French, 2004, p. 37).

7 For an overview of empirical studies see e.g. Fama and French (2004) and the literature therein.

3.4 International Asset Pricing Model and the Home Bias Phenomenon

3.4.2 IAPM

One of the criticisms of the CAPM is that not all assets are included in the market portfolio. This is encountered by the International Asset Pricing Model (IAPM) theoretically and in empirical applications. Although the CAPM is mostly applied to national markets in empirical studies, this does not reflect investment reality. Investors theoretically have access to all tradable assets in the world. Considering these thoughts, Solnik (1974a) derived the IAPM on the basis of the CAPM.

The main difference compared to the CAPM is the explicit incorporation of international capital markets – to be exact, the world market. The market portfolio therefore consists of all assets with a proportion of each country according to its asset-capitalization in the world market (Solnik, 1974a, p. 512). The basic idea is that there is a national systematic risk that can be further reduced by investing internationally. The country markets themselves (the country proportions in the portfolios) are already diversified with regard to unsystematic risk. Analogously to the CAPM, risk premiums in the IAPM are proportional to their international systematic risk. Exchange rate risk is considered to be either hedged or, in the case of bonds, the correlation between exchange rate risk and return is explicitly modelled in Solnik's model. The logic of this model implies that all investors in the world hold the same (world) market portfolio[8] and a risk free asset.

Implicitly, this model assumes that international markets are not completely correlated; otherwise, a diversification would not reduce risk. This implicitly includes that idiosyncratic shocks are not completely transmitted from country to country. If shocks hit all countries uniformly, diversification gains would not be observable.

Solnik (1974b) provides some empirical evidence that international diversification indeed reduces risk. However, his investigation period comprises the years 1966-1971. Doubts are in order if the increasing integration of international capital markets still provides room for a deeper diversification until today.

Although today markets co-move closer, there is still no perfect correlation (Kim, Moshirian, and Wu, 2005; Brooks and Del Negro, 2004). This should

8 Solnik (1974a) in his intertemporal model differentiates between a hedged stock market portfolio and a risk free bond portfolio. The bond portfolio is only riskless with regard to its beta, not with regard to exchange rate risk. These two risky assets are summarized in this dissertation to the world market portfolio. The risk free asset is our usual risk free asset with a beta of 0 and no exchange rate risk.

imply that international diversification is still beneficial. The average correlation of stock markets of several big countries amounts to 0.475 for a time period from 1991-2000 (Elton et al., 2007, p. 259), which offers a higher diversification than at national level. Lewis (1999, p. 576) confirms for the G-7 countries that correlations between markets are most often far away from 1; Forbes and Rigobon (2002) find correlation coefficient far lower than 1 in the Asian financial crisis of 1997 (correlation between the Hong Kong stock market and OECD countries). Brooks and Del Negro (2004) conclude that diversification across countries is still an effective strategy although recent literature emphasizes the role of diversification across industries. The authors attribute the growing importance of industry effects to the stock market bubble, especially in the telecommunication branch, and therefore it is supposed to be a temporary phenomenon. However, in Europe a growing industry diversification effect can be observed (Brooks and Del Negro, 2004, p. 670).

The literature findings are not totally clear on the question as to whether or not country effects are more important than industry effects on diversification though a good deal of literature points to the direction that country diversification is the better mean to reduce risk. One reason might be that countries represent partly industries, i.e. that countries specialize as it is expected by the international risk sharing literature. If countries experience a higher financial integration, they can specialize without bearing the income risk; as this kind of risk can be diversified over financial assets of different countries (Kalemli-Ozcan et al., 2005, p. 176). According to this literature, diversification across industries or countries should be a question of time until it loses some of its importance. Other reasons for the benefit of country diversification could be differences in economic or monetary policy.

Whereas diversification seems to be still effective today, an investor might ask whether exchange rate risk might not offset the advantages. Von Nitzsch and Stotz (2006) pursued this question and noticed that return increases by about 1% if an international investment strategy is followed, and exchange rate risk is hedged.[9] They found out as well that national capital market size influences the advantages of international diversification (von Nitzsch and Stotz, 2006, p. 113), which can be explained by a broader choice of assets and probably a lower systematic risk.

All these arguments should have the consequence that investors invest internationally. Why investors do not necessarily invest internationally is investigated in the literature as the home bias phenomenon, which is analyzed in the next section.

---

9 Schröder (2003) found a benefit of 3 % for European investors.

3.4.3 Home Bias – Empirical Background

In the sections above, the conclusion is drawn that it would be rational for investors to hold assets across countries to diversify risks optimally. Each country should have a weight in a portfolio which corresponds to its weight in the world capital market. The deviation of ideal and actual proportion of an investor's home country in the portfolio defines the home bias. Various empirical studies display that the home bias is quite pronounced in almost all countries in the world, and that there are few rational explanations for it. Hence, the great deviation from ideal portfolio weights is referred to as the home bias phenomenon.

How is the development of home bias? Is it rather declining or rising? Many studies concentrate on the US-investor, though those considering the EMU-countries come to the same conclusions.

A wide range of empirical studies on the home bias phenomenon exist. Especially in recent years; probably due to easier access to data and a growing public attention, the amount of empirical work rose substantially. Table 1 gives an overview on empirical studies that cover different aspects of the issue, though it is by far not a complete overview, but nevertheless focuses on certain aspects important to the dissertation.

One of the first studies addressing home bias empirically is the one by Tesar and Werner (1995). They use national time series data of portfolio holdings derived by accumulated capital flows out of the balance of payments and estimate home bias by opposing foreign investment to domestic market capitalization. Their main findings are that in the five OECD counties, home bias is still substantial, and that diversification of risks is not the dominant motive of portfolio composition but other motives such as geographic distance prevail. Another finding is that variable transaction costs are not the reason for a high bias. The last aspect is concluded because international capital flows and transactions grew though it did not result in higher foreign capital holdings.

French and Poterba (1991) find out that one of the main reasons of home bias is the tendency of investors to overestimate the return of their domestic market. Their study is based on a survey among portfolio managers. Neither institutional barriers such as capital controls nor differences in taxes or direct transaction costs are considered to be plausible reasons. Home bias is defined as the estimated foreign portfolio holding (approximated by capital flows) as opposed to market capitalization though the latter is corrected by inter-corporate equity holdings.

Table 1: Selection of Empirical Studies on Home Bias

Title	Authors	Data base of study (year)	Comprising countries
Home Bias and High Turnover (1995)	Tesar, Linda L. Werner, Ingrid M.	1975, 1980, 1985, 1990	Canada, Germany, Japan, United Kindom, United States
Investor Diversification and International Equity Markets (1991)	French, Kennth R. Poterba, James M.	1990	Canada, Germany, France, Japan, United Kindom, United States
What Determines the Domestic Bias and Foreign Bias? (2005)	Chan, Kalok Covrig, Vicentiu Ng, Lilian K.	1999, 2000	Australia, Austria, Belgium, Canada, Denmark, Finland, France, Germany, Greece, Iceland, Ireland, Israel, Italy, Japan, Netherlands, New Zealand, Norway, Portugal, Singapore, Spain, Sweden, United Kindom, United States
Global Bond Portfolios and EMU (2005)	Lane, Philip R.	1997, 2001	Austria, Belgium, Finland, France, Germany, Greece, Ireland, Italy, Luxembourg, Netherlands, Portugal, Spain
Financial Integration, International Portfolio Choice and the European Monetary Union (2006)	De Santis, Roberto Gérard, Bruno	1997, 2001	Australia, Austria, Belgium, Bermuda, Canada, Denmark, Finland, France, Germany, Iceland, Ireland, Israel, Italy, Japan, Netherlands, New Zealand, Norway, Portugal, Singapore, Spain, Sweden, United Kindom, United States
Home Bias and International Risk Sharing: Twin Puzzles Separated at Birth (2007)	Sørensen, Bent E. Wu, Yi-Tsung Zhu, Yu	1993-2003	Australia, Austria, Belgium, Canada, Denmark, Finland, France, Germany, Hong Kong, Ireland, Italy, Japan, Luxembourg, Netherlands, New Zealand, Norway, Portugal, Signapore, South Africa, Spain, Sweden, Switzerland, Taiwan, United Kindom, United States
Is the Home Bias in Equities and Bonds Declining in Europe? (2007)	Bosch, Thijs Schoenmaker, Dirk	1997, 2001, 2004	Austria, Belgium, Denmark, Finland, France, Iceland, Ireland, Italy, Netherlands, Portugal, Spain, Sweden, United Kingdom, United States

Mutual funds data is the base for the analysis of Chan, Covrig, and Ng (2005), which is among the first studies which uses a wider range of countries, including developed and developing countries. Similar to earlier studies, their finding is that more wealth is invested in domestic position, which is surprising because mutual funds are expected to behave more rational as individual investors. The authors identify as determinants of home bias geographic distance and different languages. Minor but significant determinants are the development status of a foreign country, taxes, and capital controls. The latter effects are a new insight as compared to previous literature, probably because developing countries are included in the study and a different time frame. Their data set of mutual funds is from Thomson Financial Securities and directly considers portfolio holdings in contrast to accumulated capital flows. Adjaouté, Danthine, and Isakov (2005) observe institutional investors as well; with the result that home bias is declining in Europe. They ascribe this development to the establishment of the EMU in the years 1997 till 2001.

Lane (2006) focuses on EMU countries, particularly their bond portfolios, using IMF data of the Coordinated Portfolio Investment Survey (CPIS). In Lane's study, the possibility of a euro bias – the tendency to overweight EMU-countries in the portfolio – is analyzed and confirmed. This is interpreted as a trend towards financial regionalization. The study confirms as well that trade linkages and geographical proximity are factors contributing to reduce home bias. Exchange rate volatility, on the other hand, shows no significant influence.

According to De Santis and Gérard (2006), the decline in home bias of equity and bonds can be mainly observed in the EMU countries and in a few other countries, but is not necessarily a global trend. Home bias is measured by opposing the actual foreign holdings to optimal foreign holdings. The main reasons for the positive development in the EMU are according to the study rational ones: the common currency and expected diversification benefits. The latter comprises diversification of fundamentals and currency (for countries outside the EMU) and is derived by weekly Datastream and JP Morgan return data, interpreting a decrease in return variance as a diversification benefit. Another reason for the fast decline is that home bias was very pronounced in the years before the study, which means that small amounts of international investment have a greater weight.

Another perspective is taken by Sørensen et al. (2007). The authors investigate the connection between home bias and international risk sharing (consumption smoothing and an equalization of consumption growth rates via international property holdings). They conclude that first of all, home bias declined fast; second, that a lower home bias and higher financial integration lead to higher income and consumption smoothing. Their estimation method is via pooled panel data regressions. The size of risk sharing is substantial: lowering (equity) home bias by 0.1 points means rising income smoothing by 4 % (Sørensen et al., 2007, p. 598) in OECD countries. For bond bias, no significance is deducted. Interestingly, for the pure EU sample within the OECD sample, neither equity nor debt home bias had a significant influence on consumption and income risk sharing. This raises the expectation for my study that portfolio similarity has less influence on the EU as on countries outside the EU.

Newer data confirms the trends already discovered in the mentioned literature, e.g. Bosch and Schoenmaker (2008) approve that home bias in EMU is declining more than outside the EMU and goes hand in hand with a euro bias. They add new explanations for the decline of home bias: significant are basically two effects. The professionalism effect supports the thesis that institutional investors tend to invest more rational. Countries with a higher proportion of mutual funds managers show a lower home bias. The availability effect states that a more developed domestic market induces local investors to invest at home and use the nearby resources.

As mentioned above, various other studies exist, e.g. about the influence of internationsal accounting standards on home bias (Beneish and Yohn, 2008) or address the cost of home bias (Bluethgen, Jansen, Meyer, and Hackethal, 2008), which is discussed more detailed starting from Section 4.6.

3.4.4 Explaining Home Bias

3.4.4.1 Rational Explanations

All empirical work confirms that home bias is declining though its amount is still substantial. The question is why individuals apparently do not hold optimal portfolios and do not hedge their risks across countries. Broadly, the explanations for the existence of home bias can be divided into two groups:

- Home bias is explainable because rational motives not included in the models exist.
- Home bias is explainable because investors do not act rational as it is assumed in the models. The explanation lies rather in psychological areas.

For the first group of arguments, several explanations are given in the literature though no completely satisfying and conclusive answers are given. The main arguments are prepared in a literature review by Lewis (1999, p. 575):

1. International diversification does not protect against all kinds of risk.
2. Home bias is measured incorrectly.
3. Transaction costs are too high.

Explanations in the first group are the existence of non-tradable assets such as labour or pension claims or (with restrictions) housing. These assets are strongly dependent on the development and shock sensitivity of the respective domestic market. Logic would imply that international diversification should even be larger as just the diversification degree suggested by the IAPM. Baxter and Jerman (1997) pursued this question and highlight that return on human capital (labour income) is highly correlated to return out of financial capital in their sample of four OECD countries. This implies that a great wealth position is not hedged against risks. Inflation risk is another explanation that is not addressed in the standard IAPM (returns are considered to be the same in all countries, therefore no inflation is modelled). Intuitively, inflation risk hedging by investing mainly at home would make sense if national inflation is negatively correlated with national asset returns. Empirical studies (Cooper and Kaplanis, 1994) do not confirm this connection; therefore, inflation risk does not provide a plausible explanation for home bias.

The second line of arguments assumes that home bias is not measured correctly because of shortcomings in the statistical estimation process, and because some information is not considered in the IAPM. The fist line analyzes the possibility that there are no gains from international diversification because markets co-move closely. If markets would be perfectly correlated, no adjustment of income out of capital could take place. Gorman and Jorgensen (2002) use different statistical approaches and argue that due to the difficulties in estimating the optimal portfolio correctly, a completely domestic portfolio is not significantly different from the optimal one. The issue of a correct calculation of the optimal portfolio arises from the fact that that return and variance are often calculated by historical data and estimation procedures. Historical data does not contain any information about future events. Standard errors are often too high for a good forecast of returns; therefore, uncertainty induces the investor to invest at home. Von Nitzsch and Stotz (2006), supported in this view by Baele, Pungulescu, and Ter Horst (2007), argue that although the market portfolio might not be efficient, the alternative measure of home bias, i.e. to calculate optimal portfolios, would not necessarily offer a more accurate measure because of the just mentioned intrinsic estimation issues.

Other literature investigates whether international diversification is already incorporated in assets of multinational companies which would mean that partly domestic assets need to be calculated as international assets. This would imply that assets of multinational companies do not co-move with their national stock market. Empirically weak evidence for just two countries in the sample analyzed by Rowland and Tesar (2004) could be found to support this argument.

Lapp (2001) finds out for Germany that barriers to a free choice of the portfolio composition from sources of workers' asset formation funds are a plausible reason for home bias. Out of this source, international portfolios are less supported as national portfolios because access to international markets is denied for the workforce within this funded measurement. In several European countries, privileges for domestic bonds or shares are provided, e.g. tax shelter for interest or dividend payments or the issue of shares for employees (Lapp, 2001, p. 143). For the countries of the sample that will be used for the econometric part of the dissertation, she lists Belgium, France, Italy, the Netherlands, Austria, Denmark and Sweden. The author explains home bias by the incentive of the extra return investors procured from the government if they invest at home. The investments at home are not restricted to bonds or shares, but may include, among others, saving through a building association. Disadvantages of home bias are compensated by the government. However, the author concludes that the dimension of home bias cannot be explained by the incentives of the government.

A third line analyses the influence of transaction costs, including information costs, international taxes, exchange rate volatility, and trade barriers. Transaction costs are analyzed by Tesar and Werner (1995). As already mentioned above, they conclude that because of the high amount of international capital flows, transaction costs are no explanation for home bias because foreign transactions tend to be much higher as domestic transactions. Fidora, Fratzscher, and Thimann (2007) find some evidence that exchange rate volatility plays a role in investing at home, especially when exchange rate risk builds the greater part of total risk. Still, even when exchange rate risk occurs, the return of investing internationally would be greater as mentioned above.

3.4.4.2 Behavioural Finance

The second broad line to explain home bias is known in the literature under the term of "behavioural finance" or, in a more general context, "behavioural economics". This line does not follow the assumption that investors solve situations strictly like economic theory would do – in other words, investors do not act completely rational. Deviations from the "ideal" are sought to be explained by psychological, sociological and behavioural aspects. Herding – like it was seen in bank runs in the past -, contagion effects, risk aversion or risk affection, self-control and patterns people are used to, are keywords for the financial world.

The individual behavioural background to these phenomena can be described with the following attributes: overconfidence, financial cognitive dissonance, the theory of regret, and prospect theory (Ricciardi and Simon, 2000). Overconfidence means that investors (or in general human beings) tend to be too optimistic with regard to their own skills, in this case about the judgement on the success of assets in their own portfolio. Overconfidence leads to a higher turnover in the portfolio which often leads to diminished returns (Barberis and Thaler, 2003, p. 1104). The overconfidence effect is strengthened, or sometimes triggered, by a financial cognitive dissonance. This means that bad experiences like earlier losses are suppressed, and humans do not learn from mistakes. An explanation offers the handling of inner conflicts between past experiences and new information which the investor tries to settle. Settlement can either result in neglecting past experience or justifying the investment decision by rational explanations. The theory of regret is a main point to explain herding behaviour. People are reluctant to sell their low performing stock because they might find (when buying new stock) out that the other stock is not performing any better. They would have to admit a wrong investment and have at the same time the emotion that the exchange towards an unknown investment might not be profitable. If many investors change their investment and buy something new recently, the emotion of changing the strategy is not that bad because there is the feeling that a disappointment would be shared by many others. Another explanation is informational asymmetry: the behaviour of others is observed and interpreted as an informational advance of the other market participant (Banerjee, 1992). The fourth aspect, prospect theory, deals with weighting different outcomes in a way that is not rational, e.g. that gaining stocks are sold but less performing stocks are hold. These decision weights often arise when a loss of money might occur (Ricciardi and Simon, 2000).

It would go beyond the scope of the dissertation to go further into the theoretical backgrounds; still, it is important to understand the (subliminal) motives of investors to find solution strategies to overcome the irrationality.

Some empirical studies address this issue although it is not necessarily labelled behavioural economics. As seen in Section 3.4.4, it was already suggested in some literature that geographical proximity or a common language are factors for an investment decision: a known environment seems to support foreign investment.

A very comprehensive survey on existing studies on behavioural finance is given by Barberis and Thaler (2003). In their essay, investor behaviour makes up only a fraction of the influence of psychologically motivated behaviour in the field of finance. Two examples are the puzzles as to why closed-end funds are not traded at a price that corresponds to their net asset value, or why companies pay dividends although the shareholder would be better off if shares would be repurchased because of tax payments. The authors stress that it is very important to understand investment behaviour. Their arguments are that there is a worldwide trend for individualized retirement plans including stock market assets, and because of the fact that trading becomes cheaper and is accessible for a broader mass (Barberis and Thaler, 2003, p. 1101). One explanation for home bias could be that investors seem to prefer a naive diversification, meaning to allocate capital evenly over different possibilities. This means on the one hand, that weights like the IAPM demands are not preferred; and on the other hand, that choice is dependent on the investment possibilities the investor perceives.

Fernandes, Peña, and Tabak (2009) put different behavioural explanations in a model to explain portfolio choice. The different elements of prospect theory are incorporated in a utility function: mental accounting (gains and losses are considered, not final wealth), loss aversion, asymmetric risk preference (individuals seem to be less risk averse after a loss and more risk averse after a gain) and probability weighting function (underestimation of high probabilities and overestimation of low probabilities). The goal is to find out about the cost in return due to non-rational behaviour compared to a rational choice. In the modelled world, only two assets (riskless and risky) and two periods exist. In the first period, two human biases – at least out of prospect theory – seem to cancel out (Fernandes et al., 2009, p. 15): loss aversion versus asymmetric risk preference. Probability weighting has ambiguous effects, e.g. a low probability of loss might be overestimated and stock is sold instead of kept. The overall picture gives the impression that biases are channelled in a situation in which risk premia (return of the risky asset) are high and induce loss adverse investors to turn towards the risky assets. In a situation of low risk premia, a higher inclination towards the risk-free asset is observed which would match the optimal allocation. In the second period, experiences from the first period are taken into account and asymmetric risk preference as well as return expectations induce different portfolio choices and return levels. The antagonistic part is the experience with gains and losses: a small loss in the first period would either lead to higher risk taking to compensate the losses; on the other hand, with a high loss, the loss aversion effect might dominate. In a second part, the authors test empirically if a behavioural model which includes return estimation risks outperforms the Markowitz model. They conclude that if a risk-return measurement (the Sharpe ratio) is considered, the behavioural models outperform the standard model, while a pure return consideration prefers the traditional model. At first sight, this sounds like a counter position to the usage of clear investment rules like the IAPM. However, first of all, the authors only took the prospect theory into account, not the other behavioural aspects mentioned above; second, they neglected the facts that their model cannot explain current portfolio compositions. If their model would apply, the real portfolios would not show lower performance and higher risk as the optimal portfolio does.

Graham, Harvey, and Huang (2009) show by using survey data that home bias can partly be explained by the "felt competence" of investors. If they feel that they are competent in trading and the better they know a market, the higher the probability of investment in this market is. This is typically applicable for the domestic market. On the other hand, investors who feel knowledgeable in the general field of finance and investment – typically male, wealthy and well-educated people – trade more often and have a higher foreign proportion in their portfolios. The reason behind this is that this type of investor trusts in his or her own judgement to judge on the international benefits, as described above with the overconfidence effect.

Kilka and Weber (2000) follow a similar line of research. The core thesis of the paper is that asymmetric expectations of domestic vs. foreign investors lead to a wrong expectation of returns. The authors show for investors from the US and Germany that the higher the felt competence is, the higher the expected return on a market is. This often leads to an overestimation of the returns on the domestic market. The same overconfidence can be observed for financial products that are considered to be more sophisticated and need a higher competence level.

A further proof for the competence thesis comes from the analysis of investment behaviour of immigrants. One should expect that their bias towards their origin country decreases over time with growing competence with the new home market. Foad (2008) extends the thesis by the thought that information on origin countries is spread in the new home countries and induces a lower home bias for countries with a high immigration proportion. This is indeed confirmed for 28 countries with different levels of immigration for averaged data in the time period 2001 till 2004.

Magi (2005) puts up a model that brings behavioural aspects and home bias together. Home bias is explained by the complexity of financial market information and the missing ability of investors to use all information that would be necessary to make use of the benefit of international diversification. Not all information is used and considered for the whole portfolio. In a new investment decision, only the risk of a single foreign position is perceived that might be higher than the domestic one if not the complete portfolio is incorporated in the decision (Magi, 2005, p. 23). There are hints from Italian data that people with higher education tend to be able to exploit information better and have a higher foreign proportion in their portfolios.

3.5 IAPM – A Plausible Starting Point?

Despite the actual behaviour of investors – is the IAPM a plausible benchmark for the measurement of home bias at all? To remind of the facts: it is still rational for an investor to follow the IAPM and diversify internationally. The main aspects that are discussed are listed in the following paragraphs:

The market portfolio is theoretically an efficient portfolio. Although it is not in all cases empirically founded, the alternative to calculate the optimal portfolio has its difficulties as well, especially concerning the use of historical data and the estimation of returns. Besides the estimation mistakes just addressed, optimal portfolios have greater deviations in the course of time. If the IAPM is considered as a long-term investment strategy in contrast to short-term decisions, it is a plausible direction for investors to take (von Nitzsch and Stotz, 2006, p. 107).

Another positive argument is that the Sharpe ratio is maximized, that is, the risk-return ratio is optimized if an investor follows the IAPM.

International diversification further reduces portfolio variance by diversifying domestic systematic risk. Even if capital markets are strongly correlated in the future, a diversification gain should still be observable.

Finally, the result of most empirical investigations is that although home bias exists, it is declining. Even if measurement and reasons for home bias still face difficulties, the tendency of a declining home bias is strong and cannot be neglected.

Although some factors like the empirically difficult proof of the market portfolio efficiency speak against the use of the IAPM, the alternatives are not convincing either. In addition to these arguments, one should keep in mind that the IAPM is the standard approach in the literature to calculate home bias, and most authors agree that international diversification would be advantageous for investors (e.g. von Nitzsch and Stotz, 2006; or Rowland and Tesar, 2004). I'll follow that tradition and use the IAPM as the starting point for further investigations. Later on, empirics support the findings in the literature.

Which implications does the choice of the IAPM as a benchmark have? I would like to recall that the goal of this dissertation is to find out about the influence of private portfolio decisions on consumption and on business cycle correlation in the EMU-countries. Thus, the first step was to find a plausible investment strategy that fits all investors in EMU regardless of their risk aversion. This is the IAPM. If all investors follow the IAPM, all portfolios in EMU look the same – the (world) market portfolio. The transmission channels then goes from the same returns out of financial wealth to similar consumption and from there to similar cycles.[10] With the acceptance that the IAPM applies, portfolio decisions can be judged in its light, and it can further be assumed that the choice of countries determines return and risk of a portfolio. The IAPM offers not only the insight that diversification is useful, but assumes as well that country diversification (opposed to industry diversification) is the relevant strategy. That international diversification is still more effective as industry diversification is confirmed by many empirical works as discussed above, especially in the light that more specialisation in countries is expected.

One may note, however, that the home bias is not the relevant measure for portfolios. The empirical work in this dissertation is not dependent on whether the IAPM is true or not although the results of the empirical work can be interpreted in the view of it. The relevant measure here is rather whether portfolios are similar.

This deserves further explanation. Consider a situation where two countries in the real world hold assets reciprocally in equal proportions. This would imply

10 Implicitly it is assumed that consumption patterns are similar in different countries.

that their portfolios are completely equal, but they do not follow the IAPM (because in the real world, no two countries make up of 100% of the world portfolio). Their consumption should correlate, and so should their business cycles if financial wealth has a sufficient influence on consumption. A similar portfolio could occur even if international correlation is worthless if investors hold inefficient portfolios or if home bias is measured incorrectly. Still, according to theory, the IAPM is a plausible investment strategy; therefore, the IAPM and the differences from the market portfolio are used as a measure for similarity in the next chapter.

Another indication is appropriate at this place. In the described framework international (consumption) risk sharing, i.e. the amplitude of consumption plays no role. Although consumption smoothing might contribute to business cycle convergence as mentioned above – here, only the similarity of portfolio returns, resulting in similar consumption – are interesting. Ideally, financial returns and consumption show similar developments. If so, it does not matter if the amplitude of the respective factor is large or small.

C. Empirical Analysis

The expectations expressed in the theory part should be confirmed in the empirical part. This includes the thesis of a declining home bias; an analysis of the development of the similarity of portfolio investment; and the focus of the dissertation, the linkage between portfolio investment and consumption correlation; and finally, a confirmation of the linkage between GDP and consumption.

For these aspects, different data is needed: national financial accounts broken down to the kind of investment (bond, shares, other), data from the IMF Coordinated Portfolio Investment Survey (CPIS), financial market capitalization, disposable income, consumption and GDP.

Due to data restrictions, 18 European countries are considered, most of them members of the EMU, including the "core countries". For these countries, the necessary data is provided: Austria, Belgium, Bulgaria, Denmark, Estonia, Finland, France, Germany, Greece, Hungary, Italy, Netherlands, Norway, Portugal, Romania, Slovak Republic, Spain and Sweden.

The time range of the panel is from 1999 to 2006[11] although data cannot be provided for all countries and for all the years. Data availability is mentioned in the text in the respective parts of the corresponding sections.

Chapter C is structured as follows. It starts with the analysis of the status quo of home bias, a topic that has been not been widely substantiated with a recent and broad range of European data so far, as discussed in the theory part. The next step is the analysis of the similarity of portfolios in the sample countries. This aspect, portfolio similarity, has been neglected by theory and empirical analysis in this context in the previous literature. Further steps are taken in the model section which retrieves insights into the question if the similarity of portfolios contributes to a consumption correlation between two countries. The concluding step is to see if the positive relation between consumption correlation and GDP correlation holds although this is an interdependence that is not questioned in the theory. In addition, a two-stage least-squares model follows the question as to how much the variables, especially portfolio similarity, influence GDP correlation via consumption correlation. This means that only the filtered influence of portfolio similarity and two other control variables on GDP correlation is measured.

---

11 The finally used sample ranges from 2001 to 2006 although in same cases lagged variables, the latest from the year 2000, are used.

4. Home Bias – Status quo in Europe

The main goal of this chapter is the investigation of the status quo of home bias in Europe as no sufficient empirical studies are available for the research purpose. On the way to this goal, several other frame data is analyzed as a base for the econometric model that is erected later in the chapter "Empirical Analysis".

The structure of Chapter 4 is as follows. First, an analysis of the general development of financial wealth and its components, e.g. the composition of bonds and shares in private portfolios, is conducted, followed by the description of the calculation of home bias. A depiction of the development of foreign investment builds the base for the calculation of home bias and the assessment of the development. Afterwards, the different portfolio strategies are analysed in the light of the IAPM with the goal to answer the question as to whether the theoretically founded advantages of this investment strategy hold in reality as well. The chapter is concluded with a short summary and a reminder of the question of the connection between home bias, the IAPM and portfolio similarity.

4.1 Development of Private Financial Wealth

The theory part assumes that private financial wealth has a growing influence on consumption because it is supposed to rise further in the future. Indeed, private financial wealth per head turns out to be quite stable in recent years, though in the time period of investigation (2001-2006) a steady increase is recorded. Private financial wealth is calculated from Eurostat data, to wit: from the financial accounts balance sheet. It includes the net positions of cash, deposits, bonds, shares, insurance accruals, and miscellaneous positions.

On average, private financial wealth (measured by the deflated amount of the mentioned positions per capita) increased by 13 %. In earlier periods, the influence of the new economy hype, and the burst of the stock market bubble can be observed in the data as well. In the graph below, averages of private financial wealth over all countries per year are represented by bars. The graph shows that average financial wealth went through a valley starting in 1999 and increased steadily from 2002 on – this is interpreted as a clear sign for a growing influence of private wealth. In 2006, the level of the year 2000 could be reached again. The richest countries are Belgium (around €63k financial wealth per capita), and the Netherlands (€52k) and Italy (€48k) in the time period of 2001 till 2006. The poorest inhabitants can be found in Eastern Europe, in the new EU-member states: in Romania (€1k), Bulgaria (€1k) and the Slovak Republic (€2k).[12]

12 For reasons of a clear arrangement only a selection of countries is denoted in the graph.

The level of private financial wealth has very different starting points, and the development seems to be at first sight roughly speaking the same across countries. The influencing factors of private wealth seem to be similar, which leads to the deduction that a general convergence of private wealth cannot be observed.

However, a closer look at the growth rates of financial wealth of the countries in the sample reveals very different pictures. Particularly the Eastern European countries, they show an astonishing catch-up race to core Europe. Estonia has a growth rate of private financial wealth of about 270 % from 2001 till 2006, Romania 184 %, and Bulgaria 164 %; outside Eastern Europe Denmark's wealth rose by 170 %. On the other hand, in some countries, inhabitants lost money per capita and showed negative growth rates like the Slovak Republic (-41 %), Greece (-9 %) or Portugal (-7 %). An explanation could come from the stock markets: If the proportion of stock market wealth was high on the eve of the new economy bubble, it should have had more influence on the level of wealth.

Graph 7: Private Net Financial Wealth per Head

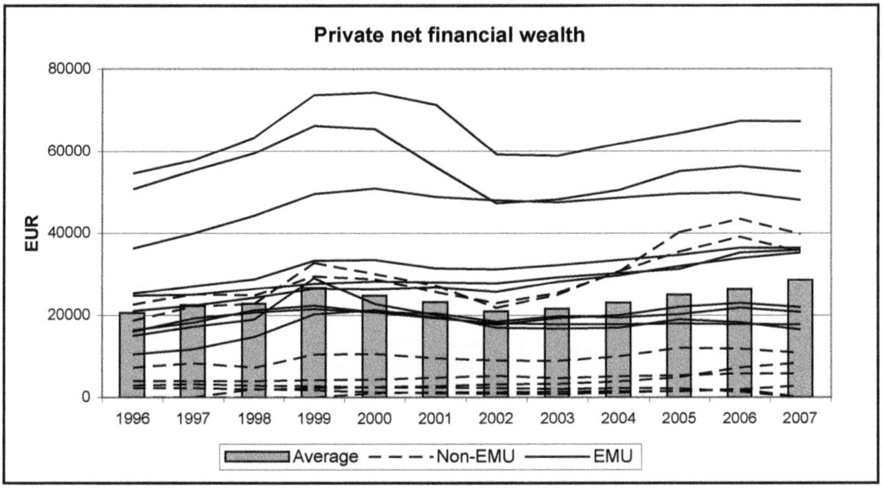

Note: Columns are average values over all countries in the respective year. Lines are individual countries. For reasons of clearness, only selected countries are labelled. Dotted lines specify Non-EMU countries.

Database: Eurostat; own calculations

The different sources of net financial wealth are displayed in Graph 8.

In the time of investigation in the EMU-countries, private financial wealth per capita stayed roughly on the same level (on average €34.2k in 2001 to €36k in 2006). This means, on the other hand, that all changes in country positions of financial wealth sources should be attributed to a re-balancing of the portfolio.

In the EMU-countries, no major shifts in the proportions of the net positions can be observed. The inhabitants of the Non-EMU-countries are less wealthy on average, but as expressed above, they show a great growth rate (average private financial wealth increased from €9.3k in 2001 to €14.1k in 2006). For these countries, an investment tendency towards shares goes to the account of cash and deposits. The other aspect that is revealed by the graph is that, in general, bonds seem to play only a subordinate role in the investment strategy of private households.[13]

Graph 8: Sources of Net Financial Wealth

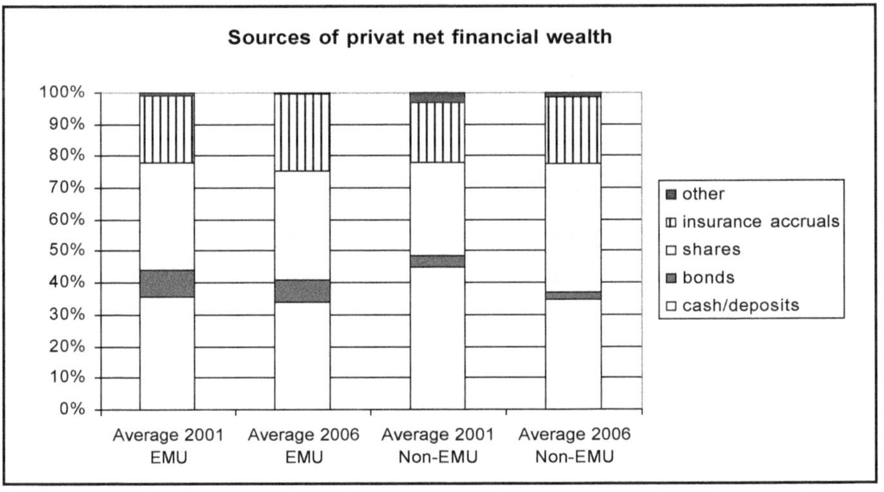

Database: Eurostat; own calculations

Though the picture of investment is quite different in the different countries, Graph 9 shows the proportions of bonds and shares as a part of total private wealth in 2001 and 2006. Only direct investment is considered, not indirect investment in these assets through, among others, pension funds.

Above the thought was expressed that countries whose investing inhabitants lost money might have lost money because of a greater proportion of shares in the portfolio. For the Slovak Republic, no major influence of stock markets can

13 Insurance accruals, a position that (potentially) contains bonds and shares, are not considered in this statement as their exact composition is not available.

be expected though Portugal and Greece showed at least above average proportions. However, their proportion is not much above average. The decline of wealth in these countries must have other backgrounds, e.g. dissaving.

Graph 9: Proportion of Bonds and Shares of Private Net Financial Wealth

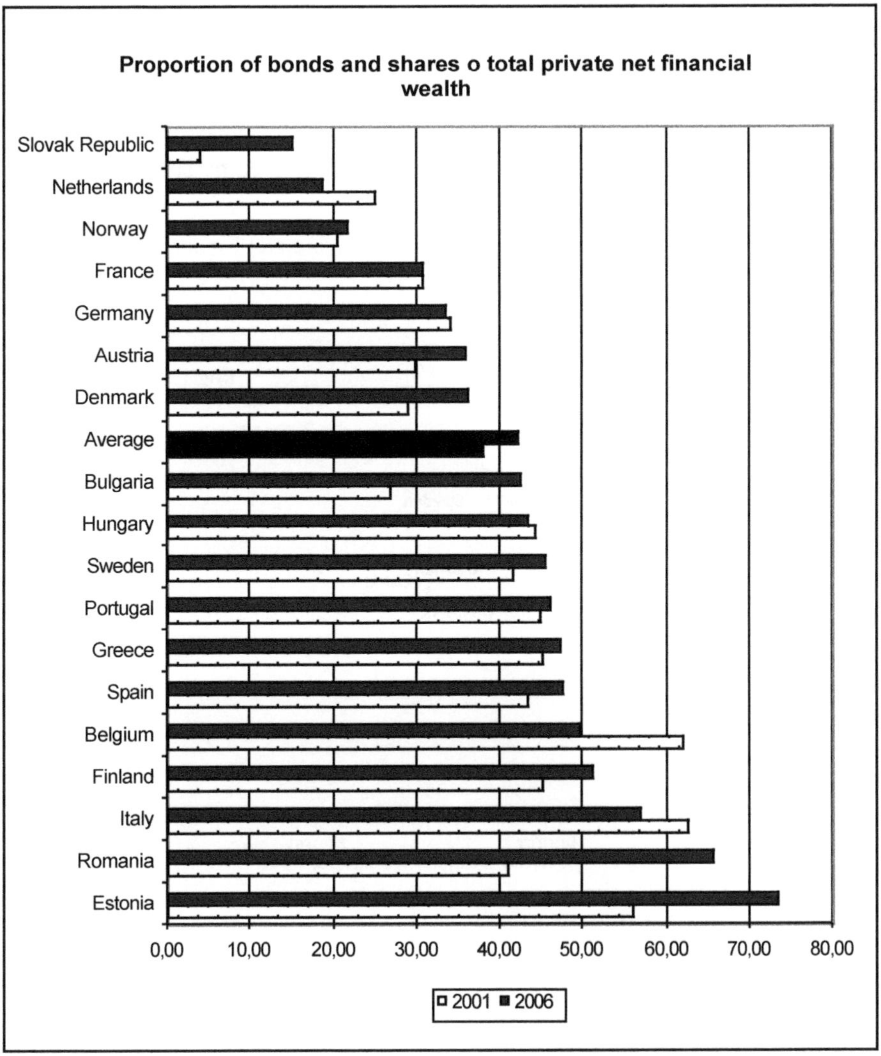

Database: Eurostat; own calculations

On the other hand, the general growth of financial wealth in Estonia or Romania, for example, is reflected by a much higher bond and share proportion in financial wealth if the two years are compared. One can conclude that at least for these countries, a positive stock market development contributed to the increase of financial wealth.

The proportion of bonds and shares in comparison to total private net financial wealth show different characteristics in the different countries. A study concludes that the importance of indirect investment into capital market products via retirement plans and pension funds impairs the importance of direct investment (Bundesverband deutscher Banken, 2004), e.g. in the Netherlands where retirement plans have a long reaching history which is mirrored by small proportions of direct investment.

Graph 10: Proportion of Bonds and Shares vs. Private Net Financial Wealth per Head

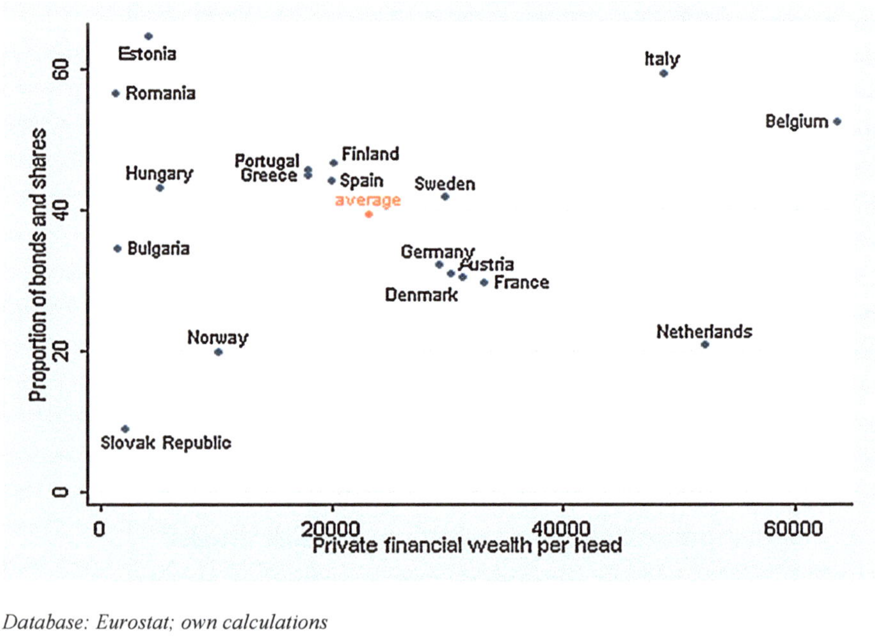

Database: Eurostat; own calculations

Other things equal, the higher financial wealth and the higher the proportion of bonds and shares in the private wealth portfolio, the higher should be the influence of the similarity of portfolios on consumption. The relationship is depicted in Graph 10. Countries like Italy or Belgium (high financial wealth, high proportion of bonds and shares) should therefore exhibit a greater sensitivity towards changes in the stock market, but the sensitivity greatly depends on the diversification qualities of the respective portfolio.

Graph 10 leads to the conclusion that in general, a higher financial wealth per head is usually accompanied by a higher proportion of bonds and shares in the portfolio. However, this statement might not be appropriate for the Eastern European countries. For them, the conclusion might be not applicable because these investment categories started to gain importance in these countries between 2001 and 2006 (as Graph 8 indicates). The investment in bonds and shares needs time to develop and are considered as long-term investments. The preferred investment category in the time before, cash and deposits, do not contribute much to financial wealth.

4.2 Development of Foreign Investment

The first section, development of private financial wealth, shows that wealth has an especially growing influence on bonds and shares, increasing contributors to financial wealth for many countries. The second step is to show the direction of investment – where do countries invest? A first precondition for a declining home bias is that investment in foreign countries increases. Graph 11 shows the averaged proportion of home country and foreign investment. Apart from a slight decline in 2005 foreign investment increased in the countries of the sample. In 2007, foreign and home investment split almost in halves.

Are there pronounced differences between the countries of the EMU and the countries outside? Whereas in the years 2002 till 2006, EMU-countries clearly decreased their home country investment; the Non-EMU-countries did so as well but less severe as the EMU countries. A change is observed in the year 2007, the first year in which compared to 2001 the Non-EMU-countries have a higher growth rate of foreign investment proportions as the EMU countries. This is probably due to a greater financial harmonization between EMU and Non-EMU countries that took place and finally gained ground. In 2006, EMU countries had a proportion of foreign investment 3.16 times as large as in 2001 (2007 compared to 2001: 3.95 as large), and in Non-EMU countries, the proportion was 3.04 times as high (2007: 4.20 times).

Split in countries,[14] the country with the lowest home country investment on average between 2001 and 2007 is Norway (41 %) followed by Austria (49 %) and Belgium (51 %). The other side of the range is built by the Eastern European countries (Romania 99 % home country investment, Hungary 97 % and Bulgaria 92 %).

---

14 Tables can be found in Data Appendix 1.

Graph 11: (Unweighted) Average Proportions of Home Country and Foreign Investment

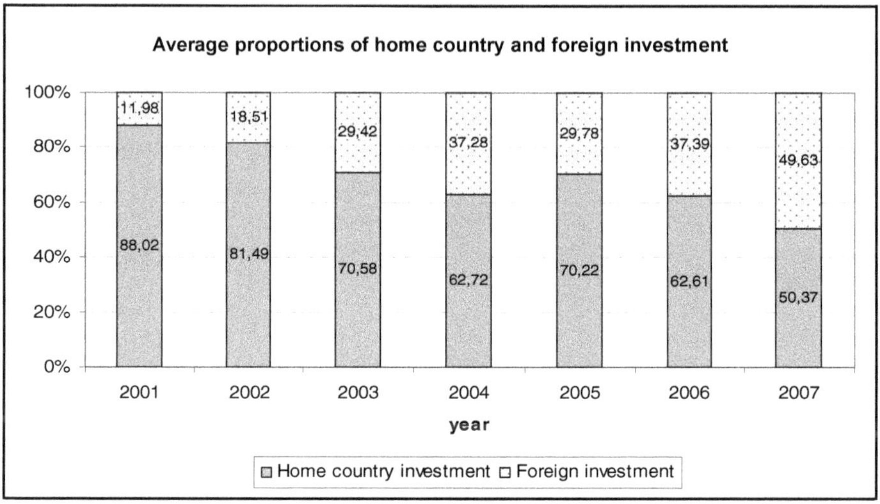

Database: Eurostat; IMF; own calculations

Graph 12: Comparison of Foreign Investment

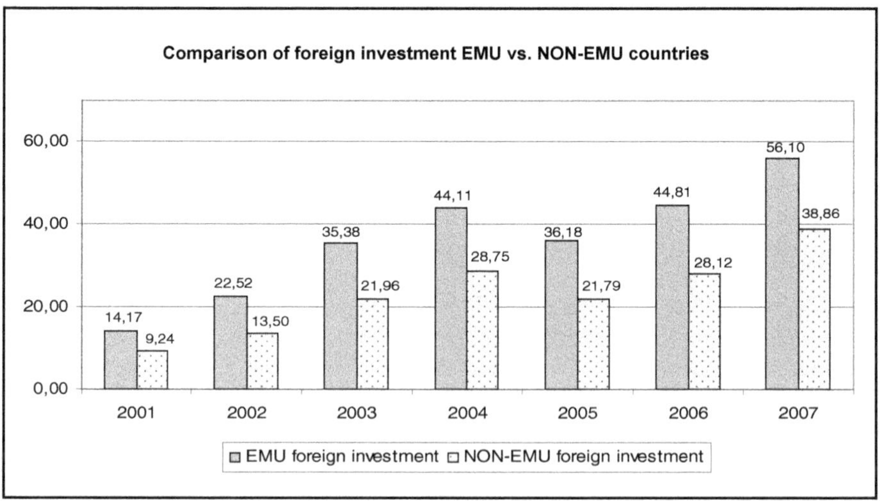

Database: Eurostat; IMF; own calculations

A question that is only initially a simple question is: What should be considered as the home country? "Home" in investment categories is not necessarily just within the political borders, but it can be considered as a financially integrated area as well. An option is to consider the Eurozone as "home country investment" with the justification that the financial markets within the EMU are open and have the same currency. It is expected that EMU countries tend to invest increasingly within the EMU and exhibit an EMU-bias (as stated in Section 3.4.3, see the therein mentioned studies of Lane (2006) or Bosch and Schoenmaker (2008)). To see whether this approach is justified for the EMU countries, the proportion of investment within the EMU, but excluding the home country, is calculated. Graph 13 below shows that indeed an EMU-bias can be observed. The proportions of investment inside EMU, but outside the home country, increased clearly over the time period 2001 to 2007. The consequence of this development is that it should be considered if home bias is calculated as a bias towards the Eurozone opposed to a calculation of home bias in the "classical sense". In the light of Europe and especially an EMU that grows together and the fact that the EMU seems to be growingly accepted as the home market, the definition of the EMU as the home country should be a plausible approach and is tracked in the next sections.

What about the population of the eight countries in the sample which are outside the EMU? What is their attitude towards the Eurozone as an investment-zone? Most of these countries are in the meanwhile already using the euro as a currency (e.g. the Slovak Republic), aiming to join the Eurozone (e.g. Bulgaria), or are being part of the exchange rate mechanism (Denmark, Estonia). As Graph 14 demonstrates, for most countries, the expectations of an increased investment inside the EMU are fulfilled, with the exception of countries like Romania which show a distinct home bias over the whole period. Other countries like the Slovak Republic or Denmark show a declining trend after years of a more pronounced investment into the Eurozone.

Graph 13: Investment Inside EMU – Outside Home Country

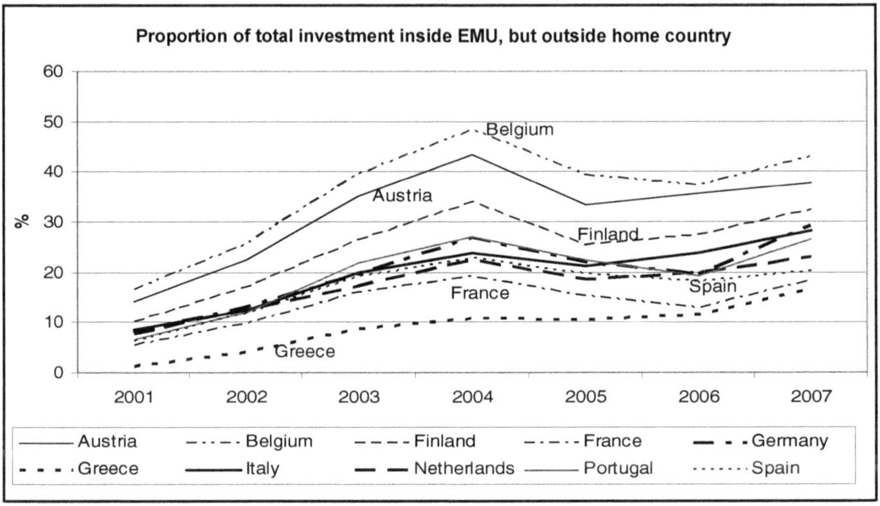

Database: Eurostat; IMF; own calculations

Graph 14: EMU-investment of Non-EMU Countries

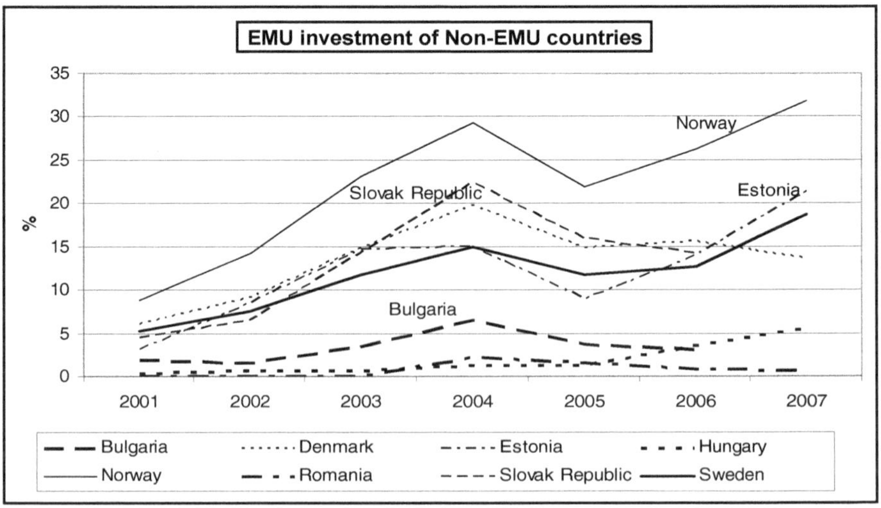

Database: Eurostat; IMF; own calculations

To gain more insights into the investment behaviour and strategies, an interesting feature is to know where the money of the countries in the sample goes if it does not flow into the EMU. It can be deducted from the portfolio tables in the Data Appendix 2 that investment flows mainly to other EU-countries (on average over all years and countries 37 % of total investment) and to the Americas (7 %). In recent years, proportions of the Americas raised significantly, whereas the EU-countries lost proportions. This can be interpreted as a tendency of re-allocation of investment from EU to Americas, which would be consistent with the IAPM because the Americas are so far underrepresented in portfolios (see Section 4.5). Other regions of the world make up only minor proportions of the portfolios.

Graph 15: Factor of Foreign Investment in Neighbour Countries to Other Foreign Countries

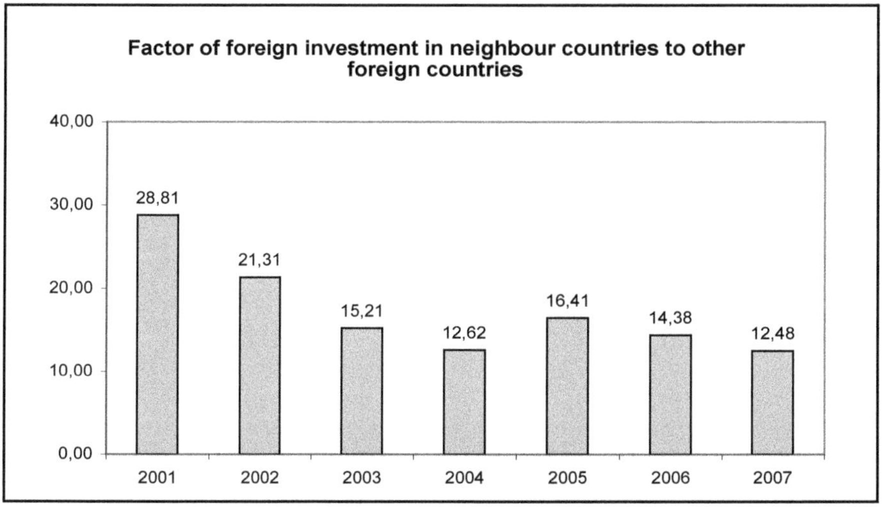

Database: Eurostat; IMF; own calculations

As discussed in Section 3.4.4.2: one of the explanations of home bias is that investors feel more competent to invest at home because they feel better informed about the market and the issuing businesses. It would be a logical consequence that investment in neighbouring countries is more pronounced as compared to overall foreign investment because a similar effect of "felt knowledge and competence" of investors could at least be a plausible consequence. Graph 15 shows that on average, investments in a neighbouring country is about twelve to twenty-eight times higher (depending on the chosen year) than those in another foreign country. This kind of "neighbour bias" is declining over the years with our already familiar contrary evolution in 2005. This leads to the conclusion that the financial links to neighbouring countries tend to be closer as compared to other countries although their importance declines with a proceeding investment abroad as demonstrated above. Reasons for international investment behaviour could be the globally growing financial integration and a higher interest in portfolio strategies, leading to more investment abroad. As a consequence, investors are closer to the recommendations of the IAPM.

In the table below, the development of foreign investment in neighbour countries and non-neighbouring countries are listed for the countries of the sample. It is expected that countries which have several borders tend to invest more in neighbour countries. The reasons are first, the "felt competence" ranges over all neighbour-countries; second, if the IAPM is followed, not too much weight should be put on just one neighbour country (depending on its market size) to gain diversification effects. To compare countries with different numbers of borders and to level out the corresponding effect, the average investment in one bordering country is calculated and compared to average investment in other foreign countries.

Table 2: Proportion of Average Investment to Foreign Investment

Proportion of average investment of total foreign investment in ...

Investing country	2001			2002			2003			2004		
	a) (all)	b) (one)	c) (another)	a) (all)	b) (one)	c) (another)	a) (all)	b) (one)	c) (another)	a) (all)	b) (one)	c) (another)
Austria	35.05	4.38	0.17	36.99	4.62	0.26	37.58	4.70	0.39	36.60	4.57	0.45
Belgium	51.06	12.77	0.10	51.18	12.79	0.15	51.84	12.96	0.21	52.13	13.03	0.25
Bulgaria	0.52	0.09	0.50	6.68	1.11	0.28	5.31	0.89	0.37	6.22	1.04	0.40
Denmark	14.32	14.32	0.17	18.80	18.80	0.19	17.76	17.76	0.31	19.06	19.06	0.37
Estonia	1.40	1.40	0.25	4.70	2.35	0.29	3.63	1.82	0.61	4.19	2.09	0.63
Finland	13.29	6.65	0.68	11.33	5.67	1.12	12.35	6.17	0.75	11.27	5.64	1.07
France	38.26	6.38	0.07	42.51	7.09	0.08	43.56	7.26	0.13	41.62	6.94	0.16
Germany	43.19	4.32	0.09	44.10	4.41	0.14	45.55	4.56	0.19	44.21	4.42	0.24
Greece	2.01	0.50	0.07	0.89	0.22	0.21	0.45	0.11	0.41	0.99	0.25	0.49
Hungary	7.15	0.89	0.03	9.28	1.16	0.03	7.23	0.90	0.03	8.87	1.11	0.05
Italy	8.08	2.02	0.12	9.43	2.36	0.18	9.50	2.37	0.28	9.90	2.47	0.32
Netherlands	17.78	8.89	0.15	22.58	11.29	0.21	20.97	10.49	0.26	20.58	10.29	0.31
Norway	4.64	4.64	0.40	5.45	5.45	0.66	4.96	4.96	0.82	3.59	3.59	0.73
Portugal	6.47	6.47	0.25	5.19	5.19	0.55	5.43	5.43	0.91	5.80	5.80	1.14
Romania	0.00	0.00	0.01	0.00	0.00	0.02	0.00	0.00	n.a.	0.00	0.00	1.06
Slovak Republic	0.70	0.23	0.19	0.83	0.28	0.26	20.95	6.98	0.64	16.96	5.65	0.67
Spain	12.98	6.49	0.15	11.15	5.58	0.23	13.44	6.72	0.34	13.52	6.76	0.41
Sweden	6.20	3.10	0.18	5.60	2.80	0.21	5.51	2.75	0.34	5.55	2.77	0.40
Average	14.62	4.64	0.16	15.93	5.07	0.24	17.00	5.38	0.35	16.73	5.30	0.42

Only non-maritime borders are considered.

a) ... investment in all neighbour-countries. Proportion of investment in all neighbour countries.

b) ... in one neighbour-country. Investment in one neighbour-country is the average of investment in neighbour countries to compare countries with different numbers of neighbour countries.

c) ... in one foreign country that is no neigbour. Investment in one foreign country is the average of investment in a foreign country that is no neighbour country.

Database: Eurostat; IMF; own calculations

Table 2: Proportion of Average Investment to Foreign Investment (continued)

Proportion of average investment of total foreign investment in ...

Investing country	**2005**			**2006**			**2007**		
	a) (all)	b) (one)	c) (another)	a) (all)	b) (one)	c) (another)	a) (all)	b) (one)	c) (another)
Austria	34.20	4.27	0.35	33.06	4.13	0.42	33.16	4.15	0.41
Belgium	53.82	13.46	0.19	53.38	13.34	0.17	52.16	13.04	0.32
Bulgaria	7.48	1.25	0.16	12.67	2.11	0.20	n.a.	n.a.	n.a.
Denmark	16.51	16.51	0.29	15.45	15.45	0.34	12.42	12.42	0.32
Estonia	7.07	3.54	0.30	7.09	3.54	0.50	8.42	4.21	0.62
Finland	12.63	6.31	0.71	12.54	6.27	0.94	14.67	7.33	1.05
France	41.36	6.89	0.13	41.48	6.91	0.16	41.40	6.90	0.19
Germany	42.36	4.24	0.18	40.77	4.08	0.23	42.57	4.26	0.32
Greece	1.14	0.28	0.47	1.54	0.38	0.63	1.58	0.40	0.95
Hungary	11.05	1.38	0.05	11.07	1.38	0.09	12.28	1.53	0.14
Italy	10.19	2.55	0.22	12.34	3.09	0.26	12.95	3.24	0.28
Netherlands	18.52	9.26	0.28	17.37	8.69	0.29	13.98	6.99	0.40
Norway	3.85	3.85	0.55	3.51	3.51	0.79	3.87	3.87	0.89
Portugal	5.42	5.42	0.81	8.36	8.36	0.49	10.18	10.18	0.76
Romania	0.02	0.01	0.14	0.00	0.00	0.20	0.35	0.12	0.08
Slovak Republic	8.58	2.86	0.49	5.81	1.94	0.52	n.a.	n.a.	n.a.
Spain	16.14	8.07	0.30	14.47	7.23	0.36	15.92	7.96	0.38
Sweden	6.21	3.10	0.43	8.30	4.15	0.35	7.91	3.95	0.44
Average	16.47	5.18	0.32	16.62	5.25	0.37	17.74	5.66	0.45

Only non-maritime borders are considered.

a) ... investment in all neighbour-countries. Proportion of investment in all neighbour countries.

b) ... in one neighbour-country. Investment in one neighbour-country is the average of investment in neighbour countries to compare countries with different numbers of neighbour countries.

c) ... in one foreign country that is no neigbour. Investment in one foreign country is the average of investment in a foreign country that is no neighbour country.

Database: Eurostat; IMF; own calculations

The trend towards a lower neighbour bias is not the same in all countries. A high decline in neighbour bias is shown by, for example, Norway, Finland, and Austria (development of column b)). Negative developments (i.e. a higher neighbour bias compared to other foreign investment) can be observed in Bulgaria, the Slovak Republic or Estonia. However, for the latter countries, the foreign investment is that small that it is difficult to draw significant conclusions. Are there common driving factors for the development of Norway, Finland, and Austria? Common factors could be the initial level of foreign investment or the proportion of bonds and shares. In 2001, all of the three mentioned countries exhibited a higher proportion of foreign investment as the average in this year (average foreign investment: 11.98 %). Another interesting characteristic is the proportion of bonds and shares. As depicted in Graph 9, the only country above average is Finland; Norway and Austria are below average. The inclusion of both characteristics as candidates for common factors are motivated by the idea that investors with high foreign investment and high proportions of bonds and shares are expected to be more concerned about portfolio theory as others. At least, a general conclusion cannot be drawn.

One more common driving factor for the development of total foreign investment could be private financial wealth. Countries that are richer, like the EMU-countries, tend to invest more internationally (see description of Graph 7 and Graph 12). This leads to the conclusion that wealth itself is important for portfolio strategies, probably due to the significance of wealth and the easier access to financial markets. The significance of financial wealth is therefore considered explicitly in the econometric model.

Summarized, foreign investment grew substantially. A pronounced tendency to invest within the EMU is observed and leads to the assumption that the whole euro area should be considered as the home country for the EMU countries. The development of foreign investment is probably influenced by the amount of financial wealth per capita, which can be deducted by the differences between EMU and Non-EMU countries. The proportion of bonds and shares does not provide unambiguous effects for the development of foreign investment.

4.3 Calculation of Home Bias

As discussed in the theory part, there are not many recent studies on the status quo of home bias in Europe – a gap that is filled by the following two sections. Broadly speaking, home bias is defined by the deviation between the home country proportion of the optimal (i.e. the market) portfolio and the portfolio held in reality. The market portfolio consists of country proportions that correspond to their respective weights in the world capital market.

Literature follows different ways to calculate the optimal weights of each country. The approach of De Santis and Gérard (2006) was used in accordance to former studies, e.g. by the IMF or in a later study of Bosch and Schoenmaker (2008). These studies use the Foreign Asset Acceptance Ratio (FAAR). This index measures the proportion of total foreign holdings in a portfolio to ideal foreign proportion in a portfolio.

$$HB_{it} = 1 - \frac{fs_{it}}{fs_{it}^{*}} \qquad \textbf{F 18}$$

with HB = *home bias*
i = *country index*
t = *time index*
fs = *held proportion of foreign investment in the portfolio*
fs^{*} = *optimal proportion of foreign investment in the portfolio*

The optimal proportion of foreign investment for a country is determined by its share in the world market:

$$fs^{*} = \frac{mc_i}{\sum_{it}^{n} mc} \qquad \textbf{F 19}$$

with n = *number of countries in the world portfolio*
mc = *market capitalisation*

The higher the optimal foreign portfolio share is, the more pronounced other things equal the home bias is. To take into account that the Eurozone is considered as one country, that is, that the share of all EMU countries (inside and outside the sample) is taken as the optimal home country investment, the market capitalisation of all EMU countries is summed up. Consequently, foreign investment is the investment outside the Eurozone. For Non-EMU countries foreign investment is the investment outside the home country.

The ideal proportion is derived by the IAPM. Consequently, a country should invest an amount abroad that corresponds to one minus the optimal home country share. The optimal share fs^{*} is determined by the weight of a country in the world market; to be more precise, the weight is the market capitalization of a country. Put in other words: The optimal (market) portfolio proportion corresponds to the proportion of the market capitalization of the respective country. There are basically two data alternatives as possible proxies for the true market capitalization: indices or stock market capitalization data.

De Santis and Gérard (2006) use the Datastream Equity World Index, but two countries, Estonia and the Slovak Republic, are not represented in the Datastream Equity World Index. Indices might be constructed in a way that do not reflect the market capitalization but that are optimized with accordance to the return situation. Unfortunately the Datastream index seems to comprise implausible data for some countries, e.g. the market weight of Indonesia does not correspond to its share of the world market capitalization for the given time horizon of the study.[15]

An alternative is to use stock market capitalization data. World wide data is available from the World Federation of Exchanges. The federation comprises the stock market capitalisation of 54 stock exchanges (including the biggest exchanges like the New York Stock Exchange, NASDAQ, and obliged to use the same statistics definitions (World Exchange Federation, 2012). The data is used by several studies, e.g. by a Bank of International Settlement publication (Garcia-Herrero and Wooldrige, 2007) and other authors (e.g. Sercu and Vanpée, 2007). The usage of this data has two drawbacks:

First, some stock exchanges of the 18 sample countries are not part of the World Federation of Exchanges. For this reason the data of Bulgaria, Romania and the Slovak Republic had to be amended with the stock market capitalization data of Eurostat.[16] Although the definitions of market capitalization differ slightly between these two data sources it seems to be the better way to amend instead of neglecting theses countries completely.

The second challenge is that several countries share one stock exchange. One example is the NYSE Euronext, a market that comprises Belgium, France, the Netherlands and Portugal. This means that the market capitalization of these countries cannot be allocated to different countries anymore. As I treat the Eurozone as one country and the mentioned countries of the NYSE Euronext are all part of the monetary union this issue can be solved. On the other hand the NASDAQ OMX Nordic Exchange comprises Finland as an EMU country and among others Denmark and Finland as Non-EMU-countries of the sample. Single data on the countries of the Nordic Exchange is available for three years (2001-2003) in the time range of the study. I assume that the mean proportion of Finland in these three years in relation to the other countries of the Nordic exchange stayed the same in the years 2004 to 2007. With this value Finland was integrated as part of the market capitalization the whole EMU has. The alternative to neglect Finland probably produces higher deviations from the true market weights compared to the assumption of a static proportion.

---

15 I am grateful for this insight by my second supervisor, Prof. Dr. Hans-Peter Burghof.

16 Eurostat data only comprises parts of the world wide markets and is only used as an amendment for this reason.

To sum up: The world market portfolio is estimated by the sum of stock market capitalization of the World Federation of Exchanges and amended by Eurostat stock market data that is not covered by the World Federation of Exchanges. For the Eurozone assumptions with regard to Finland as a part of the Nordic Exchange have to be allowed.

One question unanswered so far is how the proportion of home country investment is measured exactly. To calculate home bias (and later in Section 5.1 the specialisation index SPEC), the proportion of domestic shares in a portfolio must be known. The major data source, the Coordinated Portfolio Investment Survey (CPIS) coordinated by the IMF (see Section 5.1 for more details), does not contain information about home investment since its focus is on foreign investment. The domestic share needs to be calculated as follows:

Total foreign portfolio investment of a country as denoted by the CPIS is aggregated and converted to euro. The year's end exchange rate from US-dollars to euro as denoted by Eurostat is used because the CPIS is conducted on year's-end levels. Domestic wealth is calculated as the difference between total portfolio investment (from Eurostat data) and foreign wealth (from CPIS data).

The total wealth of portfolio assets of residents can be derived from the financial accounts balance sheet from Eurostat. The used values are approximately consistent with the CPIS data and contain bonds, shares and insurance accruals. In the case of the insurance accruals it is ambiguous as to whether or not they should be taken into account. They account on average 13.5 % of total financial wealth in the 18 countries of the study. The question at hand is whether life insurances or pension funds mainly invest in portfolio assets, and therefore, represent a part of portfolio wealth that should be considered in total portfolio wealth. Investment regulations for insurance companies usually allow bonds and shares as means to invest the technical accruals (e.g. in Germany, the Netherlands, or Norway). Shares may represent at least a certain proportion of accruals, whereas bonds are usually unrestricted. For these reasons – investment possibility and the importance of this asset class for total wealth – investment accruals are considered in the calculation. The consequence is that the domestic share of total investment might be somewhat overestimated.

For the calculation of total investment, only the asset side of the balance sheet is taken into account. The reason lies in the view of an investor. Only the personal investment is from this point of view the relevant factor and the criterion to decide according to the CAPM. Net views (compensation with liabilities, i.e. investments from abroad in the home country of an investor) are not appropriate in this case because an investor will not probably take the liability side into account for investment decisions.

The Eurostat financial accounts balance sheet is much more detailed as the CPIS. The holders of wealth can be identified and are chosen according to the CPIS criteria corresponding to the data manual of the study (International Monetary Fund, 2002) to match the data. Security holders include corporate entities (financial and non-financial), insurance companies, government entities, non-profit institutions and individuals. Their financial wealth is aggregated to total financial wealth.

Domestic wealth is total financial wealth according to the Eurostat balance sheet minus foreign wealth according to CPIS. This output quantity is used in the portfolio tables to calculate the proportion of domestic wealth to total wealth. This procedure has the advantage that it is consistent in itself – foreign and domestic wealth must aggregate to total wealth.

The corresponding calculation appears as follows:

$bonds_i + shares_i + insurance\ accruals_i = total\ wealth_i$
$total\ wealth_i - foreign\ wealth_i = domestic\ wealth_i$
i = country index

Examples for other approaches from the literature (De Santis and Gérard, 2006) are to take the sum of domestic equity and bond market capitalization plus the foreign holding of the country minus foreigners' holdings in the respective country identified by CPIS data. This method has the disadvantage that different data sources are needed (Datastream for equities and data from the Bank for International Settlements for bonds), and that securities held as reserve assets are included in the market capitalization sums. Reserve assets are not included in the CPIS data used for the calculation of foreign wealth. For this reason, an inclusion of reserve assets in the calculation of total wealth would mean an overestimation of domestic assets.

Calculations of the domestic portfolio value are the last step before calculating the proportions of investment in each country and apply it to the formula to calculate home bias. The approach has the great advantage as compared to earlier studies that no assumptions on prior allocations of capital are needed. In earlier studies, it is often assumed that net capital flows represent the actual holdings of capital in the respective beginning year; the prior allocation is therefore considered implicitly as zero or according to the market capitalisation (see Lapp, 2001, p. 67 et seqq. and the literature therein).

4.4 Status quo of Home Bias

Many empirical studies consider due to data limitations only a few countries with regard to home bias or with a very limited time series. Two exceptions considering the analyzed countries are the already mentioned studies of De Santis and Gérard (2006) or the one by Lane (2006) (see Table 1 above for an overview). Still for most countries in my sample, either no recent information on the status quo of home bias is available, or information is not detailed enough for my purposes. This section closes the gap in the literature and provides a detailed overview over the developments in recent years. The question posed and answered is whether home bias really is declining. A decline is taken as a sign for a growing financial integration. A special focus should be put on the EMU countries because their home bias is expected to decline significantly, especially if the results of the Section 4.2 (rising financial wealth and proportions of foreign investment) are considered.

Although it is expected that a decrease of foreign investment and home bias would go hand in hand, the main difference is that the concept of home bias considers that it might be optimal to invest (mainly) in one's home country if the respective market capitalization is high enough.

Table 3: Home Bias – EMU Countries

	2001	2002	2003	2004	2005	2006	2007
Austria	0.89	0.84	0.78	0.73	0.79	0.73	0.73
Belgium	0.94	0.91	0.88	0.87	0.90	0.85	0.79
Finland	0.91	0.87	0.80	0.73	0.79	0.70	0.58
France	0.95	0.93	0.89	0.86	0.89	0.85	0.81
Germany	0.94	0.92	0.88	0.86	0.89	0.84	0.76
Greece	0.98	0.93	0.86	0.76	0.78	0.70	0.52
Italy	0.92	0.91	0.87	0.85	0.88	0.87	0.85
Netherlands	0.90	0.87	0.77	0.73	0.78	0.74	0.67
Portugal	0.94	0.90	0.86	0.83	0.87	0.82	0.79
Spain	0.96	0.92	0.87	0.84	0.88	0.84	0.81

Database: World Federation of Exchanges; Eurostat; IMF; own calculations

Table 4: Home Bias – Non-EMU Countries

	2001	2002	2003	2004	2005	2006	2007
Bulgaria	n/a	n/a	n/a	0,90	0,93	0,94	n/a
Denmark	0.83	0.78	0.64	n/a	n/a	n/a	n/a
Estonia	0.96	0.89	0.79	0.74	n/a	n/a	n/a
Hungary	0.99	0.99	0.99	0.98	0.98	0.95	0.92
Norway	0.75	0.61	0.43	n/a	n/a	n/a	n/a
Romania	n/a	n/a	n/a	n/a	0.98	0.99	0.99
Slovak Republic	n/a	n/a	0.76	0.60	0.74	0.74	n/a
Sweden	0.85	0.81	0.71	n/a	n/a	n/a	n/a

Database: World Federation of Exchanges; Eurostat; IMF; own calculations

Table 3 and 4 and graphs 16 and 17 below show that – as expected – home bias declined substantially. Especially in the EMU countries, the trend towards less home bias is clear. The average (unweighted) home bias of EMU countries in 2001 amounts to 93.22 % compared to 73.34 % in 2007 (Table 3). The trend throughout the EMU countries of the sample is very similar though the dimension of decline is different. In Greece home bias drops by 45 %. This enormous decline is partly achieved because of the treatment of the Eurozone as one country. Greece still invests more than 40 % at home but increased investment outside EMU (especially in the UK) substantially. The smallest reduction can be observed in Italy with roughly 6.8 % decline. The results confirm that home bias is declining even if "foreign" means outside the EMU. In sum the development shows that financial integration takes place globally and that investors indeed seem to follow the basic ideas of modern portfolio theory: it is not neglected that an investment abroad, including outside the EMU, is favourable.

Graph 16: Development of Home Bias (EMUcountries)

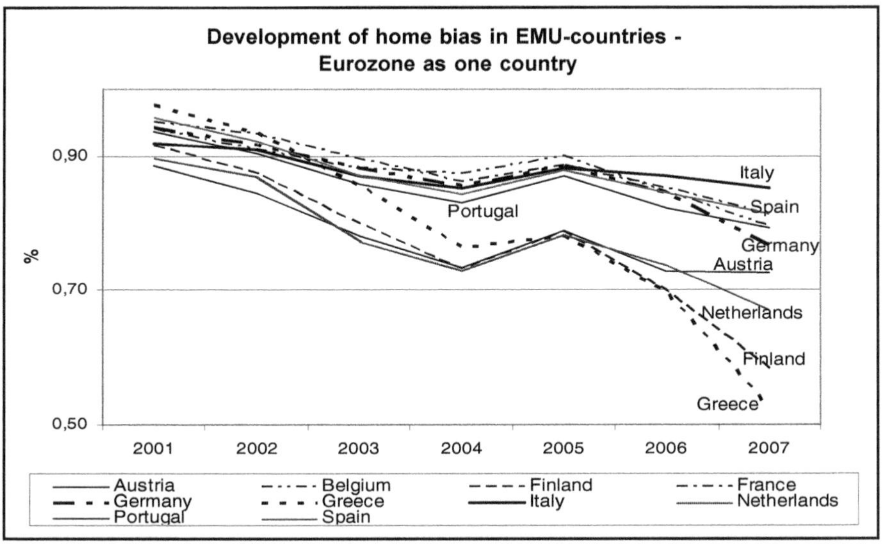

Database: World Federation of Exchanges; Eurostat; IMF; own calculations

For the Non-EMU countries a comparison of home bias in percent is not adequate because the data base differs too much as Graph 17 and Table 4 show. Still, a first indication of the results is a declining home bias in most countries. Especially the Scandinavian countries, Norway, Denmark and Sweden are to be mentioned. Estonia displays a similar development towards a lower home bias. In contrast the astern European countries, Bulgaria, Hungary, Romania and the Slovak Republic are far more reluctant with investment abroad.

Graph 17: Development of Home Bias (GDP Weights)

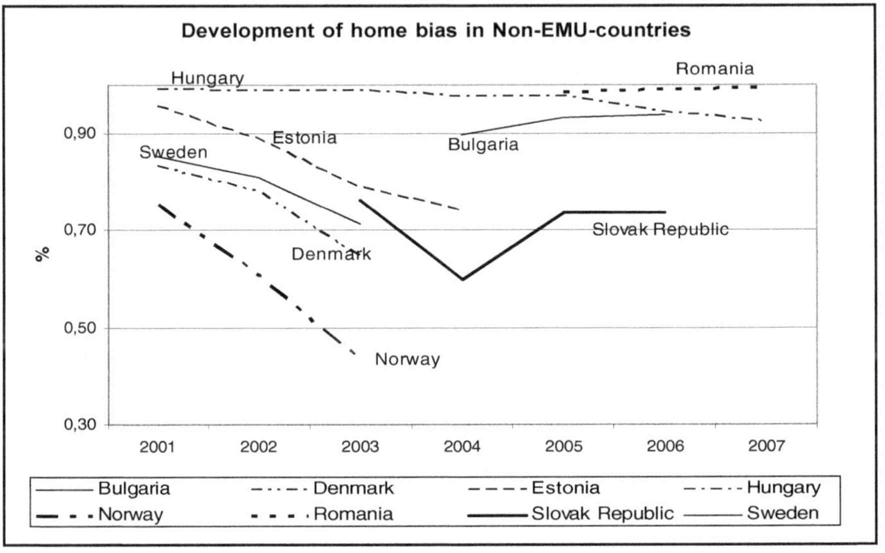

Database: World Federation of Exchanges; Eurostat; IMF; own calculations

4.5 The Market Portfolio as the Ideal Portfolio

The optimal portfolio is according to the IAPM the market portfolio and should be held by all countries. What does it look like, and how much do the countries deviate from this ideal? The question is interesting because it asks whether private investors follow the basic ideas of portfolio theory and adjust their portfolios accordingly. This would imply as well that a re-balancing of portfolio weights towards the market portfolio should be observable.

The market portfolio is determined as stated above in the section "calculation of home bias". The world market is defined in different ways in the literature (e.g. only the countries with a certain market capitalization are considered (Bosch and Schoenmaker, 2008) or all countries). As mentioned above I use the stock market capitalization of the stock exchanges that are members of the World Federation of Exchanges as a proxy for the true market capitalization.

The highest proportion for a single country is for the United States of America although they lose weight between 2001 and 2006.[17] The winner in proportions from 2001 to 2006 is the regions of Asia and Arabia (as a single stock market the Hong Kong Stock exchange is the major market). Africa (major market: Johannesburg stock exchange) and Australia and Oceania (major market: Australian stock exchange) are not very important for the word market. For the EMU countries not much change took place in the time range of the observation.

Graph 18: The World Market Portfolio

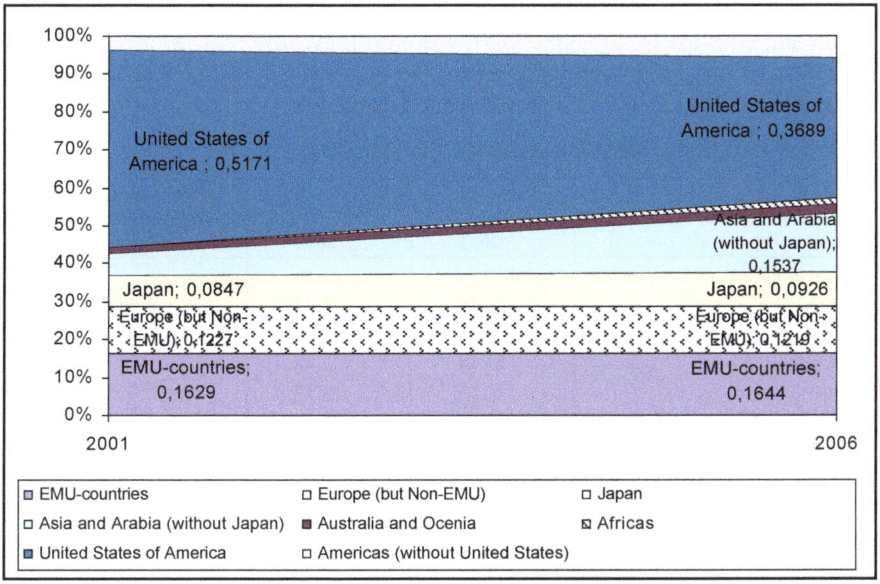

Database: World Federation of Exchanges, Eurostat; IMF; own calculations

The question as to how over- and underweight country-proportions are, present in the portfolios, is investigated by calculating the deviations from actual proportions to ideal proportions. Because over- and underweight country-proportions sum up to zero, the absolute deviations are taken as a measure if portfolio theory is taken account of.

Indeed, portfolio weights changed according to theory, the absolute deviation from the optimal weights decreased if the years 2001 and 2006 are compared. Outside the EMU, the changes have been slightly more pronounced as in the

17 The time period of 2001 to 2006 was chosen although data for 2007 is available. The reason is that econometric model bases on the shorter time period due to other data restrictions.

other countries of the sample. On average, deviation decreased by 33.92 % in Non-EMU-countries compared to 32.89 % to EMU-countries. The Scandinavian countries (Norway, Denmark, Sweden,and Finland) are the countries that show the greatest changes, while an even negative change (a re-balancing of portfolios against the principles of the IAPM) can be observed in Bulgaria. The permanence of the portfolios in the Eastern-European countries (Hungary, Romania and Bulgaria) show that financial integration and the benefits of diversification are not established principles yet. The exception is the Slovak Republic with a re-balance of the portfolio above average. On average and absolute levels the departure from the ideal portfolio is comparable between the country-groups (EMU and Non-EMU) though countries are on quite different levels concerning the effort to copy the world portfolio. The general picture is that investment strategies become closer to the world market portfolio.

Table 5: Deviations from Optimal Portfolio Weights

	2001	2006	change of absolute deviation from optimal portfolio weights
EMU-countries			
Austria	50,74	26,13	24,61
Belgium	52,69	27,56	25,14
Finland	53,18	27,43	25,75
France	53,25	31,19	22,07
Germany	53,34	30,91	22,43
Greece	54,91	25,77	29,13
Italy	52,08	32,96	19,13
Netherlands	50,30	26,27	24,03
Portugal	52,71	28,19	24,52
Spain	53,93	31,56	22,37
Average EMU-countries	*52,71*	*28,80*	*23,92*
Non-EMU-countries			
Bulgaria	50,51	40,65	9,87
Denmark	50,93	25,01	25,93
Estonia	55,37	36,91	18,46
Hungary	55,20	41,46	13,74
Norway	48,44	11,69	36,75
Romania	55,54	42,59	12,95
Slovak Republic	54,89	33,43	21,46
Sweden	50,34	28,01	22,33
Average Non-EMU-countries	*52,65*	*32,47*	*20,19*
Average overall	*52,69*	*30,43*	*22,26*

Database: World Federation of Exchanges; Eurostat; IMF; own calculations

The detailed investment strategies behind the aggregates presented in the table above are shown by the two graphs below. For a better overview, the deviations of investment are aggregated to regions of the world.

Several details are noteworthy:

- The general allocation to regions
- The shifts observed in the time range of the two years 2001 and 2006.
- The different developments of EMU and Non-EMU-countries.

The graphs are first separated into the two country-groups (EMU vs. Non-EMU), and in a second step, into the years 2001 and 2006. The most exact investment is achieved in the regions Africa and Australia and Oceania with the simple explanation that the respective market capitalization is small compared to the rest of the world and does not play a major role in the actual portfolios the same time. It is no surprise is that the EMU-countries exhibit the highest overweight in the EMU-countries due to the still existing home bias phenomenon.

Graph 19: Deviation from Market Portfolio – EMU-Countries

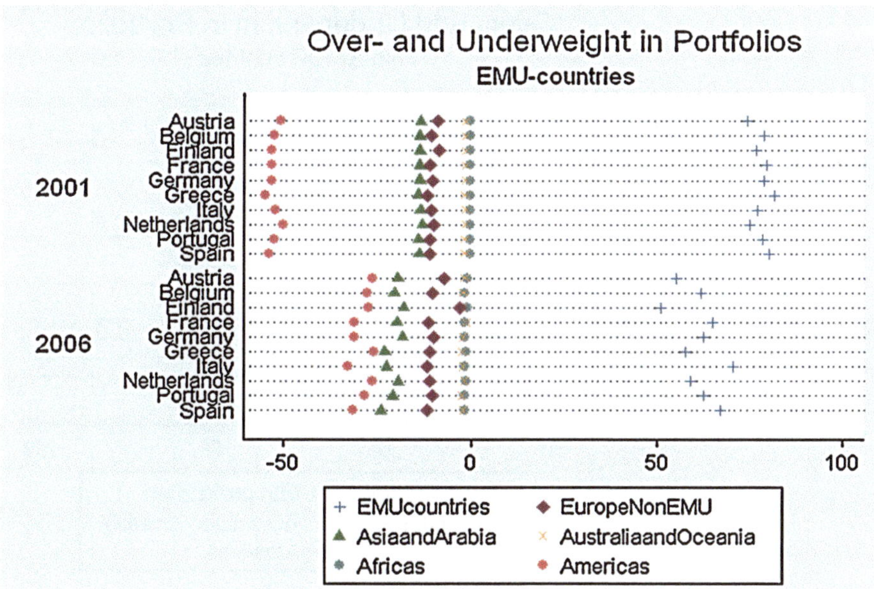

Database: World Federation of Exchanges; Eurostat; IMF; own calculations

A substantial underweight of the region Americas and partly Asia and Arabia is observable. The growing importance of the Asian market, especially the Chinese market including Hong Kong, is the reason for the greater underweight in 2006 compared to 2001 although investment stayed rather stable. It seems as though it takes some time for investors to accept new markets. Probably, the same reasons as the reasons for home bias are decisive (especially psychological dimension of investment behaviour into markets that are seemingly known better).

A comparable development applies for Non-EMU countries with respect to investment in the EMU. A comparison between the two years shows augmented investment into Americas in exchange to home country investment. The exceptions are Bulgaria and Romania with constant proportions of Non-EMU investment. If the two parts of the graph are compared, the second graph shows a less uniform picture with regard to home bias development. Especially in Norway, increased investment in Americas and Asia is substantial. Norway is the country with the lowest deviation. In general, the Scandinavian countries reduced investment in their home region severely and adopted rather international portfolio strategies.

Graph 20: Deviation from Market Portfolio – Non-EMU Countries

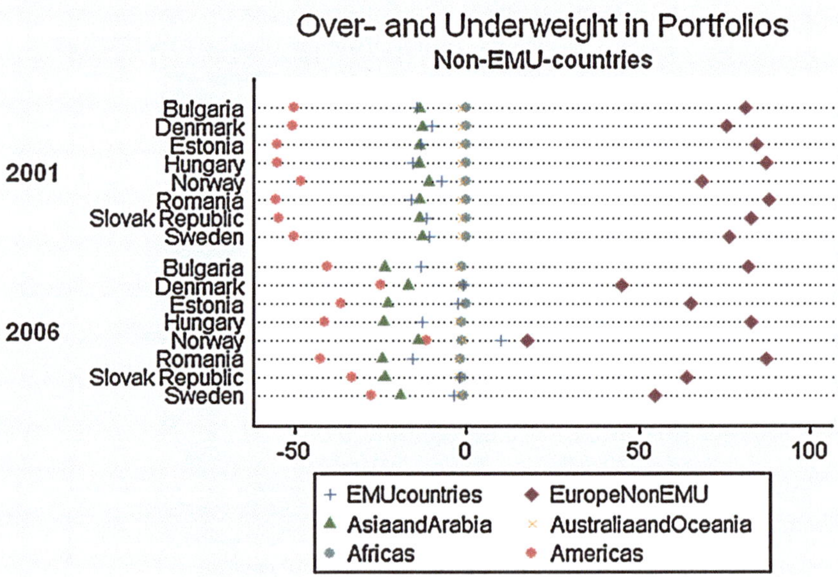

Database: World Federation of Exchanges; Eurostat; IMF; own calculations

The general impression is that the dimension of misplacement became smaller in the comparison of these two years and that all countries tend in most regions (exception is Asia and Arabia) to a investment closer to the world market. The graphs show that investors do not ignore the principles of the IAPM, but re-balance their portfolios accordingly although all countries are far away from pursuing a complete copy of the market portfolio. An open question is whether investors have any (financial) disadvantages if their own investment strategy is compared with the market portfolio. Only when a disadvantage of the personal portfolio return can be observed, the IAPM can have any guiding function. The next section has a closer look at this important question of return and loss.

4.6 Return on Investment of the Country Strategies

The issue of returns is at the same time the question whether home bias is important at all. If there are hardly any differences in return between the market portfolio and the individual portfolio, home bias would be less significant from an investor's perspective. However, even if the conclusion is drawn that the market portfolio return is not higher, the risk diversification argument could still be valid.

If portfolios are more successful as the market portfolio is analysed over the time period from 2001 till 2007, the total return index of the Datastream DS Market portfolio is used. The weights for the returns of the world market portfolio come from our known market portfolio of the World Federation of Exchanges data calculated above. The return index assumes that investors hold their portfolios over the whole time period and reinvest dividends. The output of the index is its value that would be achieved if this investment strategy of reinvestment is conducted. As equity is usually considered as a long-term investment, it is justified to use a longer time period as just single years. Apart from these arguments, in the literature, time periods of several years are usually taken as the investment horizon to prove the advantages of the market-capitalization weighted portfolio (Tesar and Werner, 1995; French and Poterba, 1991; Lapp, 2001; Pástor, 2000). As the focus of investment of the sample countries lies strongly on equity (see Section 4.1), it is justified to consider only equity indices in this section.

The return of each of the constituent country-indices within the Datastream index is calculated by the following formula:

$$R_{i,t} = \frac{country\ index_{t+1}}{country\ index_t} - 1 \qquad \textbf{F 20}$$

with $R_{i,t}$ *being the return of country-index i in year t*

To compare the success of the different investment strategies in the different countries, the average and the cumulative return per year is calculated and compared with the market portfolio. The average return is computed by weighting the returns of the single country index with the proportion of each index in the portfolio as realised by the investors. Afterwards, the geographic mean over these weighted returns is built.

$$R_C = \sqrt[n]{\prod_{t=1}^{n}\left(1+\sum_{i=1}^{m} w_{i,t} R_{i,t}\right)} \qquad \text{F 21}$$

with: *R_c as the return of the portfolio of country c,*
n is the number of years observed (seven in this case from 2001 to 2007),
t is the year index,
m is the number of constituent indices within the Datastream index,
i is the index for the respective country index,
w is the proportion of the country index i within the country-specific portfolio and
R is the return as calculated above in formula F20

Most of the countries that are destinations for investment for the countries of the sample are considered in the Datastream index. Only about 2.01 % of total portfolio investment (average over all countries and years) could not be assigned to a country of the index. For these destinations, the average of the region they belong to is used as a proxy for return. For similar reasons, Estonia and the Slovak Republic could not be computed. Both countries are not part of the index, and it is questionable as to whether a proxy of the average European investment would be justified. Bulgaria was not included either because portfolio data for 2007 is not available, or the different investment horizon until 2006 would not be comparable to the other countries or to the market portfolio.

Cumulative returns are calculated by

$$R_{cum} = \prod_{t=1}^{n}(1+R_{C,t})$$

with: *$R_{C,t}$ as the return of a country portfolio in year t.*

Results are presented in Table 6.

Table 6: Comparison of Portfolio Returns

	average return per year	deviation from market portfolio	cumulative return 2001-2007
market portfolio	**9.64**	-	**190.42**
average of sample	**9.68**	**0.04**	**243.88**
Netherlands	2.83	-6.80	121.61
Italy	3.68	-5.95	128.81
France	3.75	-5.89	129.38
Germany	3.92	-5.72	130.87
Finland	4.35	-5.29	134.72
Sweden	6.19	-3.45	152.28
Greece	6.54	-3.10	155.81
Belgium	6.88	-2.76	159.28
Spain	7.36	-2.28	164.35
Denmark	7.70	-1.94	168.04
Portugal	7.95	-1.69	170.83
Norway	9.11	-0.53	184.06
Austria	13.38	+3.74	240.86
Hungary	16.97	+7.33	299.58
Romania	44.53	+34.90	1317.65

All values are percentage points.
+ indicates a better performance as the reference portfolio, – indicates a worse performance.

Database: World Federation of Exchanges, DS World Market Index (total return index); Eurostat; IMF; own calculations

Interestingly, the market portfolio does not outperform the real portfolios on average but shows a slightly weaker performance of 0.04 percent. A closer look reveals that some outliers like Romania determine the high average return of the sample portfolios. Only three countries outperform the market portfolio. For most countries still holds: If investors had decided to follow the ideas of portfolio theory, i.e. to invest in the market portfolio as the reference portfolio, a clearly better return would have been the result. One may note, however, that transactions costs (including, among others, information costs and exchange rate risk) are not included in the calculation. Still, an outperformance of 0.53 to 6.8 % should be a sufficient advantage in a growingly financially integrated world with declining transaction costs to conclude that return is higher in the internationally diversified portfolio. Besides that, transaction costs are not likely to be the reason for home bias as stated by Tesar and Werner (1995) because turnover in capital markets is so high that it cannot be a serious barrier. Their view is confirmed with more recent data by Mishra (2007) who investigates 38 countries. In the study, no country displayed a significance of the transaction cost variable. On the other hand, e.g. Kalra, Stoichev, and Sundaram (2004), using a dataset of the time period between 1988 till 2000, find out that for a US investor who invests his or her portfolio in five different, little correlated foreign countries, has higher transaction costs as the international benefit could earn. The study is limited to the US market – this means the US is the benchmark. This is plausible because the US has a stock market that is well-diversified in it. In contrast to Kalra et al. (2004), in the study at hand, not purely domestic portfolios are compared to portfolios with an assumed foreign proportion, but real portfolios with the theoretically optimal ones.

It might be argued that there is another snare in the calculation of optimal portfolio composition: risk aversion is not considered. I would like to recall from the theory part that the optimal portfolio composition with regard to bonds and shares does not change with risk aversion; instead, the proportion of the risk free asset steers risk aversion. Seen from this point of view, the return advantage measured above can only acknowledge the merit of the risky part of the portfolio. Total return might differ depending on the return of the risk-free asset, but this does not change the superiority of a portfolio of an investor who chooses a composition of the risky part according to the IAPM as compared to another investor with the same risk aversion who chooses a composition like it is done currently.

As seen above, only three countries, Romania, Hungary and Austria exhibit higher returns as the market portfolio. The reason for the two Eastern European countries is – as surprising as it may sound – due to their high home bias. In contrast to most other countries, the country indeces of Romania and Hungary showed positive returns in almost all years (besides 2007), whereas the reference portfolio showed negative returns in 2001, 2002 and 2007 (but positive returns in all other years). In the case of Romania, home bias was the better investment strategy since risk (the volatility of return) was not considered. The highest deviation can be observed in the Netherlands and in Italy. In both countries, the strongly negative returns of their respective country indices in the years 2001 and 2002 could not be caught up in the following positive years. The foreign destinations of the Netherlands are mainly the United States, United Kingdom, and Italy; but these countries follow the same return patterns as the Netherlands, and therefore did not bring diversification benefits. The same is true for Italy with the highest proportion of foreign investment into the United States and Luxembourg. This hints to the argument in the literature that the Western stock markets are strongly correlated and do not bring as much of a diversification effect as would have been expected.

The cumulative returns over the whole time period 2001 till 2007 consequently show the same underperformance as the average returns with the exceptions of

Romania and Hungary. The dimension of the loss is made more transparent if the values in euro are utilized (Table 7). The average investment over the put time period is multiplied with the average deviation from the market portfolio return in the same period and divided by number of inhabitants. This approach has the advantage that the average values are relativised by the number of possible investors which allows a better analysis of the dimensions of gains and losses. For the sake of simplicity, the calculation per head is conducted with the complete population although there is probably a high proportion of the population that does not have any wealth at all and can not participate in the gained wealth even if new investment strategies are applied. Social politics is an interesting field though is not the focus of the dissertation. Therefore, this simplification is considered sufficient for the purpose of this study. Bulgaria, Estonia and the Slovak Republic are not considered in the calculation of the averages for reasons mentioned above.

The numbers in Table 7 show that on average each inhabitant of each of the countries would gain roughly 1,200 €[18]. If this amount is opposed to private loans, which sum up to about 13.000 € per head (Eurostat data, own calculations) in this time period, the advantages and dimensions become even more tangible. The country with the highest loss, the Netherlands, has on average the highest private loans per head (around 31.000 €), but could pay these off within only six years by investing internationally (interest of loan not calculated). The prima facie high gain of Romania and Bulgaria is relativised – judged by the euro amount of just seven or 31 euro respectively per year because of the small investment sums.

The investors in the countries of investigation definitely pay in the form of forgone returns for their insistence of investing mainly at home and partly in neighbour countries with the exception of Austria. However, there are signs that a rising attention towards this topic induces investors to change their behaviour (Bluethgen et al., 2008, p. 25). Their study finds a smaller disadvantage for German investors of 2.4 % return per year as compared to 5.7 % that have been calculated here. The reasons lie in different time horizons (30 years for the Bluethgen et al. study) and a different calculation of the optimal portfolio (their portfolio consists only of seven countries). The disadvantage, in return, should only be accepted by investors if the actually held portfolios exhibit a much lower volatility as the market portfolio.

---

18 The average value is determined by dividing the sum of gains/losses by the average number of inhabitants of the countries in the sample.

Table 7: Average Absolut Loss

	Average value of investment in millions of EUR (average 2001-2007)	**gain/loss in millions of EUR (average 2001-2007)**	**gain/loss per year and head in EUR (average 2001-2007)**
Netherlands	1,212,673	-82,497	-5,086
France	2,219,938	-130,738	-2,102
Finland	186,698	-9,873	-1,890
Belgium	651,054	-17,977	-1,727
Sweden	360,581	-12,424	-1,383
Germany	1,928,410	-110,289	-1,338
Italy	1,120,718	-66,729	-1,152
Denmark	224,645	-4,359	-808
Norway	360,026	-1,909	-417
Spain	620,035	-14,148	-334
Portugal	146,496	-2,472	-236
Greece	75,522	-2,339	-212
Romania	438	153	7
Hungary	4,273	313	31
Austria	325,148	12,170	1,492
sum	**9,436,655**	**-443,116**	**-15,153**

Database: DS World Market Index (total return index); Eurostat; IMF; own calculations

4.7 Volatility of Return

Risk is usually the price for extraordinary returns, or, to express it differently, more security is the reward for lower returns. Because the returns of most market participants are lower as the market portfolio, the result of the analysis of portfolios should be a smaller risk. Usually, as risk measurement, a lower volatility of returns is taken.[19]

19 I would like to mention that the volatility of return is not the only way to judge risk. A more sophisticated risk measurement used by banks is the measurement of the so-called value at risk. This figure tells the maximum loss with a certain probability in a certain time period, e.g. one year. This approach is future oriented and includes expected risk influencing factors such as interest rates structures or the liquidity of the positions in the portfolio. For two reasons I stay with the volatility of returns as a risk measurement: Value at risk is probably too complex to be understood for private investors and the second reason is that it gives out maximum risk. For private investors the maximum loss is important, although a sustainability of returns, measured by the volatility, is probably more important.

Volatility is measured as the standard deviation of returns on the basis of the yearly returns calculated above. This basis is chosen to ensure the comparability of risk and return. Standard deviation is calculated by:

$$\sigma_{C,t} = \sqrt{(R_{C,t} - \overline{R}_C)^2} \qquad \textbf{F 22}$$

with: $\sigma_{C,t}$ *as the standard deviation of country c at year t*

$R_{C,t}$ *the yearly return of country c at year t*

$\overline{R}_C$ *the weighted arithmetic mean of returns of the portfolio per year calculated by F23*

$$\overline{R}_C = \frac{1}{n}\sum_{n=1}^{n}\left(1 + \sum_{i=1}^{m} w_{i,t} R_{i,t}\right) \qquad \textbf{F 23}$$

with *n as the number of years (2001 till 2007)*
t as the year index
m is the number of constituent country indices within the Datastream index
i is the index for the respective country index
w is the proportion of the country index i within the country-specific portfolio

The average volatility of a portfolio of one country in the sample is the arithmetic mean of $\sigma_{C,t}$ over all years.

Results are presented in Table 8. The expectations as expressed above – that the relatively low returns are rewarded by stable returns – could not be fulfilled. The market portfolio is less risky as the individual portfolios although the return is higher. This finding is an important argument for the IAPM and a sign that investors gain from following the portfolio theory. The market portfolio is much better diversified, and at the same time accumulates higher returns. On average, volatility of the country portfolios is 9.11 % higher. To assess the interrelation of risk and return more easily, the portfolios are displayed in a risk-return diagram (Graph 23).

Table 8: Comparison of Portfolio Volatilities

	average volatility per year	deviation from market portfolio
Market	**18.90**	-
average of sample	**32.34**	**-13.44**
Romania	42.97	-24.08
Sweden	34.36	-15.46
Hungary	33.49	-14.60
Finland	32.53	-13.64
Norway	32.07	-13.17
France	31.80	-12.91
Portugal	31.67	-12.77
Greece	31.59	-12.70
Germany	31.49	-12.59
Spain	30.84	-11.94
Denmark	30.83	-11.94
Belgium	30.62	-11.73
Italy	30.45	-11.55
Austria	30.37	-11.47
Netherlands	29.96	-11.06

All values are percentage points.
+ indicates a better performance as the reference portfolio, – indicates a worse performance.

Database: World Federation of Exchanges, DS World Market Index (total return index); Eurostat; IMF; own calculations

A look at the graph reveals that one cannot necessarily conclude that risk automatically goes along with higher returns as the examples of e.g. Sweden and Hungary, or the Netherlands and Austria show. If we have a look at the country-pair Sweden and Hungary, Hungary's portfolio clearly outperforms the one of Sweden because it has a much higher return and lower risk. The portfolio held by private investors in the Netherlands has a small advantage in risk stability compared to Austria. However, this advance is brought by high losses of return which could only be explained by an extraordinary risk aversion. The only country portfolios that meets expectations with regard to the market portfolio is Romania because its outperformance in comparison with the market portfolio is accompanied by higher risks. For the two other countries that outperform the market portfolio, Austria and Hungary, applies that they have a substantial higher risk with moderate return gains. The only plausible explanation for this investment behaviour, a very low risk aversion, which in turn seems to be not plausible for private investors.

Graph 21: Risk Return Plot

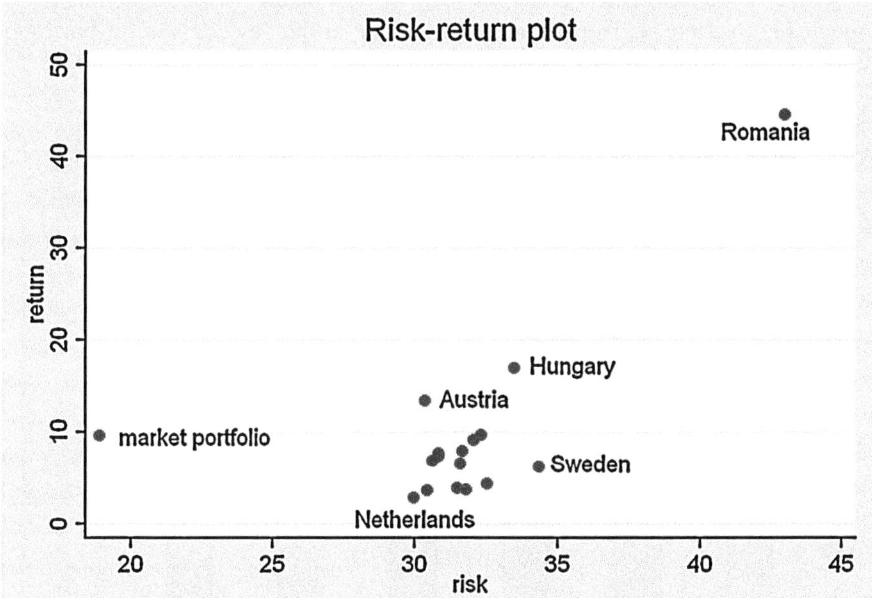

Database: World Federation of Exchanges, DS World Market Index (total return index); Eurostat; IMF; own calculations

Altogether, the findings in the literature with regard to the advantages of the IAPM (Sections 3.4.2 and 3.5), is confirmed by my own empirical analysis for the European sample. For these reasons, hypothesis number two is considered as true.

Hypothesis 2:	*The IAPM is a plausible investment strategy. It is likely that investors behave according to it; therefore the optimal portfolio weights derived by the IAPM can act as a benchmark to measure home bias.*

4.8 Contribution of Portfolio Returns to Consumption Convergence

The sections above answer the question of the advantages of the IAPM, except for returns contributing to consumption convergence. In the theory part several preconditions for a contribution to consumption convergence are listed that can be summarized as follows: Portfolio returns have to become more similar; there are no opposite influences like earned income development and implicitly, the assumption that the marginal propensity to consume out of financial wealth is the same over countries. Income development is accounted for in the econometric model (see Section 7). This section takes a look at the development of portfolio returns in the years 2001 till 2007 (annual returns).

Graph 22: Average Difference of Annual Portfolio Returns

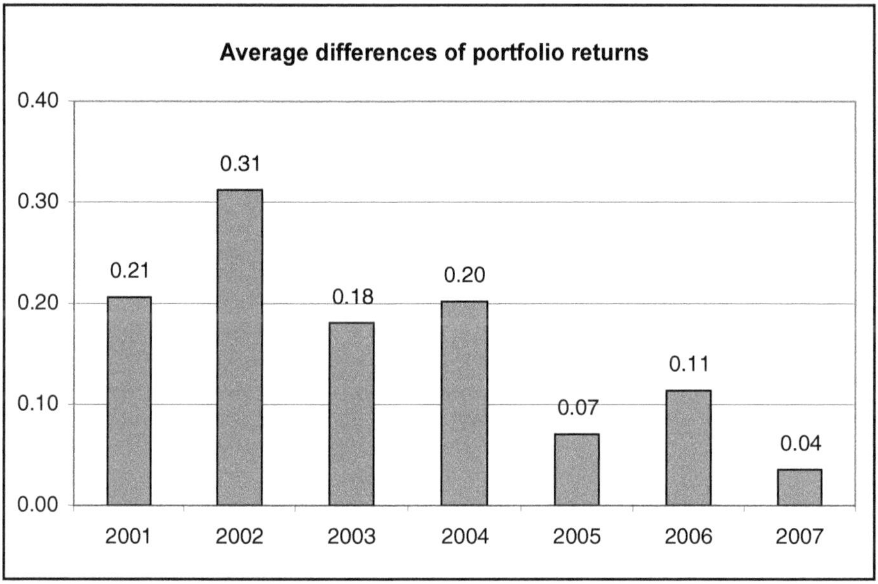

Database: DS World Market Index (total return index); Eurostat; IMF; own calculations

Graph 22 shows the average difference in annual portfolio returns over all country-pairs in the years 2001 till 2007. The differences in returns of the different countries are taken and averaged. The numbers can be interpreted as the difference of returns expressed in percentage points. Clearly, annual returns are exhibited to a great volatility as Section 4.7 shows and can therefore only be an indication. The development of the numbers hints to more similar returns while the question of the source for the similarity – portfolio similarity or a convergence of stock markets – cannot finally be answered here. Later on, only the similarity of portfolios is analysed, and for stock market convergence, I refer to the relevant literature mentioned above and the indication from the sample: the stock markets in the sample countries at least showed the same development in the last years (Graph 23) although they do not completely converge; i.e. have exactly the same return. In the years 2001 and 2002, three countries of Eastern Europe, Hungary, Romania, and

Bulgaria, showed positive returns in contrast to the other countries of the sample. In the following years, however, a similar development as the other countries can be observed, although in the case of Bulgaria, on a higher level. One may note that the annual returns are in percentage points and that Bulgaria started from a much lower level of country index performance as other countries.

Graph 23: Annual Portfolio Returns per Country

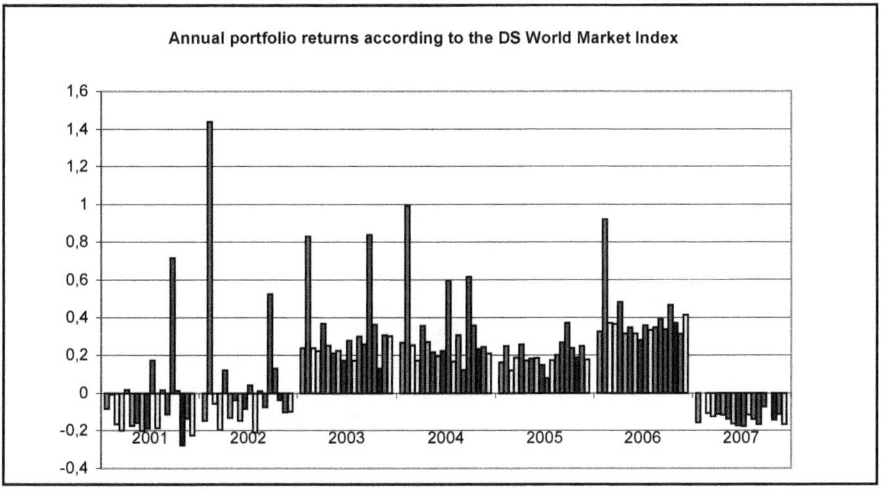

Source: DS World Market Index (total return index); Eurostat; IMF; own calculations.

In a more detailed picture Graph 24 provides an overview over the development of all country-pairs (all countries in the sample are opposed to each other, this means 153 pairs are built) and indeed, great differences in returns in some countries can be observed but with a general trend towards a higher similarity. High amplitudes in the years 2002, 2004 and 2006, which represent greater differences in returns, are the result of an extraordinary development of the already mentioned Bulgarian country index, which outperformed other countries by far. Hence – combined with the home bias of Bulgarian investors – the portfolio return of Bulgaria was much higher compared to other countries. Data from Bulgaria is not available for 2007, which is the reason why the time series suddenly ends in 2006.

Countries that come from a fairly common economic environment like the EMU countries only show slight differences in portfolio returns. On average, country-pairs that consist of two EMU-countries differed by 0.08 % in 2001 and by 0.02 % in 2007. For country-pairs in a different constellation, with EMU and Non-EMU-countries the difference diminished in absolute terms much more, from 0.24 % in 2001 to 0.13 % in 2006 (due to missing data 2007 data would not be meaningful). This history is an indication that not much influence of portfolio returns can be expected within the EMU.

Graph 24: Difference of Annual Portfolio Returns in All Country-pairs

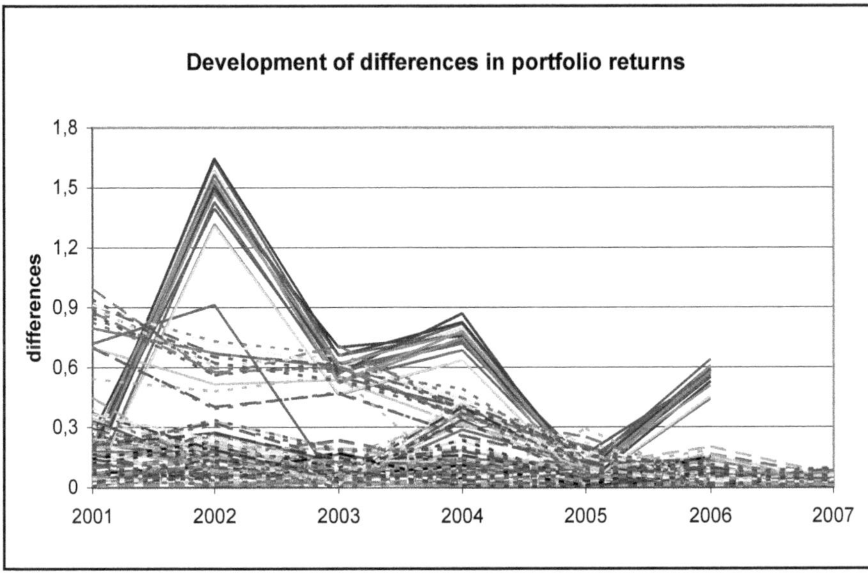

Database: DS World Market Index; Eurostat; IMF; own calculations

4.9 Concluding Remarks

This chapter confirms several expectations about investment strategies and portfolio theory. Firstly, private financial wealth rose in the countries of the sample on average and includes a growing proportion of bonds and shares. This is fundamental in the assumption that financial wealth and portfolios, especially, should have a growing influence on consumption.

Foreign investment increased over the years while home bias declined. Combined with the analysis of the deviation of the optimal portfolio this indicates that investors tend to invest more internationally and follow the recommendations of portfolio theory accordingly. The advantages of following the analysed portfolio theory are demonstrated by the superiority of the market portfolio with regard to risk and return. These are interesting insights that have not been investigated for this time period and these countries before.

However, the major goal of the dissertation is to show that portfolios become more similar and that would mean, with other things equal, countries tend to converge in their consumption behaviour supported by financial returns. Via consumption correlation a GDP correlation is achieved.

A clear distinction between home bias and portfolio similarity is in order: Less home bias only means that countries tend to invest in foreign countries, which does not necessarily mean that portfolios become more similar. The similarity of portfolios is crucial for further investigation, not a declining home bias. Led from economic intuition, only similar portfolios are an indication for similar returns. This means that a country with similar home bias tendencies does not necessarily have similar return structures. However, it is expected that quite often a low home bias and portfolio similarity go hand in hand (see Section 5.3). There is no clear distinction as to what "similar portfolios" exactly means or what "similar returns" are. Still some examples can underline the statement above: Italy and France is one example. Their portfolios are quite similar[20]; similar returns are achieved (Table 6) and a similar home bias can be observed (Italy 0.88, France 0.90) (Table 3). However, there are other examples: The country-pair Denmark and Spain shows similar portfolios[21] and similar returns. However, their average home bias differs (Denmark 0.75, Spain 0.89).

As it is beneficial and therefore likely for investors to follow the IAPM the market portfolio is used as the benchmark for the similarity of portfolios. It is expected that countries that tend to invest abroad show more similar portfolios. Similarity with the IAPM as a benchmark is defined with regard to similar country proportions in a portfolio. This leads to the conclusion that the positive relationship of a declining home bias, the IAPM and portfolio similarity is expected but the relationship of a declining home bias and portfolio similarity is not essential for the linkage of return and consumption and business cycle correlation.[22]

5. Similarity of Portfolios in Europe

As demonstrated in the last section, home bias decreased substantially within just a few years. Further financial integration is likely to contribute to more investment abroad. As already posed in the theory chapter and in the previous chapter, a declining home bias alone is not necessarily sufficient for portfolio similarity.

---

20 Details will be explained in the next section: The specialisation index of this pair is 0.07. This is well below the average 0.15 of all country-pairs which consist of two EMU members. The lower the index; the higher the similarity.

21 This country-pair shows a low specialisation index of 1.59 compared to the average of 1.71 of country-pairs which consist of one EMU member and one Non-EMU member.

22 See theory part Sections 3.5 and 4.8.

If portfolio similarity features the same development as home bias, it is one of the aspects investigated in the next sections.

5.1 Calculation

The analysis is conducted on a bilateral basis, that is, the relationship between two countries is measured. For 18 countries in the panel this means that

$$\binom{18}{2} = 153 \text{ country-pairs}$$

are constructed for each year, from 2001-2007[23]. The reason for this approach is to uphold as much information as possible. The country-pairs build the database for all further examinations, including the estimation methods in Section 7.2.5 that formally test the relationship between portfolio similarity and correlation.

To measure portfolio similarity, an index was adapted which had been used in the context of industry patterns before (Belke and Heine, 2006, 2007; or Clark and van Wincoop, 2001). It is constructed as a specialisation index, herein called SPEC. This means that the index of a country-pair with less similar portfolios is higher than the index of countries with more similar portfolios. The criterion for similarity is that country shares in the investment portfolio are similar with the assumption in mind that country shares represent on average the whole country. Country shares are represented by country indices. Transferred to the IAPM, this means that a country shares incorporates all diversification possibilities to completely diversify unsystematic risk (intra-national risks are "diversified away" in each country). The same time a country index represents the profit per country.

SPEC is calculated as follows:

$$\text{SPEC} = \sum_{i=1}^{n} \left| a_i - b_i \right| \qquad \textbf{F 24}$$

with: n = number of countries
i = country index
a is the share of country A in country i and b is the share of country B in country i
SPEC ranges from 0 (complete similarity/same portfolio) to 2 (complete dissimilarity)

23 Data availability for 2007: all countries except Bulgaria and the Slovak Republic

With regard to the high economic and financial integration, EMU was considered as one country as argued above. SPEC development, however, showed the same direction regardless as to whether the EMU was taken as the home country or not.

The data used for constructing SPEC comes basically from two sources: from the Coordinated Portfolio Investment Survey (CPIS) coordinated by the IMF and from Eurostat.

CPIS has the goal to provide data on cross border holdings of equities and bonds on an annual basis, each year at the end of December. Investment is broken down by country of the issuer of an asset. The first survey was conducted in 1997 with 29 countries participating. The second survey took place in 2001 and builds the first year of the data base for this dissertation. The originally reported values in the survey are market values in US-dollars.

In the context of this dissertation, CPIS data is used to allocate portfolio holdings to the different countries. Because of a lack of data, it was assumed that private investment has the same breakdown as the whole country including bank investment; reserve assets are not considered. The conclusion from banks investment behaviour to private behaviour is conducted in other studies as well, e.g. Lapp shows that the estimated banking investment is comparable to private investment (Lapp, 2001, p. 68). Most major countries participate in the study although countries have a growing influence, such as the P.R. of China, they do not disclose their investment abroad. Still, the CPIS offers the best overview and approximation for portfolio allocation on country level available. The participating countries obliged themselves to deliver data according to the compilation standards by the IMF to ensure that data is comparable (International Monetary Fund, 2002).

The following steps summarize the procedure how to calculate portfolio similarity:

1. From the financial accounts balance sheet of Eurostat total financial wealth in bonds and shares of a country is derived (Section 4.3 provides further details). The denomination is in euro.
2. The CPIS data shows the end-of-year proportions of investment in bonds and shares in US$.
3. The end-of-year exchange rate for the euro and the US-dollar provided by Eurostat is taken for the conversion.
4. Now, it is possible to calculate domestic investment as the difference between total wealth out of step one and the foreign investment out of step three.
5. The breakdown to foreign and domestic investment is needed to calculate the specialisation index: the proportion of investment of the 18 countries in the sample towards the countries in the world is calculated.

6. Taking the differences between the proportions between each country and summing up the differences amounts to the specialisation index SPEC, calculated for each country-pair.

5.2 Results

The overall development of SPEC satisfies the expectations (as discussed in the theory part): SPEC has a downward tendency over the covered time period 2001-2007. That means portfolios indeed became more similar with respect to country proportions.

Graph 25 shows the specialisation index averaged over all country-pairs per year.

Graph 25: Averaged SPEC

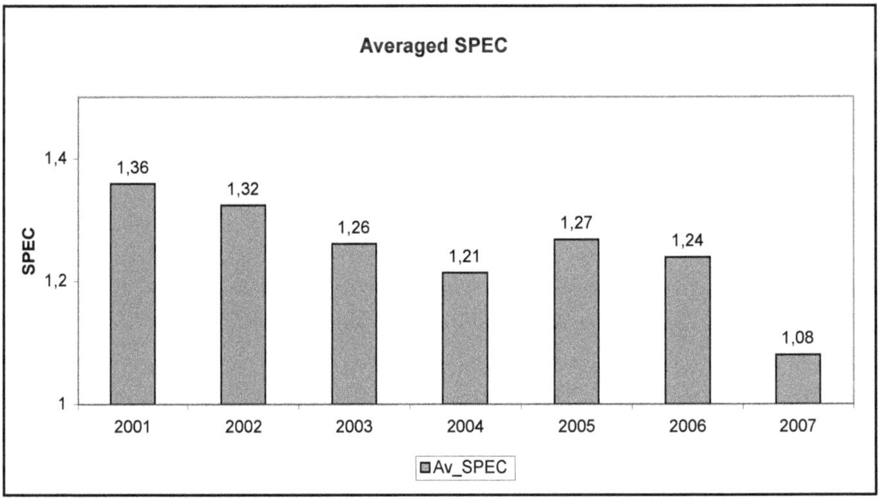

Database: Eurostat; IMF; own calculations

In the Appendix 3, the indices for all pairs are provided. For the sake of clarity, the presentation of the investment proportions per country-pair and year is in country groups: EMU-countries (all countries are shown in the Data Appendix 2); EU-countries (Non-EMU), other Europe, Asia and Arabia, Africa, Americas, Australia and Oceania, and Others.

To explain the development of SPEC, the main drivers of it need to be analysed first.

First of all, the general development of SPEC was not dominated by the trends of single countries as Graph 26 indicates.

Graph 26: Development of SPEC for All Country-pairs

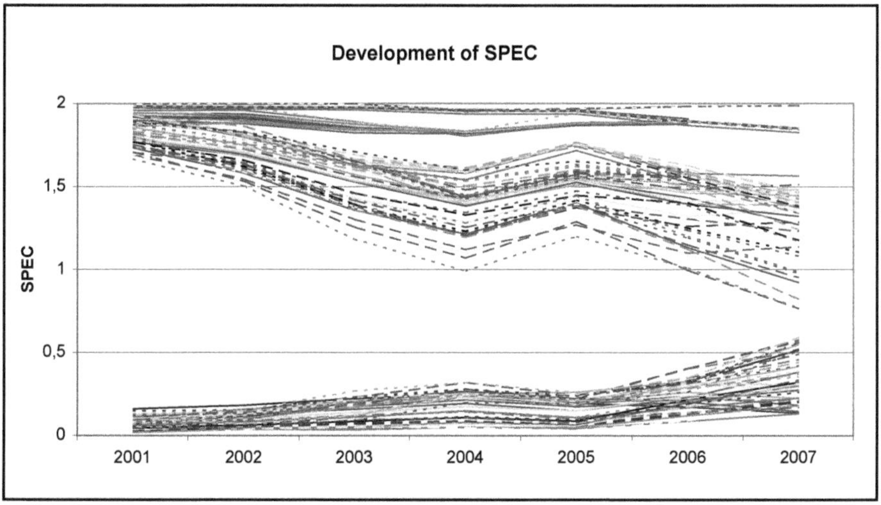

Database: Eurostat; IMF; own calculations

Clearly, two groups can be distinguished: one group emanating from a rather high level of dissimilarity, directing towards more similarity, and one group with very similar portfolios with a slightly growing dissimilarity.

The first group consists mainly of country-pairs that combine one EMU member with one Non-EMU member (called EMU1, the 1 indicats that there is just one EMU member), or two countries that are both not part of the EMU (called EMU0). This means that countries that are still outside the EMU increasingly invest inside the EMU with the exemption of the year 2005. If countries outside the EMU invest in the EMU, the difference between foreign investment of these countries and the "home zone" investment of EMU countries becomes smaller and SPEC declines. There are a few exceptions that show strong dissimilarity over the whole time range; mainly, the Eastern European countries like Rumania or Bulgaria with rather narrow financial markets in their history.

Within this first group, a declining home bias corresponds to more similar portfolios. This is not accidental – home bias and SPEC usually should take the same direction in the current stadium of a high home bias. The reason is that SPEC is calculated as the difference of country proportions in the portfolio. If the home proportion of a country A is low, the difference to country's B investment in country A is smaller, leading to a smaller SPEC and higher similarity. Naturally, a corresponding investment of country B in country A further reduces the difference though this contribution might be much smaller than the declined home bias. The temporary rise of the SPEC-index can be attributed to the higher proportion of home country investment in the year 2005. Possible and plausible reasons are various – e.g. a better economic development of the home country, a strong euro – and are not covered by this investigation.

Graph 27: Development of SPEC for Non-EMU Country-pairs

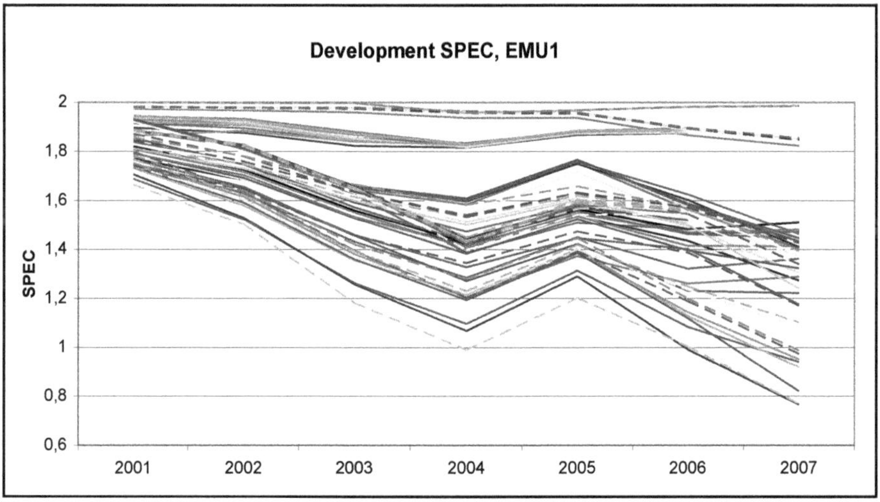

Database: Eurostat; IMF; own calculations

The other group (Graph 28) consists of country-pairs in which both countries are joined with the European Monetary Union (called EMU2). Interestingly, the investment pattern within the EMU seems to exhibit a different trend. The reason why the portfolios of these countries become dissimilar is that the EMU-bias is declining, and that countries tend to invest abroad, especially in the US. As not all countries share the same foreign investment strategy outside the EMU, the portfolios become more dissimilar.

One needs to distinguish between these two groups with regard to home bias. In both groups, SPEC has the same interpretation – country-pairs become more dissimilar if SPEC is increasing. However, in the first group consisting of EMU1 pairs, less home bias means a lower SPEC; in the second group with EMU2 pairs, less home bias means a higher SPEC. This is due to the specification of the EMU as one country with regard to portfolio shares. One cannot conclude that a declining home bias automatically leads to a higher or a lower portfolio similarity (for a further discussion see Section 5.3 below).

Graph 28: Development of SPEC for EMU-country-pairs

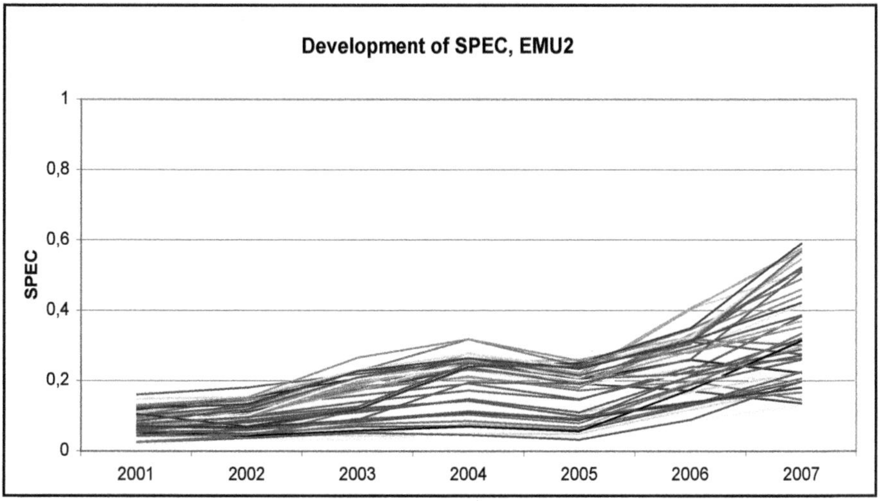

Database: Eurostat; IMF; own calculations

On average, the most similar portfolios are those of Austria and Germany (average SPEC 1.22), Norway and The Netherlands (1.32), and Denmark and Norway (1.33); the most dissimilar ones are Austria and Romania (1.98), Romania and The Netherlands (1.98) and Portugal and Romania (1.98) due to the high home bias in Romania. The last country-pairs with a high SPEC are those mentioned above in Graph 27 with highly dissimilar portfolios.

Although within the EMU2-group, a slightly growing dissimilarity can be observed the general tendency of more similar portfolios – e.g. shown through a lower average SPEC – can be assumed. Therefore, it is considered that hypothesis three is true.

Hypothesis 3: Portfolios in the sample became more similar.

The specialisation index is used in the econometric model in the next sections to provide more insight in the correlation between portfolio similarity and business cycle conversion.

5.3 Portfolio Similarity and Home Bias

The assumption that portfolio similarity and a declining home bias co-move is motivated by the idea that less home investment (ideally but not necessarily combined with a higher investment in a country by the other partner of a country-pair) leads to a smaller difference of the investment proportions, i.e. a greater portfolio similarity. Less home bias is necessarily accompanied by a higher foreign investment by definition of the measure (FAAR, see Section 4.3).

An example illustrates the context of home bias and portfolio similarity. For illustration purposes and as a starting point, the year 2006 of the country-pair of Greece and Finland is chosen. In a simulation, the proportion of the domestic investment of just one country, Greece, is decreased by 10 % and the proportion of foreign investment increased accordingly. The sum of investment is held stable; only redistribution takes place. For Greece, the simulation would imply that roughly 18.6 billions € are reallocated.[24] How is the redistribution allocated? In a first simulation, the 10 % decreased domestic investment is allocated proportional to the existing foreign investment structure of Greece. In a second simulation, portfolio similarity is increased by adapting the structures of Greece to those of Finland. Finland's structures are held stable throughout the example. This second approach results in allocating all of the "new" foreign investment to Finland if EMU is not considered as one country. If the EMU is considered as one country a reallocation according to the patterns outside the EMU must be simulated. In this case an optimized results is achieved by reallocation the "new foreign investment" to Sweden..

The results, summarized in Table 9, show that first of all, an increased foreign investment means less home bias but not necessarily a lower portfolio similarity. The example strengthens the observations made in Section 5.2. SPEC decreases as expected on a single country base (by 4.4 %) but increases if the EMU is considered as one country (by 18.7 %). Different investment strategies outside the EMU are emphasized by the reallocation. In this case the higher investment proportions of Greece into the UK market are emphasized by this approach. The smaller difference of investment in Greece could not compensate the simulated foreign investment pattern outside the EMU. The second approach to invest completely in Finland or Sweden respectivly instead of using existing patterns results in a higher portfolio similarity by -6.1 % or 14.7 % (EMU one country). Of course, a rather extreme example with regard to the immovability of Finland's portfolio was chosen and the assimilation of the Greek portfolio towards the Finish one. This assumption was just made to make the results graspable.

24 Total investment of a country, this means the 18.6 billions € include e.g. bank investments.

Table 9: Interdependence of SPEC and Home Bias

	Finland	Greece
Initial data		
Proportion of Foreign investment	60%	38%
Home Bias	0.70	0.70
SPEC	1.521	
SPEC (EMU one country)	0.293	
Reallocation according to existing investment structure		
Proportion of Foreign investment	60%	41%
Home Bias	0.70	0.65
SPEC	1.454	
SPEC (EMU one country)	0.348	
Reallocation to minimize SPEC		
SPEC	1.428	
SPEC (EMU one country)	0.250	

Database: Eurostat; IMF; own calculations

One may note that the effort to increase portfolio similarity differs widely in the country-pairs. It depends on the initial level of home bias, the respective portfolio structures and the size of countries. Take France and Romania as extreme examples in size and SPEC (their SPEC in 2006 is 1.98). To achieve an 14.1 % decrease of SPEC (to 1.70), Romania would have to re-allocate capital to France at about 14.4 % of its total domestic investment. In the real world, a one-sided convergence would not work because the bonds and shares of a country can only be held once. If, e.g., France would try to allocate its capital according to the Romanian pattern (98 % of its total assets in Romanian assets), this could not work because Romanian bonds and shares would need to be multiplied (other things equal). The IAPM, on the other hand, considers this issue by proportioning bonds and shares according to the world market proportion. This procedure ensures that only 100 % of a country's asset can be held.

Moving back to a more general level, the whole sample: to get an indication for the relationship, the three variables home bias, portfolio similarity (SPEC) and foreign investment (FAAR) are averaged (arithmetic mean)[25] over all country-pairs and pictured in the graph below. The theoretical links are confirmed in hypothesis four.

25 The same results are derived if the median is taken.

Hypothesis 4:	*A lower home bias is an influencing parameter for a higher similarity of portfolios.*

Put in other words, when foreign investment increases, home bias increases, and portfolio similarity increases.

Graph 29: Home Bias vs. Portfolio Similarity vs. Foreign Investment

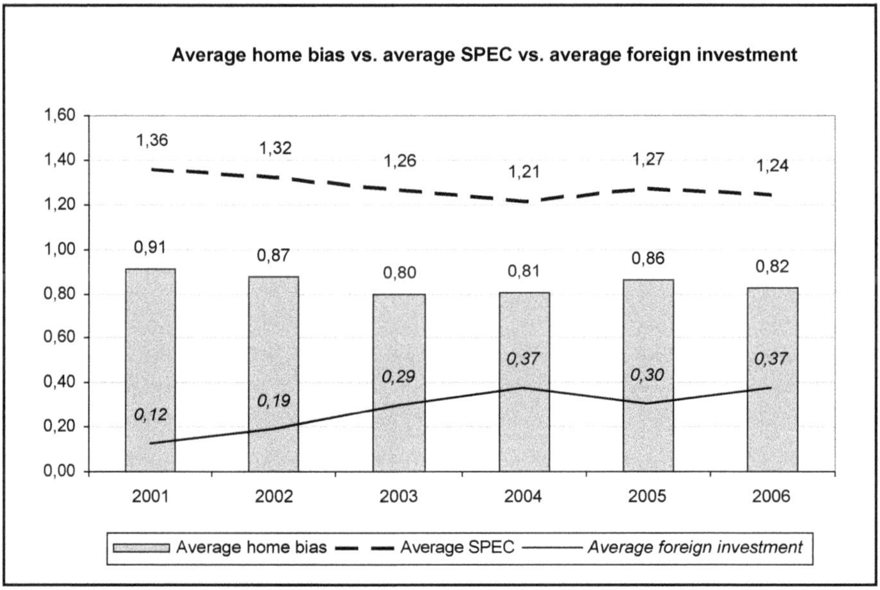

Database: World Federation of Exchanges, Eurostat; IMF; own calculations

The picture emerging is that the variables stay quite stable over the years, but one needs to keep in mind that the general investment behaviour of private investors is usually not changed within just a short period of time. The other factor is that the average covers a broad range of countries with different access to financial markets and different backgrounds of investment. Hence, the average will usually not change rapidly.

One thesis that arises in this context has not been answered so far: the question as to whether a higher similarity of portfolios and more similar returns out of this investment go hand in hand. If portfolios become more similar with regard to the country proportions, it is plausible to assume that the returns measured by the country indices become more similar as well. If this assumption is true, it is likely that the transmission channel runs from portfolio similarity to portfolio returns, to consumption convergence; and from there, to business cycle convergence. If this link does not hold, i.e. that portfolio similarity and return do not have the same development, either the transmission chain would be broken or portfolio similarity would not contribute to a convergence of returns. The other possibility is that another transmission channel exists which runs from similarity to consumption. Other transmission channels to contribute to a convergence of returns could be the convergent financial wealth, the same economic settings due to the advancement of the EMU or reasons emerging from higher intra-industry linkages.

Graph 30: Portfolio Return vs. SPEC

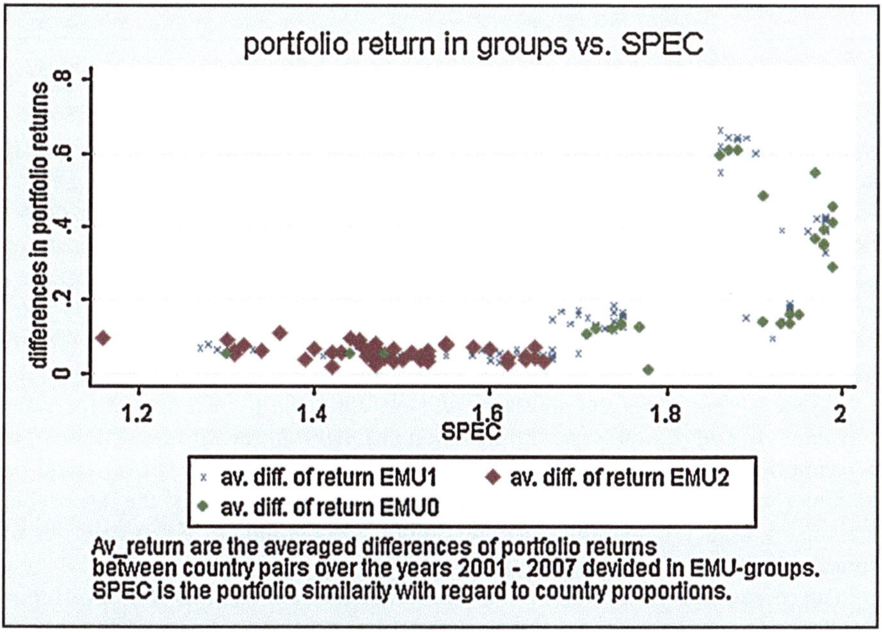

Database: Eurostat; IMF; own calculations

The foundation for the linkage has been made in Section 4.8 (contribution of portfolio returns to consumption convergence) and is now combined with portfolio similarity. It was already concluded that the different EMU groups probably show different characteristics because of their different (financial) backgrounds. To consider these characteristics, the countries should be analysed in different groups. Graph 30 shows the different EMU-groups and the relation between SPEC and portfolio return. As expected, a higher similarity of portfolio in the sense of country proportions (i.e. a low SPEC) is usually combined with similar returns, indicated by a low difference of portfolio returns. The groups behave differently. While the EMU2 group has in general quite similar returns, SPEC still differs by a few points. Contrarily, the EMU1 group behaves as expected: it exhibits a trend of less similar portfolios, but if SPEC is low, return differences are low as well. On the other hand, high dissimilarities are accompanied by high return differences. The fitted values are demonstrated in the Data Appendix 4; the context seems to be clear enough to renounce from a diagram at this place and to consider hypothesis five to be true.

Hypothesis 5:A higher similarity of portfolios results in more similar returns out of this investment.

A note considering objections about the necessity of thesis five is in place here. Is the similarity of returns really a precondition for the main thesis, that business cycles become more similar due to return similarity? It is a logical consequence if investors have completely similar (the same) portfolios, and if we are talking about return correlation on stock markets. No matter how much returns on markets correlate, the returns of identical portfolios are the same. Therefore, the similarity of returns is a logical consequence from the similarity of portfolios. Still, the similarity of returns can be achieved if portfolio structures are not converging, but only market returns are converging. In this case, return similarity is achieved even if portfolio structure is not assimilated. The second argument deserves a closer look:

When talking about the similarity of portfolio returns, it is true if (private) consumption correlation is the transmission channel that runs from portfolios via consumption to GDP. If returns would not become more similar, there would be no direct impact on private households because returns are part of the disposable income. A higher disposable income should – according to the propensity to consume – lead to more consumption.

But there could be another, more direct transmission channel from portfolios to GDP that is not the focus of this dissertation. Portfolios do not only have an impact on the asset holder's side, but investments means financing companies and represent a companies' value. No impact on a single asset would be expected if investors would really behave like the IAPM because industry risk would be completely diversified, and country risk would be at least minimized (it would develop like the world economy). Therefore, all countries are – as far as their bonds and shares are concerned – exhibited to the general world economy. However, if investors do not behave like the IAPM, what can be empirically observed, an effect on single countries or industries is plausible. Examples are economic facts or rumours inducing herding effects, and investors withdrawing money or investing money in single branches and countries. Then, a direct effect on GDP could be the consequence, depending on the financial market structure and the finance model of the respective companies. A banking based finance model would have less impact in this case. A positive effect would occur if investors would invest according to the IAPM because all branches and countries would benefit according to their shares. Although talking about country shares, in a European context, the close linkages of countries probably shifts the focus of investors to industries and branches compared to countries.

Put these arguments together, the following preconditions have to be fulfilled to make hypothesis five necessary: a convergence of returns contributes to consumption convergence in the sense of the arguments of this dissertation if

- dissimilar returns could be observed in the past,
- portfolio composition is converging,
- portfolio returns in two countries contribute to a different proportion, though noticeable to disposable income (otherwise no effect on consumption would be observed),
- no other income sources induce a counter-trend.

For convergence, it is not necessary that countries with less financial income gain more in the sense of catching up. For convergence, it is only necessary that returns become more similar. This is indeed observed in Section 4.8. Implicitly, it is assumed that all countries have the same propensity to consume. The next steps are to investigate the interdependence of portfolios and the real economy.

6. Consumption and Business Cycle Correlation

6.1 Data and Estimation Method

Data concerning consumption and GDP is derived from the Eurostat-Database. The GDP of all 18 countries is available from 1998 on; for consumption, this applies from the year 2000. The following table gives an overview.

Consumption and GDP data are deflated by the harmonized consumer price index (derived from Eurostat) and de-trended by a Hodrick-Prescott filter (Hodrick and Prescott, 1997). The general idea of this kind of data filters is to distinguish between a cyclical component (e.g. seasonal trends, business cycle) and a trend component (growth). The cycles are measured by the deviation from growth to trend. In the case at hand, the cyclical component is the interesting part. The reason is because with the background of European common interest rates, this study is interested with whether cycles are more similar or not, and not whether the long-term (growth) trend becomes more similar. The result after de-trending is a smoothed time series that approximates the cyclical component without the trend component. The more technically motivated aim of using filters is to transform the non-stationary variables consumption and GDP into stationary variables. Stationary variables show the same mean and variance in different time periods. Without the data characteristic of stationarity, an interpretation of results would be more difficult because, for one, the starting point of the time series would already influence results. The chosen parameter for de-trending is 6.25, as recommended by Ravn and Uhlig (2002), to avoid the high smoothing effect that derives from a parameter of 100 that is often used for annual data.

Table 10: Data Availability GDP and Consumption

Country	GDP	Consumption
Austria (AUT)	1976-2008	1976-2008
Belgium (BEL)	1995-2008	1995-2008
Bulgaria (BUL)	1990-2008	1990-2008
Denmark (DEN)	1971-2008	1971-2008
Estonia (EST)	1993-2008	1993-2008
Finland (FIN)	1975-2008	1975-2008
France (FRA)	1974-2008	1974-2008
Germany (GER)	1991-2008	1991-2008
Greece (GRE)	1995-2008	2000-2008
Hungary (HUN)	1991-2008	1991-2008
Italy (ITA)	1974-2008	1974-2008
Netherlands (NET)	1971-2008	1971-2008
Norway (NOR)	1974-2008	1974-2008
Portugal (POR)	1995-2008	1995-2008
Romania (ROM)	1998-2008	1999-2008
Slovak Republic (SLO)	1991-2008	1991-2008
Spain (ESP)	1980-2008	1980-2008
Sweden (SWE)	1980-2008	1980-2008

Database: Eurostat, own compilation

A correlation coefficient measures the relationship between two variables and takes values from -1 to 1: a value of 1 means that the variables co-move completely; -1 means a development in the totally opposite direction. For the correlation coefficient, the commonly used Bravais-Pearson coefficient is calculated on a 5 year rolling time window. Moving time windows are used to smooth short-term variations in the data in order to avoid misinterpretation of exceptional years. The window should be used in a way to reflect the real situation in the data.

Later on, the correlation coefficients will be opposed to the specialization index SPEC. Therefore, it is reasonable to assign the rolling time windows of consumption according to the effect of SPEC on consumption. The economic model is mainly designed with a subsequent role of consumption after portfolio-wealth-effects come into force; or put in other words, that portfolio similarity is followed by consumption correlation. However, it cannot be precluded that anteceding years of consumption correlation do have an effect on portfolio choice. This situation might occur if cycles are at different levels in the years before, and the weaker country receives, e.g. transfer payments from a European fund. Consumption cycles assimilate, and people start to participate in foreign investment because financial barriers are lowered and additional money comes into the country. The result would be a growing consumption correlation, decreasing home bias and a lower SPEC. Due to the very limited data availability of SPEC, a compromise would be to choose a centered time window with the corresponding SPEC year as the center.

At the same time, autocorrelation of the data should be avoided. Autocorrelation means that the error terms of two time periods are correlated and might lead to an inefficient estimation. In a rolling time window of, say, 10 years, 9 years of proceeding coefficients are the same and might be serially correlated. To minimize that effect, a window of 5 years is chosen with the additional advantage that five years are a reasonable approximation of the time span of one business cycle.

6.2 Results/Correlations Coefficients

The correlation coefficients of both consumption and GDP reveal an ambiguous picture as the graphs below show. According to theory, those countries showing a declining SPEC should offer higher consumption and GDP coefficients. As most countries show a higher portfolio similarity, as it was shown in the section dealing the specialization index, a general tendency to higher correlation coefficients is expected. The tables in the data appendices 4 and 5 provide both correlation coefficients for each year and country-pair.

A general outline of the development of the correlation coefficients is provided below with descriptive statistics. For a more thorough analysis, the countries are divided into groups, as already conducted in Section 5.2 for the SPEC analysis: All country-pairs (denoted with "overall"), pairs where just one or no country is an EMU-member (denoted as "EMU1") and pairs of countries which share the euro as a means of payment (denoted as "EMU2"). This denotation is used throughout the remainder of the dissertation. The distinction makes sense for several reasons:

1. It is expected that members of the EMU have more correlated cycles for the reasons of a higher (price) transparency due to the common currency and the common framework these countries share (e.g. the Maastricht criteria).

2. The division of countries into groups makes it easier to check for the development of home bias vs. SPEC if one keeps in mind that for the calculation of SPEC, the euro area was treated as one country (see Section 5.2).
3. The main interest lies within the EMU, with the motivation of the optimal currency discussion. However, it is important to know how (potential) members of the EMU can be integrated and are correlated with the Eurozone-countries.
4. A higher propensity to consume is found in rather market-based economies outside the EMU (Slacalek, 2006, p. 21 et seqq.); a higher effect of SPEC should be anticipated for this group of countries.
5. Countries outside the EMU are poorer on average. When countries become richer, they tend to have a diminishing marginal increase of GDP correlation as mentioned explicitly by an earlier version of Imb's paper of co-fluctuations (Imbs, 1998, p. 11; Imbs, 1999). A separation of the poorer countries (mostly, but not all those outside the EMU) could provide some insight into this aspect.

Graph 31: Median Development of Consumption Correlation Coefficients

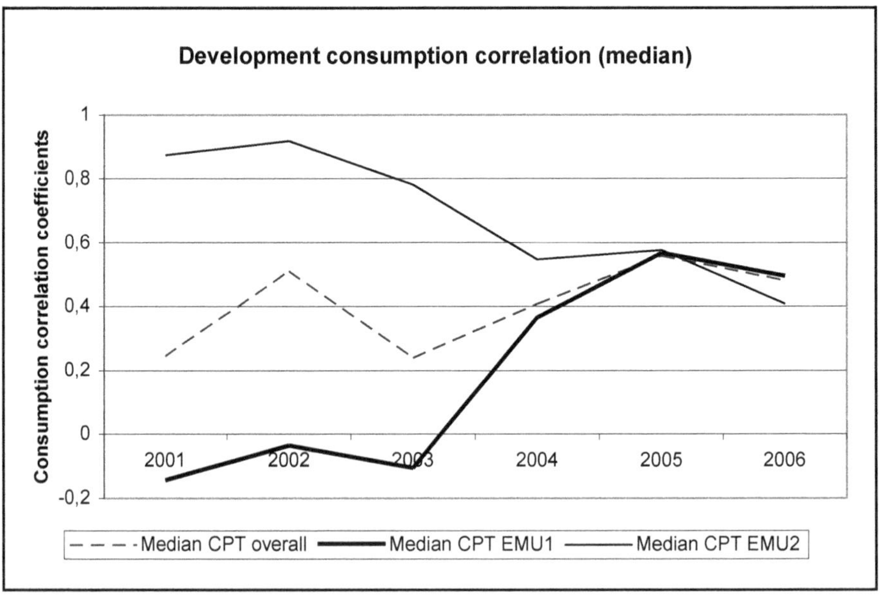

Database: Eurostat; own calculations

Graph 32: Median Development of GDP Correlation Coefficients

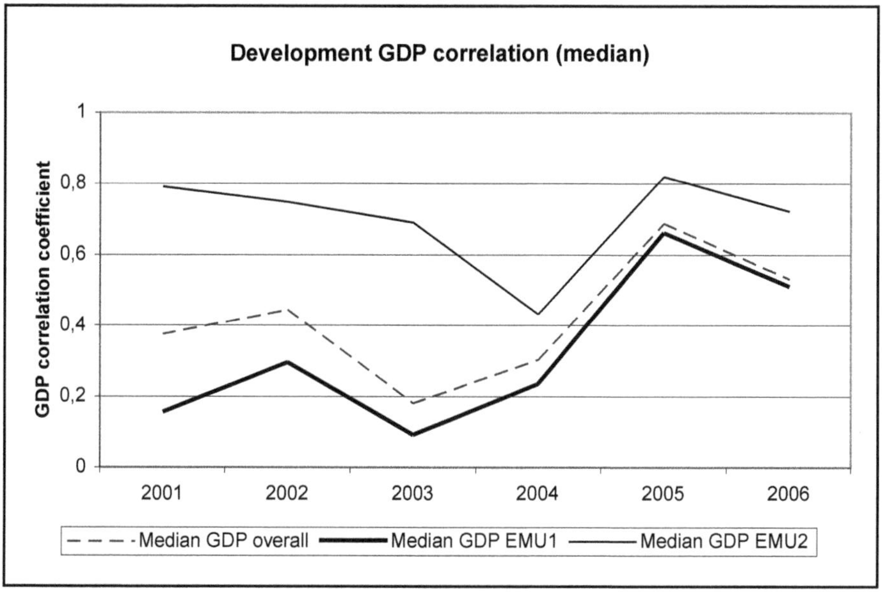

Database: Eurostat; own calculations

The impression that derives from the graphs is that consumption correlation is on similar levels in EMU2 and EMU1-pairs. The overall trend gives an indication for a higher consumption correlation, which confirms other studies (Darvas and Szapáry, 2008). On the other hand, GDP correlation follows the same influences and shows similar devolution in the different pairs though on different levels. This is an indication that consumption and GDP are not exhibited by completely common influencing factors. This finds the necessity of a different treatment in the econometric analysis for the two correlation coefficients – GDP and consumption. With regard to the monetary union, the EMU pairs are of special interest. These pairs exhibit a GDP correlation above the other countries. For the future, the decreased consumption correlation might lead to a decreased GDP correlation as well.

In disaggregating the correlation coefficient, some country-pairs showed particular strong correlations. One would expect that the core EMU countries and neighboring countries especially have rather high coefficients. The averaged data for the two groups (EMU1 and EMU2) confirms the general expectations: the unweighted average consumption correlation is 0.62 (0.55 GDP correlation) for the EMU2 group, and 0.12 (0.22) for the EMU1 group. If the average over the five-year-rolling window coefficients is taken, it comes as a surprise for the EMU2 countries that Germany and the Netherlands have the most dissimilar consumption cycles with both countries being core countries and neighboring countries. The "opposite" surprise applies to France and Finland being the most similar countries with regard to consumption correlation. However, the picture is relativised when GDP correlation is considered. Here, Greece and the Netherlands have the most dissimilar cycles, and France and the Netherlands the most similar ones. For the EMU1 group, Finland and Hungary show little correlation in consumption (Greece and Norway for GDP correlation); Spain and Denmark, on the other hand, have a high consumption correlation of 0.83 (Austria and Denmark for GDP).

The fact that EMU1-pairs tend to have increasing consumption correlation coefficients, whereas EMU2-pairs show a declining coherence, is interesting and should, other things equal, be reflected by the SPEC-development. This had been indeed approved in the previous section.

6.3 Summary of Results for Portfolio Similarity and Correlation

The following maps give a quick overview which countries show on average (between 2001 and 2006) the expected behaviour: a high portfolio similarity (i.e. a low specialisation index SPEC) should go hand in hand with a high consumption correlation (CPT) and business cycle correlation (GDP). Only the average of the years 2001 to 2006 was chosen because of the congruency with the used data in the econometric model.

How are the country-pairs labelled to have a "high" portfolio similarity or a "high" consumption correlation? The countries are divided according to the 0.7 and 0.3 quantile of the highest or lowest values, respectively. The values for the quantiles where chosen to have an approximate trisection of the countries, but still at the statistically interpretable value of a quantile (instead of an absolute ranking of the countries). Of course, these pictures only have an indicative meaning; for a thorough analysis, the econometric model is indispensable. Still, one could learn from a perspective of single countries.

The first map shows portfolio similarity. It is not much of a surprise that the so-called core countries of the European Monetary Union are among those that have the most similar portfolios (in descending order of average portfolio similarity): Germany, Belgium, France, Italy, Austria and the Netherlands. They invest mainly in the European Monetary Union and in return, countries outside the EMU often concentrate their investment in these six countries.[26] For example, in the year 2006 the percentage of total investment into the six countries of the

26 One may note that I count fifteen countries as EMU countries because the Slovak Republic joined 2006.

EMU by the Non-EMU countries amounts to 63 %.[27] Another reason for the high portfolio similarity is that the financial markets within the EMU are well integrated. Just the opposite can be found in the countries of Eastern Europe with their pronounced home bias.

Graph 33: Consumption per Head

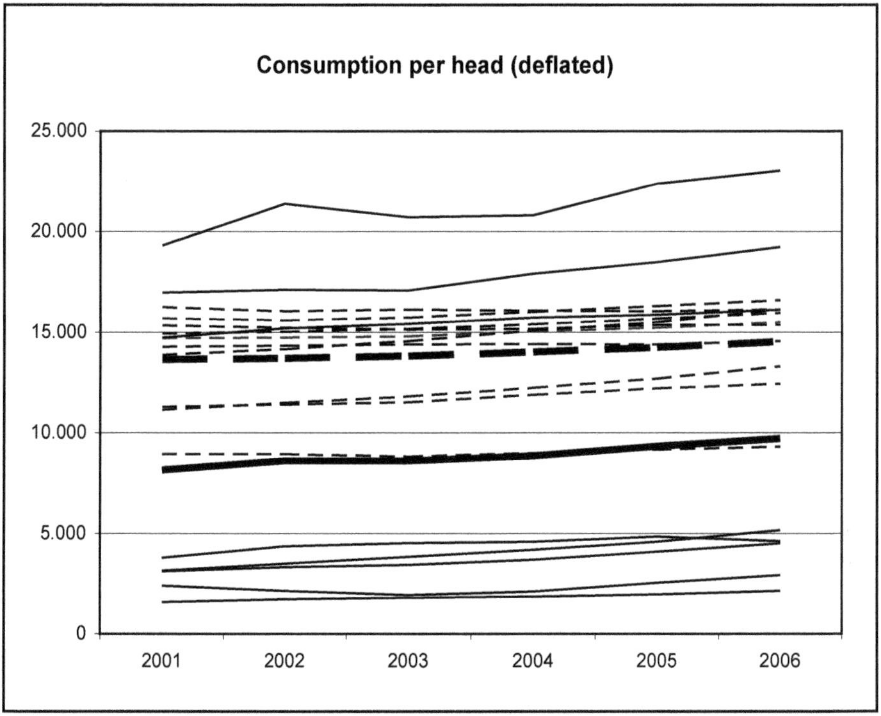

Database: Eurostat; own calculations

Consumption correlation again shows the highest values in the EMU which speaks for similar influencing factors in this area, and a high integration. However, the country with the highest portfolio similarity towards all other countries, Germany, is not even in the middle group of countries with values between the 0.3 and the 0.7 quantile. The ranking order of countries emerges as follows (in descending order of consumption correlation): France, Greece, Italy, Portugal,

27 Investments into other countries flow mainly to Spain and Luxembourg, and to a smaller extend Finland.

Spain, and Belgium. Again, the Eastern European countries, besides Romania, do not seem to be very integrated in the consumption correlation cycle of the EMU countries. This is not negative per se and could mean as well that consumption of these countries is quite stable instead of going through cycles. In general, consumption is supposed to be quite stable, especially if annual data is considered. Graph 33 shows the countries that belong to the European Monetary Union (dashed lines) and the other countries (constant lines). The averages are displayed with bigger lines. It is noteworthy that the average consumption differs more than 5,000 euro per head between the two country-groups although the countries with the highest consumption per head, Norway and Denmark, are not members of the EMU. Altogether, a small upward trend can be observed of about 1,000 euro per head over the whole time period from 2001 till 2006. Cyclical components can hardly be found and if so, only small amounts; e.g. in the case of Norway and Romania, a decline between 2002 and 2003 can be observed or in the Netherlands from 2001 till 2003. In almost all cases, a quite constant, though small increase, of consumption is noticed.

The deciding factor from the perspective of the European Monetary Union and the European Central Bank should be business cycle correlation. Astonishingly, this time the core countries of the EMU do not seem to be as correlated as expected. Only France, Austria and the Netherlands share on average the same business cycle with other countries in the sample (descending order: France, Finland, Portugal, Austria, Netherlands, Denmark). This first sight onto the countries already shows that consumption correlation and business cycle correlation do not necessarily coincide.

The two following maps show whether countries with a relatively high portfolio similarity exhibit a high correlation with regard to consumption and GDP, respectively. The countries that are both times (for SPEC and for CPT or GDP) in the same quantiles are marked with the same colour. No match of quantiles leaves the country colour blank. Whereas for consumption correlation, eleven matches (same quantile for both variables) could be found, the relationship towards GDP seems to be weaker with only eight matches. Altogether, there are three countries with lower GDP correlation as consumption correlation: Belgium, Italy and Norway. Although this is only a rough indication the direction points to a slightly stronger connection between portfolio and consumption correlation, as between portfolio and business cycle correlation. However, there are some countries that have (seen in quantiles) a higher business cycle correlation as consumption correlation (e.g. Austria, Denmark or the Netherlands). The most stable group is the one of the Eastern European countries. This group proved to have a small portfolio similarity, but consequently a low business cycle and consumption correlation.

Graph 34: Map: Quantiles of Portfolio Similarity (Specialisation Index SPEC)

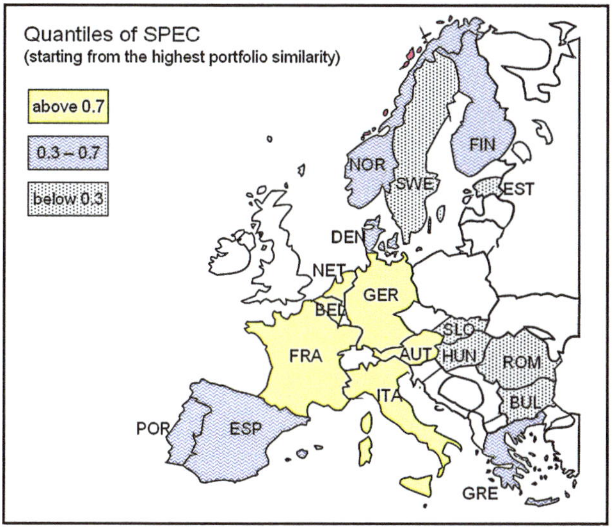

Database: Eurostat; IMF; own calculations

Graph 35: Map: Quantiles of Consumption Correlation

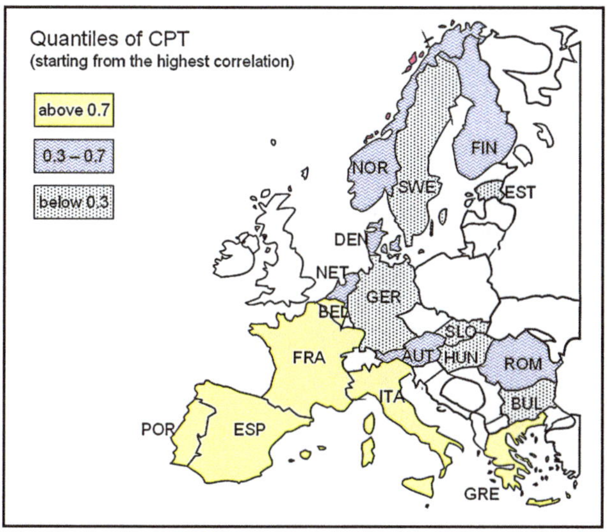

Database: Eurostat; IMF; own calculations

Graph 36: Map: Quantiles of GDP Correlation

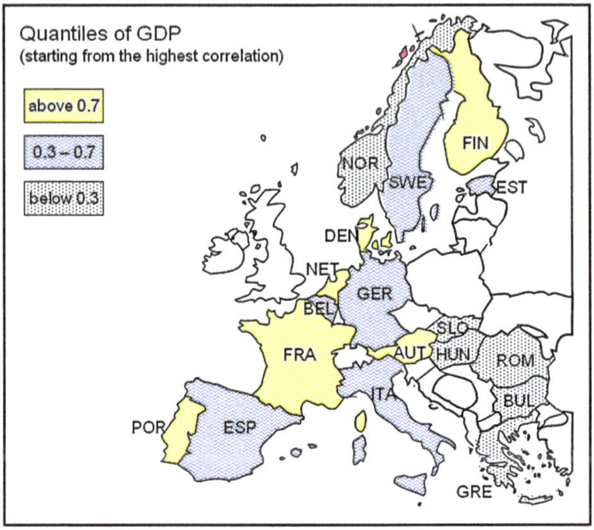

Database: Eurostat; IMF; own calculations

Graph 37: Map: Portfolio Similarity and Consumption Correlation

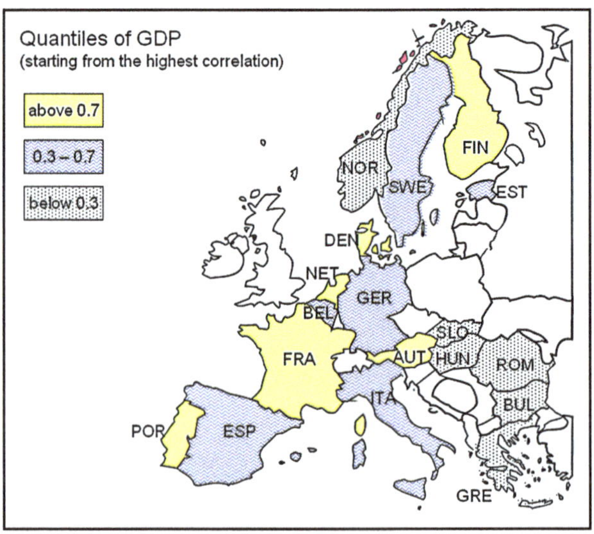

Database: Eurostat; IMF; own calculations

Graph 38: Map: Portfolio Similarity and Business Cycle Correlation

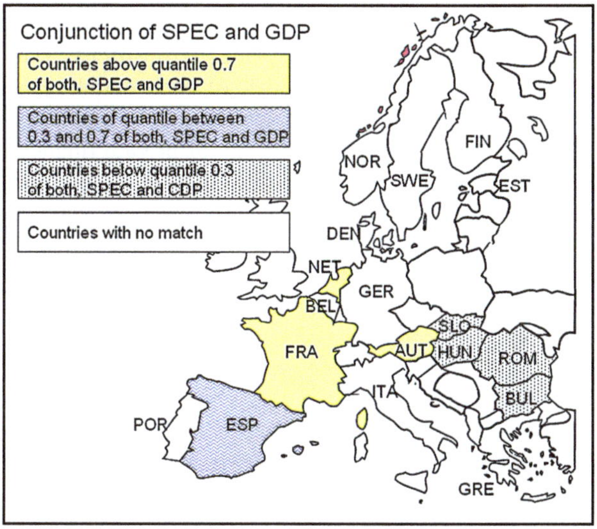

Database: Eurostat; IMF; own calculations

7. Model

7.1 General Outline and Variables

The econometric model explains the relationship between portfolio similarity and consumption correlation or GDP correlation, respectively.

Two additional control variables are included: financial wealth and income. Private financial wealth is implemented, founded by the consumption-wealth linkage and the insights of Imbs (2004) that similar wealth situations contribute to correlation of business cycles. Imbs (2004) measures wealth by GDP and attributes GDP (i.e. wealth) correlation to similar industry structures because similar industries are exhibited to similar influences on the world market. In this dissertation, wealth is measured by private financial wealth; however, it also stresses the linkage between wealth and consumption by private persons. Seen in this light, the consumption-wealth linkage is stressed and not an industry linkage. The more similar financial wealth becomes in two countries; the more consumption correlation is expected to increase. As indicated by the consumption-wealth linkage and the consumption function, a direct positive link from changes in financial wealth to changes in consumption is expected.

The corresponding variable for the similarity of financial wealth, RELFW was calculated by taking the net financial wealth of private households as reported by the financial accounts of Eurostat. Financial wealth consists of cash, deposits, bonds, shares, insurance accruals and miscellaneous positions. Data was deflated by the corresponding consumer price index of each country and calculated per capita. Taking the differences of the logarithms of the country-pairs results in the used variable that expresses the similarity of private financial wealth between these two countries. The lower the variable RELFW is, the more similar are the countries with regard to financial wealth. The general development of private financial wealth is already demonstrated in Section 4.1.

The variable RELINC stands for "relative income" and is built by the logarithm of the absolute deflated differences of disposable income per head of the respective country-pair. Net savings are conducted from disposable income because net savings are already included in financial wealth. The inclusion of income is motivated by the traditional consumption function (as indicated by the theory part) and the insight that consumption out of wealth might be endogenous because consumption and wealth are determined simultaneously through income (Slacalek, 2006, p. 3).

Table 11 summarizes the variables.

Table 11: Variables

Variable	Description
SPEC	Specialisation index as described in Section 5.1: $\text{SPEC} = \sum_{i=1}^{n} \lvert a_i - b_i \rvert$ *with: n = number of countries* *i = country index* *a is the share of country A in country i and b is the share of country B in country i* SPEC ranges from 0 (complete similarity/same portfolio) to 2 (complete dissimilarity)
RELFW	Logarithm of the absolute difference of private financial wealth per country-pair. Financial wealth was deflated by the consumer price indices of the corresponding country.
RELINC	Logarithm of the absolute difference of disposable income less net savings per country-pair. Disposable income was deflated by the consumer price indices of the corresponding country.
CPT	Statistical (Bravais-Pearson) correlation coefficient of consumption; range: -1 to 1. A moving average window of 5 years, centred, was chosen. Consumption per head was deflated by the consumer price indices of the corresponding country.
GDP	Statistical (Bravais-Pearson) correlation coefficient of GDP; range: -1 to 1. A moving average window of 5 years, centred, was chosen. GDP per head was deflated by the consumer price indices of the corresponding country.

Before starting with the formal model, for a quick overview and an indication as to whether the general theory holds, graphs that oppose consumption correlation coefficients (respectively) to SPEC are prepared. All values were averaged over the time period of 2001-2006 as far as data is available and complemented with a regression line.

Graph 39: Consumption Correlation vs. SPEC Index

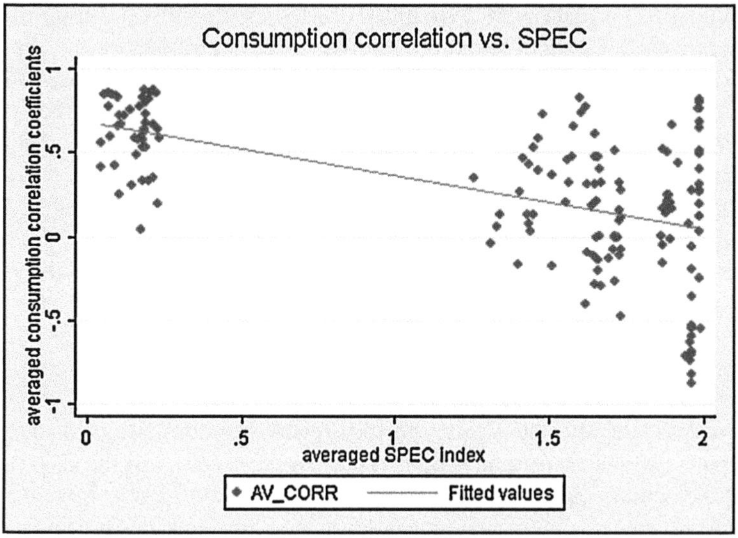

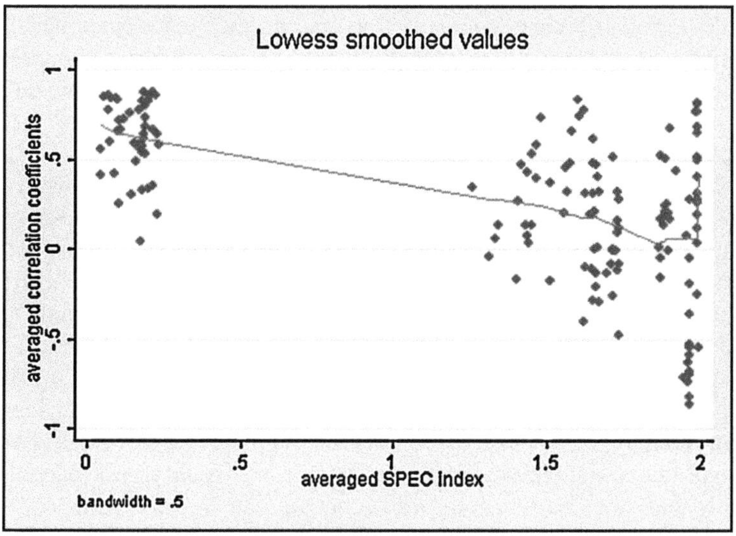

Database: Eurostat; IMF; own calculations

The graphs illustrate the expected interdependence: a lower SPEC (i.e. a higher portfolio similarity) leads to higher consumption correlation. The Lowess-smoother used in the graph on the right is used to emphasize visually the connection of SPEC and the respective correlation coefficients. The technique is based on a polynomial fit to the data with a weighted least squares method. Large residuals have less weight as small residuals to achieve higher variations not distorting the results. This is the main advantage of this visualization as opposed to OLS, which is quite sensitive to outliers. The higher the smoothing parameter, the smoother the fitted values are. Following the recommendation of Cleveland (1979) for visualizing data, a smoothing parameter (bandwidth) of 0.5 is used. However, the general relationship seems to be clear, though not very strong and is more formally analyzed in the model section.

The graphs provide additional insight into the characteristics of the country-pairs: there is a highly correlated group of countries that exhibit similar portfolios structures, and another group with a less distinct picture. The second group features sometimes highly correlated cycles, but are characterized with less similar portfolios (i.e. high SPEC) on average.

The first group on the left with similar portfolios and high correlation consists mainly of the pure EMU country-pairs (both countries are member of the EMU). About 64 % of the country-pairs with an average correlation coefficient above 0.5 share the common currency. On the other hand, there are a few countries with a low SPEC that are not very well correlated. Their amount is limited. Most often a lower SPEC with little correlation corresponds to Norway and the Netherlands which seem to invest abroad, but are still not taken along with the countries situation they invested in. The reasons behind this constellation might be a time issue due to the limited time series, individual investment strategies, or other reasons that determine consumption correlation such as the development of income.

Typical representatives of the second group on the right of the two graphs, with a high correlation but high SPEC, are often Denmark or Estonia. Both countries take part in the exchange rate mechanism (ERM II) of the EMU. These pairs, however, often do not have a similar portfolio structure because their investment in the EMU is not as pronounced as their home bias. An interesting aspect is that Romania is well-correlated with most of the other countries although it shows a deep home bias and therefore a high SPEC. Probably, this attribute can be interpreted as the result of long reaching prearrangements of Romania on the eve of joining the European Union in 2007, and catching up in consumption after the sharp income decreases after the break-down of the Soviet Union. If only the framework would be considered, this would imply that other Eastern European countries like Bulgaria show comparable patterns to the Romanian development. This is not reflected in the real situation though further research on the special characteristics of the Eastern

European countries would be necessary. This dissertation concentrates on the question as to whether the general theory holds.

Graph 40: GDP Correlation vs. SPEC Index

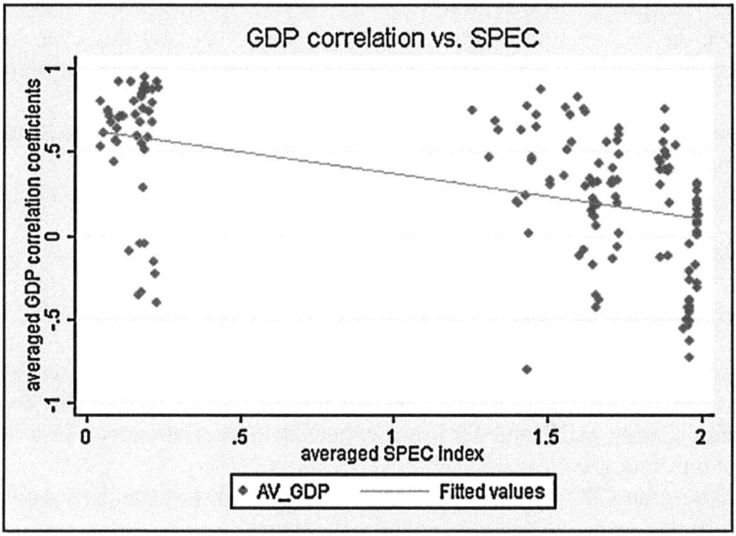

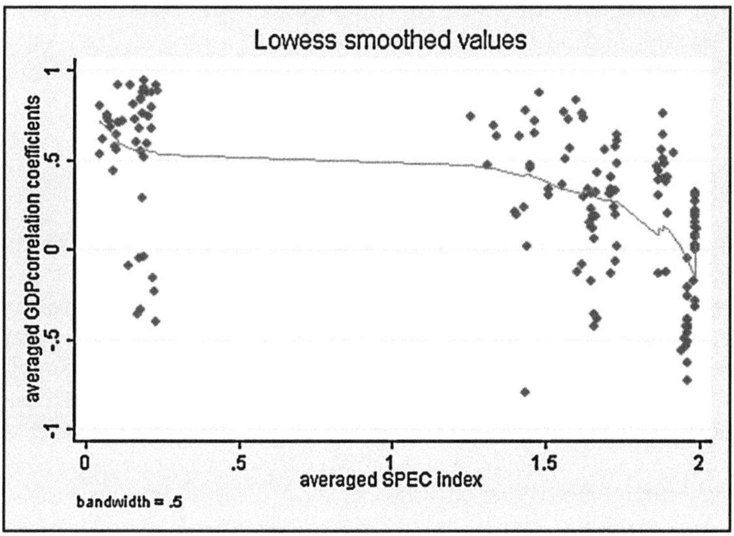

Database: Eurostat; IMF; own calculations

To give a richer picture of the relationship of SPEC to macroeconomic variables, another plot with the comparison of averaged SPEC and GDP correlation values is provided. Here, the connection is expected to be weaker because SPEC is supposed to have a direct relationship only towards consumption and in an indirect way, via consumption, towards GDP.

As expected, the relationship seems to be slightly less steep and less clear in the overall picture in the case of GDP correlation as compared to consumption correlation.

The next section deals with the more formal depiction of the data and analyses whether the empirical findings above are confirmed by the econometric model.

7.2 Econometric Model

7.2.1 Formal Analysis and Model Specification

The formal analysis is initiated by tests of the non-stationarity of the time series. Estimates are in levels instead of differences because due to the use of the detrending technique, only GDP and CPT are expected to be stationary. This is confirmed by a unit root test.

The one of Pesaran (2007) is applied, which is based on the standard Augmented Dickey-Fuller test. The test has several advantages:

- Cross-section dependence is considered. Although the time span is quite low, which is assumed to lead to a smaller exhibition of temporal persistence (Wooldridge, 2002, p. 175 and p. 250 et seq.), a cross-sectional dependence within the framework of the EMU cannot be excluded a priori.
- It can be applied to unbalanced panels, which is the situation at hand.
- A (fractional) serial correlation is accounted for.
- It is consistent for small samples.

As expected, the null hypothesis of the unit-root test, the non-stationarity of data, is rejected for all variables, even if a lag is included.

Another formal test is the one for serial correlation (following Wooldridge, 2002, p. 282 et seq., calculated by the Stata[28] routine as described in Drukker (2003)). Serial correlation is a characteristic often found in time series that shows that the variance of one time period is dependent on the last time period(s). This in turn would mean that errors would exacerbate over time. Results suggest that serial correlation is indeed a data attribute, and heteroskedasticity cannot be excluded either. Heteroskedasticity means that disturbances show diverse variances instead

28 For all econometric analysis the econometric software package Stata 10 is used.

of a constant one and is typical for cross-sectional data. If not corrected, the presence of heteroskedasticity and/or serial correlation might lead to inefficient least squares estimator. As the final time series of six years is rather small and the moving time window of the variables CPD and GDP has a span of only five years, the serial correlation problem should be less severe (Wooldridge, 2002, p. 274). The data attributes described, serial correlation and heteroskedasticity, are referred to as non-i.i.d. errors, meaning they are not identically distributed (heteroskedasticity) and/or not independently distributed (serial correlation) (Baum, 2006, p. 133). These issues can be accounted for by two measures in line with Greene (2003, p. 314 et seqq.).

Table 12: Unit Root Test Statistics

Variable	**t-bar statistic (p-value)**	
SPEC	2.368	(0.991)
SPEC (lagged 1)	39.693	(1.000)
RELFW	4.539	(1.000)
RELFW (lagged 1)	2.001	(0.977)
RELINC	5.442	(1.000)
RELINC (lagged 1)	6.290	(1.000)
CPT	5.574	(1.000)
CPT (lagged 1)	39.693	(1.000)
GDP	0.922	(0.822)
GDP (lagged 1)	39.693	(1.000)

Database: Eurostat; IMF; own calculations

First, fixed effects estimations are conducted and their standard errors corrected for both autocorrelation and heteroskedasticity.

Second, feasible generalized least squares (*FGLS*) estimations allow for both data attributes. However, FGLS is only appropriate when the number of periods is higher as the number of panels (country-pairs) (Greene, 2003, p. 322 and p. 333; StataCorp., 2007, p. 146). Therefore, it cannot be applied here, and I rely on the first technique and correct the standard errors. Whenever it is appropriate, I use the more efficient FGLS estimator used by the random effects model.

Another estimation technique would be a seemingly unrelated regression (SUR). It assumes that the error terms of different pairs are correlated and exploits this information in a generalized least squares framework. Although SUR would be appropriate in principle as well, it is technically not possible since SUR requires a longer time period as the number of cross-section (Baum, 2006, p. 236).[29]

29 All estimations correspond to country-pairs. Due to the limited data availability of a six or seven years (depending on the variable) time series an estimation based on single countries is not suggestive. For this reason the SUR approach is not chosen.

The question that needs to be answered with regard to model choice is: what are the deciding characteristics of a fixed effects model to be the chosen estimation methods?

The fixed effects model is a panel data model designed for a small time period and a clearly bigger number of unities; that means country-pairs in this case (Baum, 2006, p. 219). The preconditions for fixed effects models are quite moderate (StataCorp., 2007, p. 396 et seqq.) and require that the unit-specific residual varies only over units and not over time. This attribute – the variation of residuals over units – is the reason for another denomination of the fixed effects model: within estimator. The name comes from the understanding that the estimations are derived from variations "inside" the unit. The variations around the mean are explained, and the panel average itself is removed from the data. This is the reason why time invariant variables cannot be included. They do not change within the unit and do not contribute to the explanation of the variance around the mean (Baum, 2006, p. 220 et seqq). On the other hand, the technique of a pooled regression would assume that consumption behavior is the same in all countries and initiates from the same level (common constants are assumed). Fixed effects models allow for heterogeneity across units. This means that different intercepts for different country-pairs are calculated and that the individual (i.e. country-pair; panel) effect is correlated with the regressors. Transferred to the topic of the dissertation, this means that it is assumed that the countries start from different levels of consumption or GDP correlation respectively (country-pair specific constants are assumed). The specialization index SPEC and/or the similarity of financial wealth, RELFW and/or relative income RELINC could be correlated with unobserved effects. These unobserved effects are considered to have a roughly time-constant effect on the regressors (Wooldridge, 2002, p. 248) and could be, among others, trade variables, common language, investment, or government expenditures. These aspects probably contribute to consumption and business cycle correlation, but are not explicitly included in the equation. The different intercepts are a plausible assumption because different levels of correlation probably prevail in the sample; especially if countries inside and outside the rather homogenous EMU are compared.

Fixed effect estimation requires the assumption that the slope coefficients are the same across units. This means that the correlation coefficients of the different country-pairs are assumed to react in the same way with regard to changes in the regressors, SPEC, RELFW and RELINC. This assumption was already made earlier in the dissertation, postulating that the propensity to consume is the same across countries. The consequence is that the only way to consider different responses between country-pairs and over the time period of the analysis is the intercept (Hill, Griffiths, and Lim, 2008, p. 391).

The corresponding model for the fixed effects model is represented by the following equation:

$$y_{it} = \alpha_i + x_{it}^{'}\beta + v_i + \varepsilon_{it}$$ **F 25**

with y_{it} *as the dependent variable (consumption correlation; variable CPT),*
$x_{it}^{'}$ *and* β *are the vectors of the regressors SPEC, RELFW and RELINC,*
v_i *is the unit specific disturbance term and*
ε_{it} *the normal residual.*

The subscript i stands for country-pairs (i = 1,2,...,N), t reports the time dimension (t = 1,2,...,T). The vector β has no indication for time or countries because, as explained above, the slope coefficients are expected not to vary over time and units. The country-pair specific disturbance term v_i bears no time index because it is assumed to be constant over time.

A more detailed illustration of the corresponding model equation is represented by the following term:

*CPT = cons(1) + cons(2) * SPEC + cons(3) * RELFW + cons(4) * RELINC*

The expression “cons” stands for the constant.

The alternative to a fixed effects model is a random effects model. Random effects assume that the panel effects are uncorrelated with the other modeled influence factors; therefore, the panel effect, plus the normal error term (see below), are treated as random disturbances (Baum, 2006, p. 220). Another precondition for the application of random effects models are that the sample is drawn randomly from the population. It is more efficient as the fixed effects model if the assumption of uncorrelated panel effects holds (StataCorp., 2007, p. 185). Basically, the random effects estimator uses the uncorrelatedness of regressors and disturbance terms to reduce the number of estimations. If the assumption of uncorrelatedness does not hold, the results are not efficient.

The random effects model is represented by the following equation:

$$y_{it} = x_{it}^{'}\beta + v_i + \varepsilon_{it}$$ **F 26**

with y_{it} *as the dependent variable (GDP correlation; variable GDP),*
$x_{it}^{'}$ *and* β *are the vectors of the regressors CPT,*
v_i *is the random effect of the country-pairs (Hill et al., 2008, p. 398) and*
ε_{it} *as the overall disturbance term.*

The random effects estimator is a GLS estimator; this means that the information is ideally exploited by weighting the already known fixed effects estimation and a between estimator in the covariance matrix. A between estimator is an estimator that uses the averages of each unit and regresses the mean of the explained variable on the means of the explaining variables. While the within estimator only explains the variance of the country-pairs around their means the between estimator only uses the variations of the means themselves (Baum, 2006, p. 226). The random effects estimator combines these estimates and is therefore more efficient if the assumptions hold.

The assumption of fixed effects is verified in each regression by the Hausman test. The Hausman test shows whether the results from the fixed effects model (the consistent model) statistically differs from the random effects model (the efficient model). It is necessary to analyse whether the variables in a random effects model are really uncorrelated with the panel disturbance term v_i. If there are hardly any differences in the estimation of the estimators (consistent point-estimates), the application of one of the other approaches would be less important. If the Hausman test casts doubt on the suitability of the random effects estimation, inconsistent results would be a consequence. The null hypothesis of the Hausman test is that the random effects estimator is consistent (Baum, 2006, p. 230 et seq.). If the Hausman test indicates that the random effects model brings consistent results, the random effects estimation is implemented due to its higher efficiency.

7.2.2 Approach

Basically, there are two approaches for the design of the analysis. One approach would be to estimate the influence of the variables on consumption correlation, and in a second step, a separate estimation on GDP correlation. A second approach would be to use the more modern two-stage least-squares technique that uses the information of the variables SPEC, RELFW and RELINC by calculating the impact of these variables via consumption correlation on GDP correlation. It is described in Section 7.2.5.

Which are the reasons for the analysis of consumption correlation as distinguished from GDP correlation?

First, theory suggests that portfolio similarity and financial wealth both affect consumption directly and not GDP. It is plausible to think that higher (lower) financial wealth on private accounts leads to more (less) private consumption and only in a second step to a higher (lower) GDP. The inclusion of SPEC and financial wealth in the consumption equation responds to the thesis of Mélitz and Zumer (2000, p. 24) as well. They find that after the transfer of monetary policy to a monetary union and therefore to dispense with monetary policy as a shock smoother, the change will promote consumption and income smoothing of shocks via market channels, especially diversified property holdings as here represented by the variable SPEC.

Graph 41: Separate Estimation

A cursory view on Imbs' (2004) results might suggest a direct link of wealth to GDP over industry linkages. One should not ignore, however, that Imbs (2004) measured wealth by GDP which naturally allows a link to GDP correlation via industry linkages and specialisation. In this dissertation, wealth is measured by financial wealth of private households; therefore, no direct linkage to GDP can be assumed.

Second, consumption is a volatile GDP component. Understanding the determinants of consumption therefore helps for the comprehension of GDP fluctuations.

The estimation is conducted without dynamics. The reason is that only bonds and shares are considered in SPEC; in RELFW, additionally cash, deposits and financial accruals are considered. All of these components are rather liquid financial instruments with low transaction costs (maybe with a confinement on insurance accruals). Hence, there are little obstacles for a quick assignment of wealth for consumption, and no great time lag is expected to be motivated by transaction time. Although it cannot be excluded a priori that parts of financial wealth are just stored with the bank, the propensity to consume is assumed to be the same in two countries. A withdrawal of wealth is registered by lower financial wealth values which are mirrored in the calculation of RELFW. If the same propensity to consume is assumed, it is implicitly assumed as well that a reduction or increase of financial wealth has the same outcome in the different bilateral pairs.

It is not expected that the similarity of portfolios and private financial wealth have a dominating impact on consumption correlation, but still with non-negligible economic effects. The assessment of the dimension of the impact is derived from the consumption-wealth linkage literature (as discussed in the theory part, Section 2.3.2).

As stated above, assessing starts with a two-step-estimation. SPEC, RELFW and RELINC are regressed on consumption correlation to see whether the general theory holds as indicated above. The second step is the regression of consumption on GDP correlation with the goal to close the cycle and to check the direction of influence consumption correlation has on GDP. In the case of GDP correlation, the Hausman test indicates that random effects are appropriate in most cases; therefore, a random effects model was chosen if applicable. The focus, however, lies on the field of consumption correlation.

According to the theory, more pronounced (private) financial interdependences should lead to more synchronized consumption. More similar financial wealth should indicate a similar impact on consumption. The expected consequence is that an increased consumption correlation leads to GDP correlation. For all explaining variables, SPEC, RELFW and RELINC, negative signs are expected. A negative sign means that the more similar the countries are, the more likely they are to correlate.

The following tables give a first overview over the characteristics of the used variables:

Table 13: Variables, Descriptive Statistics

Variable	Mean, all country-pairs	Mean of EMU1	Mean of EMU2
CPT	.2457479 (.5826107)	.0538718 (.5778479)	.6722831 (.3442252)
GDP	.2727054 (.551297)	.1843981 (.5501075)	.5636564 (.4329154)
SPEC	1.254481 (.7433009)	1.690632 (.2639865)	.1820124 (.1173527)
RELFW	.5926015 (.4688719)	.7757079 (.4928413)	.2417455 (.1627629)
RELINC	.3722123 (.319188)	.4716529 (.2927319)	.1020557 (.0862881)

Standard errors in brackets

Database: Eurostat; IMF; own calculations

A quick look at the data reveals that EMU members are much higher correlated concerning consumption and GDP as compared to country-pairs where one country is not part of the EMU. The EMU countries show a smaller standard deviation as well. This result is expected because countries in the EMU have strong interdependences and similar framework requirements, e.g. through the Maastricht criteria. Stronger financial involvement is indicated by a lower SPEC of EMU country-pairs; more similar financial situations are indicated by the difference of financial wealth of the country-pair (variable RELFW). The same interpretation is valid for the variable RELINC: income per head is more similar (the differences are smaller) in the EMU2-group as compared to the EMU1-group. The pure EMU group is much more homogenous with regard to the economic circumstances that build the background for the variables as the other group.

7.2.3 Consumption Correlation

The first regression deals with the relationship between consumption and the explaining variables SPEC, RELFW and RELINC.[30] The results are shown in the table below. All coefficients show the expected negative sign: a lower SPEC (i.e. more similar portfolios, closer relationship of the countries within the country-pair) leads to more consumption correlation. Likewise, the result of the estimation confirms that similar financial situations, represented by a negative sign for the variables RELFW and RELINC, contribute to consumption convergence as well.

Table 14: Results Consumption Correlation with RELINC

First stage regression (on CPT)	**Overall**	**EMU1**	**EMU2**
Fixed effects estimation	x	x	x
SPEC	-.6156357***	-0.3279127*	-2.543656***
(t-value)	-3.79	-1.74	-6.3
RELFW	-1.206134***	-1.233496***	-
(t-value)	-5.07	-4.01	
RELINC	-1.548924**	-2.936724***	-
(t-value)	-2.13	-3.44	
R-squared	0.1180	0.1954	0.2985
F-Statistics	14.41	13.52	13.23
Hausman-test (χ-squared)	71.71	86.87	18.55
p-value	0.0000	0.0000	0.0003

Dependent variable: consumption correlation CPT
*, **, *** *indicates significance at the 10, 5 and 1 % levels, respectively*

Database: Eurostat; IMF; own calculations

30 As an additional cross-check the dummy variable for border was included. As no direct link on consumption correlation hints on border significance, it was not included in the main part of the dissertation. I argue that the border effect is already included in the variable SPEC as countries with borders tend to have closer financial linkages as well. This is confirmed by the data because the average SPEC is clearly different (average SPEC for bordering country-pairs is 0.76, for countries with no border 1.32). As there might be reasons that speak for additional border effects like a similar income level of neighbouring countries or border-commuters (indeed data shows that neighbour-countries exhibit more similar incomes), the results are shown in the Data Appendix 7. The evidence on the relationship of the variables SPEC, RELFW and RELINC stays unchanged, however. An interesting fact though is that the border dummy is negative in all cases and in most cases significant. A reason might be that during the analysed time period especially the countries outside EMU increased their financial and economic linkages with the EMU, gained income and exhibit an increased correlation with EMU.

R-squared can be interpreted as the usual R-squared that is known from "normal", non-panel regressions although there are slight differences. It explains the (squared) correlation between the explained variable and the estimations of the explained variable. The within R-squared, which is reported here, corresponds to the normal interpretation of the fraction of variance that is explained by the regression (StataCorp., 2007, p. 398). The R-squared is not too big for all subgroups, but is nonetheless sufficient. Usually, panel data R-squared-results are lower than time series results because the fit over units is usually weaker as it fits more than just one unit over time.

The F-statistics and Chi-squared statistics confirm the model validity. It was expected before that the model does not explain all variations because I constrained myself to financial variables, income, and private households. Other important variables that could explain consumption correlation like, for example, housing wealth or state expenditures are left in the unobserved part of the model. Besides that, financial wealth in bonds and shares has different traditions in the different countries, especially as far as the acceptance as a mean for retirement conditions is concerned. Some countries, like Germany, exhibit lower financial wealth per head, especially in shares because private retirement arrangements have been a topic only since 2002 when a law that regulates funded pension insurance systems came into order. In other countries like the Netherlands, it is an established way to invest in private pension systems. However, all countries in Europe have in common that direct investment in shares is subordinate. This might even be due to pension systems because an investment into shares over pension plans might replace other direct investment (Bundesverband deutscher Banken, 2004). Section 4.1 confirms the findings of the recently mentioned article for more recent years. Because of different savings behaviour in the form of shares or bonds, the explanation power of the model is expected to vary. In general, it is clear how investment affects consumption behaviour: on the one hand, savings targets like retirement indicate that consumption is postponed; on the other hand, behavioural finance suggests that "felt wealth", as could be recently observed in the US with growing housing prices or in the "New economy area" with financial holdings, leads to the feeling of being richer, which again supports consumption.

The variable of central interest, SPEC, always shows the expected negative sign and is significant at the 1 % level for the overall group and the EMU2-group. For the EMU1-group, the significance decreases to the 5 or 10 % level respectively for the different country-groups, but the negative sign is upheld throughout the estimation results. The similarity of financial wealth as indicated by RELFW shows the expected negative sign, that is, if financial wealth becomes more similar, whenever it was included in the model. The variable was highly significant at the 1 % level for the whole sample and the EMU1 country-pairs. However, the variable was not significant in the EMU2 case. A similar observation is made for income differences between country-pairs (RELINC). Probably, the already mentioned common framework, the similar starting level of financial wealth and income, and the common currency offset the influence within the EMU. A first hint towards a possibility of a smaller influence within the EMU can be deducted in Section 3.4.3: an empirical study of Sørensen et al. (2007) shows that home bias (in equity or debt) has a non-significant influence on consumption and income risk sharing for the EMU countries. However, within the EMU the similarity of portfolio shows clearly the greatest influence on consumption correlation, a result that should induce politicians to support investment abroad.

7.2.4 GDP Correlation

The second step is taken by regressing consumption correlation on GDP to check whether the assumption holds that a higher consumption leads to a higher GDP correlation. Both theory and the former results clearly indicate the positive relationship. For these reasons, only a short analysis is conducted.

Table 15: Results GDP Correlation

Second regression	**Overall**	**EMU1**	**EMU2**
(on GDP, separate estimation)			
Fixed effects estimation	x		
Random effects estimation		x	x
CPT	0.3358891***	0.3614807***	0.1394842***
(t-value)	9.62	9.84	3.85
R-squared	0.1449	0.1881	0.0075
$\chi 2$ (F-Statistics for FE)	92.46	96.74	14.81
Hausman-test (χ-squared)	4.50	0.40	0.16
p-value	0.0339	0.5262	0.689

*, **, *** *indicates significance at the 10, 5 and 1 % level respectively*

Database: Eurostat; IMF; own calculations

Not in all circumstances was fixed effects estimation necessary according to the Hausman test. As explained above, random effects estimations are partly used if appropriate. The random effects model might be the adequate method because GDP correlation is more homogenous as consumption correlation, as the descriptive statistics in Table 13 indicate. The random effects estimator is usually preferred to the fixed effects estimator. Reasons are for example that the GLS estimator of a random effect model exhibits a smaller variance (Hill et al., 2008, p. 403) and that fixed effects estimation is at the expense of degrees of freedom (Hill et al., 2008, p. 395). As argued above, it cannot be assumed that the cross-sections (country-pairs) are drawn randomly from the EMU population. For this reason, a fixed effects model seems to be more suitable if it is confirmed by the Hausman test.

The variable CPT is significant at the 1 % level and shows the expected sign in all cases. However, consumption correlation seems to explain only a little fraction of the variation in GDP as indicated by the low R-squared. The reason for the subordinate role of consumption correlation on GDP correlation might be, as already mentioned above, that the common framework of the EMU is more important to GDP correlation as compared to private consumption.

7.2.5 Two-stage Least-squares and General Method of Moments

7.2.5.1 Model

As declared above, this second approach uses (only) the impact of the variables SPEC, RELFW and RELINC on GDP correlation. The difference from the first approach is that only the effects on consumption that can be directly traced back to the three variables are regressed on GDP correlation. Other effects on consumption that are not explicitly modelled (e.g. propensity to consume) are filtered out when regressing on GDP.

Two-stage least-squares is normally used as an instrumental variable approach because some of the right hand side regressors (here SPEC, RELFW, RELINC) are assumed to be endogenous with regard to the individual country-pair effects. Endogeneity means that the covariance of the considered variable and the disturbance term are not zero; or in other words, that the outcome variable and the explaining variable are determined simultaneously. Here, it is not necessary to use instrumental variables. It is stressed that a correlation of the endogenous variables with the error term is not a necessary precondition to use instrumental variable approaches. Though, it is a sufficient precondition. Although instrumental variables are not necessary in this case, the approach is used to have the advantage of the recently described filtered effects of the three exogenous variables on GDP correlation. In the first stage regression, the specialisation index SPEC, differences in financial wealth in the country-pairs RELFW and differences in income in the country-pairs RELINC are regressed on consumption correlation CPT as their direct impact on consumption is assumed. The results of the first regression are used directly in the second regression that estimates the influence of consumption correlation on GDP correlation with the background that only the effects that come out of SPEC, RELFW and RELINC are used.

Graph 42: Two-stage Least-squares Approach

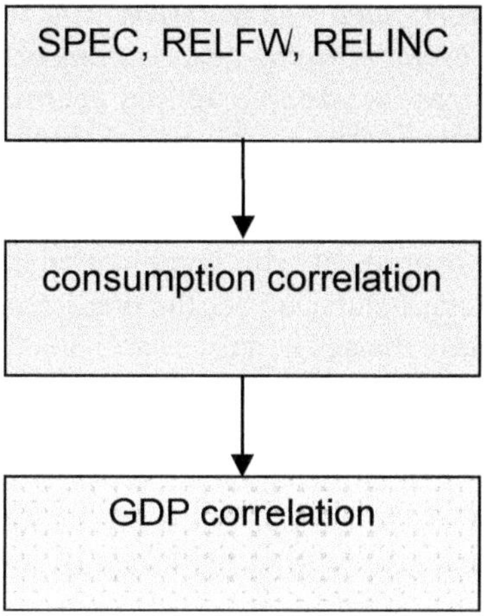

What reasons are there for and against an instrumental variable approach? The instrumental variables are necessary if the correlations of the regressors with the unobserved effects (that are represented by the individual effects) are not (roughly) time constant. Here, only financial variables are used as the explicitly modelled factors to estimate their special influence on the real business and consumption cycle. Other influencing factors are left in the individual effects and are not explicitly observed. Economic theory provides several suggestions for these unobserved effects, e.g. trade variables, common language, policy integration, industry structure, or government expenditures. Whereas it is in some cases quite obvious (e.g. common language) that a quite time-constant effect should be present, in some other cases – such as trade – the influence could change. Over the short time period of six years and due to the moving average window of the correlation coefficients, the time-invariant factor should be dominant. Still, the variables consumption correlation and GDP correlation are determined simultaneously in the same macroeconomic environment. Probably this could lead to an endogeneity issue that should be addressed if necessary. However, it is essential to note that a Hausman test on the endogeneity of the variable CPT brought the clear result that endogeneity is not an issue. The p-value for the null hypothesis that CPT is endogenous is rejected with a value of 0.3472 (χ^2 value 0.88).

The two-stage least-squares (2SLS) estimation is represented by the following equation (StataCorp., 2007, p. 184):

$$y_{it} = Y_{it}\gamma + X_{1it}\beta + \mu_i + v_{it} \qquad \textbf{F 27}$$

with y_{it} *as the dependent variable (GDP)*
Y_{it} *is the 1 x* g_2 *vector with the observations of the endogenous variable(s) (CPT), it may be correlated with the error term* v_{it}
X_{1it} *is the 1 x* k_1 *vector with the observations of the exogenous variables (no additional exogenous variable besides the instrumented CPT is used)*
and β *are the vectors of the coefficients* g_2 *and* k_1 *respectively*

The variables SPEC, RELFW and RELINC are treated as instruments of CPT by combining them into one instrument. This combination has the regression of these variables on CPT as a background and uses the predicted values of this first stage regression in the second stage; however, it uses the residuals of the original regressor in step two (instead of the residuals of the instruments) (Baum, 2006, p. 188 et seq.).

As heteroskedasticity and serial correlation might be data attributes as discussed above, a general method of moments (GMM) approach produces more efficient results as those of the normal 2SLS estimation (Baum, 2006, p. 199). The name of this approach results from the usage of the moment condition that the correlation with the error term is zero. GMM conducts the first step as 2SLS does, but estimates in the second regression in a way that the correlation to the error term is minimized, as well as accounts for the correlations between the instruments. This is done by calculation of an optimal weighting matrix of the three instruments (SPEC, RELINC, and RELFW). The standard approach of 2SLS, however, reduces these instruments to one instrument with a non-optimal weighting matrix (Baum, 2006, p. 195 et seqq.).

Preconditions to use 2SLS as a fixed effects model (as described in the Stata manual for panel data (StataCorp., 2007, p. 180 et seqq.) and in Baum, 2006, p. 185 et seqq.):

The equation needs to be identified. This means that the instruments used are valid and satisfactory in a way that the correlation between instruments SPEC, RELFW, and RELINC and the endogenous variable CPT is as high as to ensure that the estimation result is well-defined. This means automatically that the order condition and the rank condition are fulfilled:

- There are at least as many instrumental variables as endogenous variables (order condition), which is fulfilled with three instruments and one endogenous variable.
- There is no perfect linearity between the instruments, and the rank condition is fulfilled. The rank condition requires that there is “enough correlation between the instruments and the endogenous variables to guarantee that we can compute unique parameter estimates” (Baum, 2006, p. 191). If the rank con-

dition is not met, the equation is underidentified which leads to inconsistent results. The rank condition is tested by the Stata routine xtivreg2 (Schaffer, 2007) with the Kleibergen-Paap rk statistic.

- In an overidentified equation, with more than one instrument per explanatory variable (which is the situation presented here), the suitability of the instruments needs to be tested (test of overidentifying restrictions). In other words, the instruments must not be correlated with the error term (which can be tested by a Hansen test, the equivalent of a Sargan test for GMM tests (Baum, 2006, p. 198).

If the correlation of instruments (SPEC, RELFW, and RELINC) with the variable CPT is not high enough, the instruments are said to be weak. In other words, the relevance of instruments is tested. The relevance is identified by analysing the first stage regression results that are the same as the regression results already conducted in Section 7.2.3. For data with the possibility of heteroskedasticity issues and autocorrelation, a Kleibergen-Paap Wald test statistic is automatically shown in the Stata test results (see help file for the State routine ivreg2 (Baum, Schaffer, and Stillmann, 2007)). The test of correlation is necessary because the rank condition only requires a low level of correlation. This requirement is not satisfactory for useful results of the regression (Baum, 2006, p. 191). Weak instruments may cause a biased estimation of the instrumental variable approach vs. the normal ordinary least squares approach (Stock and Yogo, 2005).

For fixed effect models, the exogenous variables are allowed to be correlated with the individual level (country-pair) effects μ_i, but these effects are considered to be quite constant over time (as already mentioned above). Other preconditions are that the error term v_{it} has a zero mean and is uncorrelated with the exogenous variables and, that no time-invariant variables can be included.

The following table summarizes the necessary steps to conduct the econometric analysis:

Table 16: Summary of Preconditions for 2SLS

Issue	**Description**	**Statistical test**
Order condition	Are there as least as many instruments as endogenous variables?	Not necessary, as the order condition is sufficient though not necessary for the rank condition.
Rank condition	Is there a correlation of the excluded instruments with the regressor?	Kleibergen-Paap test as conducted by the Stata routine xtivreg2 (Schaffer, 2007)
Weakness of instruments	Is the correlation of the instruments with the regressor high enough?	Kleibergen-Paap Wald test statistic as conducted by the Stata routine xtivreg2 (Schaffer, 2007)
Correlation of the instruments with the error term	Instruments that are correlated with the error term produce inconsistent results.	Hansen-J-test as conducted by the Stata routine xtivreg2 (Schaffer, 2007)

7.2.5.2 Results

The equation is set up with GDP as the dependent variable, and CPT as the explaining variable, instrumented by the portfolio specialisation index SPEC, the differences in financial wealth of the country-pairs RELFW and the differences in income RELINC. The GMM option is chosen; the standard errors are again corrected by a robust option, for serial correlation is accounted as well.

The first-stage regressions are identical to the ones described above; for the discussion, refer to Section 7.2.3. Only the second stage results are presented with the test statistics mentioned above. For reasons of transparency, the results of the original set up are presented first; that means without regard of test indications.

First of all, as expected, consumption correlation has the expected positive sign and is highly significant. The positive sign is expected because a higher consumption correlation should lead to a higher business cycle correlation. For the EMU2 subgroup, no significant results emerged because this time the results of the first-stage regressions are used. The first-stage regression did not bring sufficient results as has already been assessed above. In contrast to the separate steps, the coefficients for CPT are higher, but show a lower significance with regard to their t-values. This is expected because the "filtered" values of the first stage regression have a smaller impact as the full size consumption correlation coefficient.

The Kleibergen-Paap statistic for non i.i.d. errors works under the null hypothesis that the equation is underidentified (see help file for ivreg2 (Baum et al., 2007), section "tests of under- and weak identification"). This null hypothesis is soundly rejected for the overall and the EMU1 case. The rank condition is fulfilled.

The test for the weakness of instruments with non i.i.d. errors is conducted with the Kleibergen-Paap test statistic of the Stata-routine xtiveg2 (Schaffer, 2007), it necessarily needs the routine ivreg2 installed (Baum et al., 2007). The used critical values for the null hypothesis, that the instruments are weak, are the ones of Stock and Yogo (2005). The test rejects if the Kleibergen-Paap test statistic exceeds the critical values that are tabulated in Stock and Yogo (2005, p. 100). The tabulation depends on the number of endogenous regressors (here, CPT), the number of instruments (here, SPEC, RELFW and RELINC), and the maximal bias of the instrumental variable estimation vs. the OLS estimation. In the table, the critical values for a maximum of 10 % bias are printed.[31] The test statistic exceeds these values, and the null of weak instruments is rejected.

31 The 10 % critical value is suggested in research papers, e.g. the one of Bleaney and Dimico (2010).

Table 17: Results of the Second Stage Regression – Original Results

Second-stage regression (on GDP)

Fixed effects estimation		Overall	EMU1	EMU2
CPT (z-value)		0.4820545 2.99***	0.7683817 3.70***	-
Rank condition (Kleibergen-Paap)	test-statistic p-value	22.104 0.0001	14.561 0.0022	-
Weakness of instruments (Kleibergen-Paap Wald test)	test-statistic critical value	14.05 9.08	13.413 9.08	-
Correlation of instruments with error term (Hansen J)	test-statistic p-value	22.806 0.0000	8.707 0.0129	-

Overall *All countries in the panel are considered*
EMU1 *One country of the country-pair is a member of the EMU*
EMU2 *Both countries of the country-pair are members of the EMU*
*, **, *** *indicates significance at the 10, 5 and 1 % level respectively*
- not implemented/not significant

Database: Eurostat; IMF; own calculations

Are the instruments correlated with the instrumented variable consumption correlation? The Hansen J statistic is built on the null hypothesis that instruments are uncorrelated with the error term and this hypothesis is soundly rejected, as the p-value of the tests show. A respecification of the equation with regard to the inclusion of all instrumental variables is adequate. However, before the specification of the new equation, one should not forget that an instrumental variable process, as indicated by the Hausman-test, is not categorical.

What are potentially suspicious variables – variables that might be correlated with the error term? According to theory, portfolio specialisation and financial wealth are related to each other. As financial wealth might be driven from factors such as government expenditures (one may think of government aid of e.g. retirement plans), a small fraction could be correlated with the error term and could be time-variant in case of changes of public financial support. Therefore, both variables are potential candidates for the correlation with the disturbance term although only a small variation is expected. As portfolio similarity SPEC is rather motivated by individual economic thoughts and experiences than by macroeconomic factors, a more plausible candidate in a macroeconomic context would be financial wealth. One potential argument for SPEC would be that the variable showed changes over the years of monitoring. A growing influence of closer relationships through trade or foreign direct investment, and thus leading to more portfolio investment abroad, could be observable. Still, it is not expected that the change of influence of the short time period is deciding. Differences in income might be a candidate because GDP and income might be determined simultaneously.

The best fitting with sufficient results of the Hansen J test is derived, if all variables are left in the equation and all variables are instrumented by their own lags. Due to the small time range of the sample the number of lags is limited to two, which produced results that are sufficient. Especially for the specialisation index (which unfortunately has the shortest time period available) and financial wealth, one could imagine that it takes some time until their changes result in real consumption. Especially against the background of retirement plans, a much longer "time-till-spending" effect is probably applicable as could not be modelled here due to the data restrictions. Income is supposed to have a much more immediate effect on consumption; therefore, it is instrumented with a maximum of one lag.

The best fit was achieved with SPEC and RELINC entering the equation with one lag, and RELFW with two lags. The subgroup of countries that are both members of the EMU did not bring significant results; for this reason, the first stage regression is not reported.

Both regression tables represent the results as expected:

A higher consumption correlation leads to a higher business cycle correlation, and CPT is significant. All tests meet the requirements: the rank condition is fulfilled, the instruments are sufficiently strong, and the null hypothesis of correlation with the error term is rejected.

In the first stage regression SPEC enters with a negative sign; that means that a rectified broader geographic diversification of the portfolios leads to higher consumption correlation. Differences in income do not appear to be significant if all country-pairs are considered. However, in the group of EMU1 country-pairs a significant negative sign (on the 5 % level) is displayed. This leads to the suspicion that the pure EMU group (EMU2) is responsible for the non-significance of the result of this variable. The reason for the less satisfactory performance of the variable might be either that within the EMU income is too homogenous to deliver measurable influence on consumption correlation (as discussed above). Another explanation might be that the influence of financial wealth is more immediate as expected or much more behind. As a consequence, a lag of two years might just not measure the right time distance for this sub-sample. The measured correlation with the error term makes it necessary to use two lags, however. Income differences enter the equation with one lag and are highly significant: more similar income leads to more similar consumption.

R-squared and the F-statistic are in both cases higher as in the equation without lags, indicating that probably deferment in consumption is the more adequate assumption. The basic results, the signs of the variables, remain unchanged.

Table 18: Results of First and Second Stage Estimation – After Adjustment

Second stage regression (on GDP)

Fixed effects estimation		**Overall**	**EMU1**	**EMU2**
CPT (z-value)		0.2913388 2.72***	0.2970682 3.70***	-
Rank condition (Kleibergen-Paap)	test-statistic p-value	31.176 0.0000	22.774 0.0000	-
Weakness of instruments (Kleibergen-Paap Wald test)	test-statistic critical value	13.058 9.08	18.883 9.08	-
Correlation of instruments with error term (Hansen J)	test-statistic p-value	3.671 0.1595	4.166 0.1245	-

First stage regression (on CPT)

Fixed effects estimation	**Overall**	**EMU1**
SPEC (1 lag) (t-value)	-1.023339 -5.37***	-0.8005302 -4.16***
RELFW (2 lags) (t-value)	-	-1.551893 -2.27**
RELINC (1 lag) (t-value)	-3.537729 -3.58***	-4.181008 -3.47***
R-squared F-Statistics	0.1608 13.0800	0.3245 18.8800

*, **, *** *indicates significance at the 10, 5 and 1 % level respectively*
- not implemented / not significant
Overall All countries in the panel are considered
EMU1 One country of the country-pair is a member of the EMU
EMU2 Both countries of the country-pair are members of the EMU

Database: Eurostat; IMF; own calculations

The summary of Section 7 leads to the conclusion that hypotheses numbers six and seven are true.

Hypothesis 6: Similar investment contributes to consumption cycle convergence
Hypothesis 7: A convergence of consumption cycles contributes to business cycle convergence.

With these last two open theses, all preconditions are fulfilled. This means in turn that the main hypothesis is true as well.

Similar portfolios contribute via a convergence of consumption cycles to a convergence of business cycles.

The main hypothesis could especially be proved for countries of the EMU-1-group. This group exhibits the characteristic that it consists of countries that have quite different income and wealth structures. The last part of the dissertation considers the questions of possible political implications that can be drawn from the insights gained by the empirical part.

7.2.6 Summary

The hypotheses formulated at the beginning of the dissertation are confirmed on a macroeconomic base. In this summary the individual country view and the country-pair view are summarized and exemplified. What are the preconditions for a country-pair to contribute to business cycle convergence via the choice of portfolio composition?

1. A high proportion of financial wealth probably leads to a higher consumption out of financial wealth. Poorer countries have smaller possibilities to use financial wealth as a mean for consumption.
2. A high proportion of stock market wealth within financial wealth strengthens the role of portfolio similarity.
3. A broad dispersion of stock market wealth over the population supports the effect on consumption. In countries with a very uneven allocation of wealth, the effect might be smaller because rich people probably show a smaller inclination to consumption. The reason for the lower marginal propensity to consume is a diminishing marginal utility of consumption. Not in all countries is micro data available. However, it seems to be plausible to assume that in market based economies, which have a long history and custom with stock markets, the dispersion of stock market wealth is greater as compared to bank based economies.
4. Portfolios of a country-pair are quite similar or became more similar in the course of time.
5. Income and income development is similar in two countries. If income rises much more in one country, a shift from consumption out of wealth towards income might be a consequence in this country. This again means that the effect on consumption out of financial wealth becomes smaller. Another impact might be a higher consumption on just one side of the country-pair, which would diminish consumption correlation.
6. Influencing factors other than the included variables that influence business cycle convergence do not change. An example is the trade linkage between two countries which is in turn probably influenced by the exchange rates for countries outside the EMU.

Which country-pairs fulfil these conditions well? Examples on the country or country-pair level are chosen as follows: first countries are selected that fulfil the criteria 1 to 5 above. Criterion 6 is kept in mind and in a next step the consumption and GDP correlation is regarded. Second, the examples are seen from the result side. This means that highly and badly correlated country-pairs are chosen and analysed with regard to the mentioned criteria. Ideally, in the second step, the country-pairs from the first step turn out to be identical.

The countries are ranked according to their proportion of financial wealth, stock market wealth, and their income per head. The countries with the highest ranks in these three criteria put together are Belgium, Italy, Sweden, Denmark and the Netherlands. The last three of the mentioned countries are market based economies. The financial system only gets a small weight (0 for bank, 1 for market) to calculate the total rank. The reasons for the reluctance with this criterion are firstly, the difficulty to classify the financial system; secondly, the probably quite different dispersion of stock market wealth in different countries although the same financial system is allocated. For the development of portfolio similarity, the specialisation index of these five country-pairs is compared. The most similar portfolios on average have Belgium and Italy; Belgium and the Netherlands and Italy and the Netherlands, all of these are EMU countries. A look at the correlation coefficients reveals whether the criteria mentioned are sufficient. A confirmation of the macroeconomic results is reached for the pair Italy and Belgium with consumption, and GDP correlation well above the average of the EMU countries (consumption correlation: 0.88 compared to an average of 0.62; GDP correlation 0.68 (average 0.55). Belgium and the Netherlands exhibit a lower consumption correlation as compared to the EMU average of 0.62, but still have a GDP correlation close to average. Contradictory to the criteria, Italy and the Netherlands show a low number in the consumption correlation coefficient (0.33) though it is well above the average of the total sample: the average consumption correlation in all country-pairs is 0.27; for GDP correlation it amounts to 0.29. GDP correlation for Italy and the Netherlands is high as expected. Why is consumption correlation for the country-pair Italy and the Netherlands that low? One reason might be that although the Netherlands are considered as a market-based economy, only roughly 20 % of their financial wealth is allocated to stock market wealth compared to almost 60 % in Italy. This induces smaller influence of the Dutch portfolios on consumption. Financial wealth and income show no major changes in their development from 2001 to 2006 in the Netherlands or Italy; the results are not influenced by these criteria. Still, the GDP correlation – the main ambition if considered in the light of ECB interest rate setting – is much higher in the Italian-Dutch case as consumption correlation. This probably means that the neglected criterion 6 – criteria influencing GDP correlation directly such as trade linkages – are important for this country-pair. Table 19 below summarizes the results.

In conclusion, the summarized results confirm that if all the criteria are fulfilled, the correlation of consumption and GDP bring out the results as expected. However, this would happen only if the average of all country-pairs is taken as the benchmark.

Table 19: Summary of Criteria

	1. Financial wealth	2. Proportion of stock market wealth	3. Dispersion stock market wealth	5. Disposable income (EUR/head)
Belgium	63,783	52.56	bank based	21,377
Italy	48,725	59.34	bank based	19,226
Netherlands	52,196	20.64	market based	22,672
Average	23,971	39.22		16,451

4. Portfolio similarity

	Belgium	Italy	Netherlands	Average
Belgium		0.0795	0.1791	1.2793
Italy			0.1979	
Netherlands				

Correlation coefficients

	Belgium	Italy	Netherlands	Average
Belgium		0.8429	0.5341	0.2717
Italy	*0.6779*		0.3345	Average
Netherlands	*0.5463*	*0.5862*		*0.2929*

Numbers in italics indicate GDP correlation coefficients
All country values are averaged from 2001 – 2006
"Average" indicates the average over all country-pairs.

Database: Eurostat; IMF; for criterion 3. Dispersion stock market wealth see Section 2.3.3; own compilation and calculations

The second step starts from the result side. The country-pair with the highest correlation (again averaged from 2001 till 2006) for consumption correlation is Belgium and Finland (coefficient 0.87) and for GDP correlation, France and the Netherlands (coefficient 0.94). Their counterparts, the pairs with the most dissimilar cycles, are Finland and Hungary for consumption (-0.87), and Hungary and Italy for GDP (-0.80).

The table below illustrates that the dissimilar pairs show high differences in wealth and income. Hungary is much poorer as Italy or Finland. The quite similar proportion of stock market wealth cannot compensate this disadvantage: a small amount of financial wealth cannot generate much financial income. Disposable income is much lower in Hungary as well. The development of income and financial wealth per head is quite similar in Hungary and Finland if the growth side of the whole period is regarded. Italy grew much slower as the other two countries, which indicates that the relatively poorer countries catch up. The picture is completed by very dissimilar portfolios derived by the high home bias of the Hungarians.

Table 20: Summary of Criteria – Result Side, Low Correlated Countries

Correlation coefficients

	consumption correlation	GDP correlation
Belgium – Finland	0.8701	0.7581
France – Netherlands	0.5335	*0.9447*
Finland – Hungary	-0.8670	-0.4221
Hungary – Italy	0.4263	*-0.7991*
Average (all pairs)	0.2717	0.2929

Numbers in italics indicate the chosen criteria – high / low GDP or consumption correlation.
Shaded areas indicate the low correlated pairs.

Low correlated country-pairs

	1. Financial wealth	2. Proportion of stock market wealth	3. Dispersion stock market wealth	5. Disposable income (EUR/head)
Finland	20,192	46.59	bank based	21,207
Hungary	5,132	43.11	market based	6,280
Italy	48,725	59.34	bank based	19,226
Average	23,971	39.22		16,451

4. Portfolio similarity

	Finland	Hungary	Italy	Average
Finland		1.9596	0.2118	1.2793
Hungary			1.9590	
Italy				

"Average" indicates the average over all country-pairs.

Database: Eurostat; IMF; for criterion 3. Dispersion stock market wealth see Section 2.3.3; own compilation and calculations

The well-integrated country-pairs (Table 21) do not only show values above the average in the respective chosen category (consumption or GDP correlation), but have high correlation coefficients in the other category as well – especially France and the Netherlands.

At a first glance, it comes as a surprise that Belgium and Finland are well correlated in their consumption because financial wealth is on quite different levels. Still, the highest impact on consumption comes from income, not finance; therefore, the very similar levels of income explain the high correlation. From the portfolios, a very similar stimulus might arise because the portfolio proportions of these countries are quite similar, and so is the proportion of stock market wealth.

France and the Netherlands as neighbouring countries have high trade linkages. Their lower consumption correlation (though still high compared to the average) can probably partly be explained by the different effects of portfolios. The Netherlands is wealthier, and the stock market wealth is probably more dispersed over the population because of the market based system.

Table 21: Summary of Criteria – Result Side, Well-integrated Countries

Well-integrated country-pairs

	1. Financial wealth	**2. Proportion of stock market wealth**	**3. Dispersion stock market wealth**	**5. Disposable income (EUR/head)**
Belgium	63,783	52.56	bank based	21,377
Finland	20,192	46.59	bank based	21,207
France	33,227	29.56	bank based	21,745
Netherlands	52,196	20.64	market based	22,672
Average	23,971	39.22		16,451

4. Portfolio similarity

	Belgium	**Finland**	**France**	**Netherlands**	**Average**
Belgium		0.1822	0.0549	0.1791	1.2793
Finland			0.1917	0.1808	
France				0.1883	
Netherlands					

"Average" indicates the average over all country-pairs.

Database: Eurostat; IMF; for criterion 3. Dispersion stock market wealth see Section 2.3.3; own compilation and calculations

We can keep hold; that the general tendency of the econometric analysis can be confirmed at the single country-pair level. A criticism is appropriate at this place: the analysis is thought for a quick and intuitive indication if the criteria hold on a more detailed base as well. A complete comparison to the econometric is not possible because the static analysis just conducted on the country-pair level does not reflect developments completely. The time series character is only caught partly in the averages. The analysis fulfils its goals, but does not go beyond it.

D. Political Implications and Summary

8. Political Implications

8.1 Reasons for Political Actions

The analysis in the previous chapters highlights different insights and aspects as to why politicians should be interested in the investment portfolios of their citizens. Summarized, the reasons present themselves as follows:

Financial wealth grew substantially in recent years. Investment in stocks gained more attention either directly or via retirement plans.

Portfolios, which are highly diversified as the ones that follow the IAPM, are less risky and more profitable. Especially in the light of the financial crisis and the breakdown of the Lehman bank, politicians and investors became more sensitive for the risk of portfolios and the risk of single shares or bonds.

The latter aspect needs to be judged against the background that (at least according to the media) many investors put most of their money for their retirement on a single address – in this case the Lehman bank. Obviously, neither the advice of their banks nor the financial education of the investors comprises the portfolio view. Another aspect is that the subordinate characteristics of the certificates are not considered in the investment decision. Probably, personal incentives of the financial advisors contribute to disregard the personal situation of their customers.

For politicians, not only is the direct impact on their citizens important, but also the indirect impact via higher taxes and debts because of the need to save banks. As a result of the financial crisis, in Germany, for example, the regulation for banks changed in a way that they cannot buy any positions for their own portfolios without surveying the default risk of a position themselves. This means that banks cannot buy a bond, or share by solemnly trusting the estimation of creditworthiness of an external rating agency as it was usual at least in smaller banks before the regulation. The idea behind the regulation is a more critical look at the characteristics of a single investment. At the same time, a more comprehensive portfolio view is the goal: how does the single investment fit in the portfolio? Does it change the portfolio risk?

One comment to the emergence of the recent financial crisis even goes so far to attribute a massive contribution to the disregard of very old insights of the capital market theory: the disregard of the CAPM with its rather simple truth that more return is only gained by more risk, and that diversification of assets is a solution (Horsch and Paul, 2009).

The macroeconomic analysis shows that portfolio similarity contributes to business cycle convergence via consumption. More correlated business cycles make it easier for the ECB to set their single interest rate to control inflation as their superior aim and to give similar impulses for the economies in the Eurozone simultaneously.

Although portfolio similarity is only one building block of business cycle convergence, this view has been neglected so far. A growing influence of financial aspects due to steadily growing financial wealth is expected.

The thoughts above can be summarized into a chain of arguments for politicians. The guiding line for political implications should be the following thoughts: the macroeconomic analysis indicates that portfolio similarity contributes to business cycle convergence. This is a positive development for the countries within the EMU and should be supported by politics. As the thought of business cycle convergence is usually not enough for investors to invest internationally, a second thought is that portfolio similarity is achieved if investors follow the IAPM. As the IAPM strategy brings more return and less risk, it will be more feasible and more advantageous for investors to follow this strategy.

For politicians, the following questions result: Why is an international investment strategy often not present in portfolios? How important is the comprehensive understanding of financial aspects in private portfolios? What are the consequences of investment and diversification? What can be done to pursue the goal of international diversification?

The aim of the following sections is to give an overview over approaches to support portfolio similarity, and to sensitive private investors for portfolio aspects. These points may differ across countries, and should therefore just give ideas how to approach the issue. As the main aspect of the dissertation is put on the general dependencies and the econometric background, a half-full policy strategy is provided.

The procedure is set up as follows:

The first step is to summarize the obstacles for a declining home bias and portfolio dissimilarity mentioned so far. In a second step, the ideas discussed to overcome these obstacles are classified. The third step combines the results of the econometric model with recently discussed policy actions.

8.2 Reasons for Portfolio Dissimilarity

In the theory part (part B), the main aspects of the reasons of dissimilar portfolios are already discussed. Complete similarity would be achieved if all investors would follow the same investment strategy. A benchmark or strategy is the optimal portfolio proportioning proposed by the IAPM. This means that ideally, all investors hold a world market portfolio and according to their risk aversion, a proportion of a riskless asset. The advantage is an ideally diversified portfolio which offers simultaneously returns which are above the currently held portfolios. Economically, it is not reasonable as to why the benchmark is not followed. Discussions of portfolio similarity always need to be judged against the background of benchmark choice.

Many investors exhibit a pronounced home bias; that means a home bias higher than the one suggested by the benchmark. Home bias and portfolio similarity, though not congruent, are closely related topics.

A quick summary acts as a reminder for the main aspects of deviation from the benchmark:

- Rational reasons for home bias do not deliver satisfying results in explaining home bias:
  - Not all risks are included in the measurement of home bias. Risks that are mainly local and not tradable are real property or human wealth (e.g. risk of unemployment or illness). Domestic non-financial risks should induce investors to diversify their financial risks even more broadly and internationally.
  - Home bias measurement does not consider the co-movement of stock markets, though empirically, a complete co-movement could not be observed.
  - Transaction costs cannot be a real obstacle because the observed turnover in markets is high.
- Behavioural finance offers explanation resulting from an individual perspective. The keywords of this topic are as follows:
  - Overconfidence, here: to overestimate ones abilities to judge financial developments.
  - Financial cognitive dissonance; not to learn from earlier mistakes and suppress bad experiences.
  - Theory of regret: not to admit that an investment decision in the past was not optimal and to take the consequences and sell the respective position because a new position is uncertain as well. Only if others, seemingly better informed investors sell, might an investor follow.
  - Prospect theory: less probable outcomes like gains are given more weight.

Interestingly, literature focuses on finding out the reasons for home bias and most often does not go the last step to find out the solutions to overcome it. Judged from the listed reasons for home bias, the real background for the reluctance of investors to invest abroad seems to be obvious: as the rational explanations – like neglecting certain kinds of risk such as human wealth risk or transaction costs – cannot be proved empirically; either private investors do not know about the advantages of international diversification, or the behavioural aspects are stronger as rational insights.

In some contributions, it is doubtful as to whether the investors – including institutional investors – fully understand the dimension of forgone returns through purely domestic investment, which is supported by empirical studies on institutional investors as well (Chan et al., 2005; Bluethgen et al., 2008; Coval and Moskowitz, 1999).

8.3 Solutions Discussed in Literature

What are the approaches discussed in the literature? The idea of Bluethgen et al. (2008) is that financial advisers use the results of affirmative studies to advise their clients accordingly. A further suggestion is a regulative or tax incentive for investment funds to invest internationally. A similar direction is taken by Van Nieuwerburgh and Veldkamp (2009) who come to the conclusion that home bias can be explained by the limited abilities of investors to learn about all details of investment. Most investors decide to generate informational asymmetries in concentrating on local stock. Although the authors do not draw policy conclusions, a consequence of their suggestion would be to educate investors accordingly. Foad (2008) stresses the positive impact of immigration on international diversification. The author wants politicians to take these – at least between high income countries – positive effects of labour mobility into account. Within the European Union[32], labour mobility is not legally restricted. Because immigration is not a wide reaching instrument because of its small effect on portfolios and is very much depending on a personal financial status, this aspect is neglected in the further discussion.

A solution from the behavioural side is more tangible: Ricciardi and Simon (2000) advice to circumvent psychological and emotional snares by keeping record on own investment decisions including reasons for buying and selling. This leads to a higher control and discipline of oneself in combination with making up objective rules for trading. The goal of this record is to help the investor

32 Besides Norway all countries of the sample are members.

to evaluate own decisions and implement a long-term strategy. In general, a buy-and-hold strategy is superior with regard to performance as compared to high turnovers in the portfolio. One clear objective rule would be to implement the IAPM in the portfolio or buy indices or mutual funds representing the world-wide portfolio.

Put together, solutions can be divided into financial education, regulation and individual investment plans. The rather short summary shows that there is an unsatisfied need for the elaboration of policy solutions. Although the solutions do not go into details, a first judgement is appropriate.

The idea to educate investors and explaining risk and return characteristics of investment seems to be plausible. This would have the advantage to bring in a portfolio view into the investment decision, and an investor's competence and responsibility for her or his money would be growingly congruent. Ideally, the cultivated knowledge finds its way to the personal investment record and results in a personal long-term investment strategy. In this case, the behavioural limitations could be overcome by giving oneself clear rules even for more difficult times. The disadvantage of this approach is the complexity of the topic and how to "teach" an investor. At the moment, there is nothing like an investor certificate to prove that the investor really understood what he or she is doing. A kind of proof would be examinations which in turn would lead to questions: Who would be responsible for the content? Who pays? Who has to be examined in which fields? At which point of time? How is examination organized? Probably, this plan would not be politically enforceable, too expensive, and would not correspond to the image of the mature consumer. Another solution start at the financial advisor's side and is discussed in the next section.

8.4 Current Political Discussion of Solutions

An approach that is already in force in some European countries (e.g. Sweden) and planed for other countries (e.g. Germany) is to "teach" the investor by educational standards of the financial advisor or financial planer. This means that certain standards have to be fulfilled to be admitted as an advisor. This would solve some of the above problems: the explanations of the advisor are directed towards a certain product and a certain investor right before an investment. The explanation at hand of a certain product makes the advice less abstract and theoretical. The advisor understands what she or he sells because all advisors went through education measurements. As a consequence, he or she should be able to explain the investment to the customer, including risk and return issues. Timing, organisation and payment issues are solved. The intensiveness of the process depends on the knowledge and experience of the customer.

The issues that are not covered within the procedure above are the ethical standards. Only if a financial advisor considers the whole situation of the investor like time of retirement, personal goals, tax issues, portfolio view, and other investments and not only the certain product can a "good" in the sense of comprehensive advice be the result. Additionally, the advisor should have the ability to explain complex facts to the investor in an easy language. These ethical standards and comprehensive view are established on a voluntary base in many European countries through different organisations. Examples are EFICERT (European Financial Certification Organisation) (European Financial Certification Organisation, 2010) with currently members mainly from insurance unions, the EPFA (European Financial Planning Organisation) (European Financial Planning Organisation, 2010) with several universities, banks and insurances as members or the Financial Planning Standards Board (Financial Planning Standards Board, 2010). In most countries, as stated above, financial advisory is on volunteer levels. This could – but does not necessarily have to mean – that education of financial advisors and planners is on very different levels.

Partly, this issue can be offset by regulation – regulation in the sense that personal incentives of the advisor, e.g. provisions, should not play a predominant role in process of the advice, and that a comprehensive view on the investor is assured.

The researcher would like to have a closer look at the solution currently discussed in Germany to check whether it could be a possible solution and blueprint for other countries to promote international diversification in the portfolios of Europe. Basically, the policy solution discussed in Germany focuses on the financial advisor and primarily addresses the risk side. Ten theses have been formulated by the German ministry that is responsible for consumer protection to support the aim of a better quality of financial advisory for private investors. These theses can be outlined as follows (Bundesministerium für Ernährung, Landwirtschaft und Verbraucherschutz, 2009):

1. The needs of investors have to be the background and reason for recommendations – not sales incentives.
2. The "average" investor is the benchmark for thoughts on how to achieve the first thesis although financial education for investors is desirable.
3. Financial advisory should follow structured lines. Coverage of the process depends on the situation (wishes of the investor, experiences, etc.).
4. Needs for living have first to be covered.
5. Recommendations for products for a financial investment should depend on the goal of the investment and the risk the investor is able to take.
6. A product sheet should inform about all costs and risks of a product.

7. Interest conflicts need to be articulated before the advisory, this means the advisor has to disclose whether she or he gets provision from the product placement.
8. The profession of an independent financial advisor or planner is established.
9. Financial planners needs to proof qualification and further training. Proof needs to be disclosed to the government.
10. Advisors need to take liability on their recommendations.

Interesting for the promotion of international diversification are the arguments that are specific to risk issues, including the comprehensive view on the investor. Risk issues are decisive because an IAPM-portfolio features low risk. Product specific themes are less important because there are several providers and products which include international diversification. Hence, these aspects, although important for consumer protection, are not directly linked to the guiding question here. In this respect, the postulations made in hypotheses numbers three, five, six, nine and ten are those that deserve a closer look.

The fifth hypothesis wants to make sure that investment strategies are made according to the situation the investor is in. This includes time dimensions as well as risk. In general, a risk adverse investor should not invest in shares in a short-term horizon. For longer periods, especially if the risk component is considered, it is safer to diversify risks. One has to keep in mind that shares are usually not considered as safe products but if one goes into this investment category, e.g. because of the returns, the diversified structure is safer.

The sixth hypothesis wants to achieve that the risks of a product can be understood by the customer. Banks in Germany already implemented the product information sheet after political pressure in the aftermath of the financial crisis. In the sense of the IAPM, internationally diversified investment should score well in risk and return categories if it is accompanied by the meanwhile mandatory protocol of the advisory process. The protocol is only for stock market investment and it should make sure that a comprehensive view on the investor is kept in mind (thesis number three).

Following thesis number nine, the certification of qualification, accomplishes the understanding complex financial products with the goal to transport the insights of the education to the customer, with a focus on risk issues.

The risk issue is further strengthened by the postulation of thesis number ten. Experience tells that punishment often works better as positive incentive. In this sense, the liability of the advisor strongly supports the risk issue.

Summarized in an ideal, a well-educated financial advisor should have a comprehensive view on an investor. If necessary, this comprehensive view is enforced by protocols and product information. Product information should enlighten the advantages of an internationally diversified portfolio in the sense of risk and return. If this investment strategy is ideally accompanied by a seriously taken measurement plan – what to do if certain events come into force such as a loss – a win-win situation should be a consequence. The advisor gains reputation, the investor gains from a higher financial income, the government from profits from well-off citizens, and the ECB transcends from a contribution to higher correlated business cycles. However, one should not forget that the risk advantage of the IAPM does not necessarily apply to all investment strategies. An investment into, for example, the savings account of a bank brings less risk – but less return as well.

One gap comes from those investors who feel competent and do not want any advice, but are not competent. A small security net comes from the regulation that usually for the first investment in a certain product type or risk type advice is mandatory. If the first advice is ensured, at least a certain level of information should be reached.

The flaw in this strategy is that the ideal world does not exist. Investors might disregard their own measurement plans, stock markets might react differently as in the past, investors do not follow pieces of advice, or shocks might distort business cycle convergence. The ideal world is still a good picture to start with and initiates the idea of diversification.

8.5 Target Group for Measurements

The improvement in financial planning aims at supporting international diversification and portfolio similarity. For which countries is the support of similarity important? Several groups can be listed:

Especially for those countries that have very dissimilar cycles as compared to other countries, it is important to support similarity. These countries should be careful not to strengthen negative impulses on correlation out of financial wealth. This is quite important for countries who want to join the EMU. They ideally already possess highly correlated cycles or their cycle converges with the EMU countries' cycles.

For countries with relatively high financial wealth, on the one hand the development out of financial wealth is more important with regard to absolute size. On the other hand, for rich countries, the propensity to consume out of wealth might be smaller. Therefore, "relative" wealth needs to be assessed with regard to income: the higher the relation of financial wealth to income is, the higher I expect the effect on consumption.

The first two points should be seen in combination with dispersion of financial wealth. A country with highly dispersed financial wealth (often market-based economies) will probably have a broader effect out of it on consumption. However, one cannot automatically conclude that portfolio similarity is not important for banking-based economies because the base of people buying stock seems to become broader. Therefore, this information is again only taken as additional information.

A third group might be deduced from the aspects just discussed: countries with small financial wealth probably show a higher propensity to consume out of wealth as rich countries. On the other hand, the influence out of financial wealth on consumption is probably too small at the moment to have great influence. For the (financial) future of those countries, they should still try to support diversification strategies.

To pick out countries according to the criteria listed, the criteria needs to be more specific. What are countries with dissimilar cycles? First of all, the final interest lies in GDP correlation and not in consumption correlation although consumption correlation is an important part of it. Second, a country perspective is taken. This means that GDP correlation coefficients of a country towards all other countries are taken into account. Third, there is the question about the size of the correlation coefficient to consider cycles as similar, or as Artis, Krolzig, and Toro (2004, p. 4) put it: [...] "question of how large correlations should be before we can talk of a European business cycle". The European business cycle is interpreted as a correlation high enough to speak of similar cycles. Following the just mentioned study (Artis et al., 2004, p. 13), I use an average coefficient of 0.5 as a benchmark for the EMU countries.

The second question is the specification of criteria for Non-EMU-countries. First, only Non-EMU countries that want to join the monetary union are considered. Here, Non-EMU is defined as countries that were not members of the EMU before 2001. In the sample, this applies to the Slovak Republic, which joined in 2009. Greece joined at the beginning of 2001 and is considered as an EMU country. Countries in the sample that officially plan to join the EMU in the future are Bulgaria, Estonia, Hungary and Romania. For Denmark and Sweden, it is not clear if they would decide to join. Norway is not a member of the European Union and cannot join the EMU. The three mentioned Scandinavian countries are not considered in the analysis. For Non-EMU-countries, a benchmark of 0.5 seems to be too high as almost no country achieves this value on average. For those countries, a positive correlation with the EMU countries (average coefficient is above zero) is used as a threshold. Within the calculation of the average correlation coefficient, only the current EMU countries are taken into account because it is not clear in advance what the composition of the EMU looks like when the respective countries join.

The importance of financial wealth is considered to be "high" if it is at least one and a half as much as disposable income.

The tables below summarize the results and the criteria and classify countries.

Table 22: Data for Classification of Target Countries

Average correlation coefficients within EMU countries

AUT	BEL	ESP	FIN	FRA	GER	GRE	ITA	NET	POR
0.6458	0.6003	0.5625	0.7167	0.6862	0.5825	-0.1532	0.5924	0.6424	0.6679

Average correlation coefficients of EMU candidates with EMU countries

BUL	EST	HUN	ROM	SLO
0.5015	0.3700	-0.4255	0.0253	-0.0040

Average Proportion of financial wealth / income

NOR	SLO	ROM	BUL	EST	HUN	FIN	DEN	GRE	SWE
0.3169	0.3962	0.4295	0.6010	0.7432	0.8095	0.9359	1.1235	1.1745	1.2303
ESP	GER	AUT	POR	FRA	NET	ITA	BEL		
1.2816	1.3799	1.4030	1.5061	1.5155	2.2822	2.5264	2.9593		

Database: Eurostat; own calculations

Table 23: Target Countries for Policy Implications

Target countries for policy implications

criteria	**measurement**	**countries**
countries with dissimilar cycles		
– within EMU	country perspective: GDP-weighted correlation coefficient to other EMU countries smaller 0.5	Greece (b)
– EMU candidates	country perspective: GDP-weighted correlation coefficient to EMU countries smaller 0	Hungary (m) Slovak Republic (b)
high financial wealth	financial wealth is 1.5 as high as disposable income	Belgium (b) Italy (b) Netherlands (m) France (b) Portugal (b)

Information on financial system:
(m) = market based
(b) = banking based

Database: Eurostat; for financial system see Section 2.3.3; own compilation

The results do not come as a surprise. The financial wealth criterion is only fulfilled by EMU countries. These countries should have a closer look at their portfolios, especially the Netherlands because of their market-based system. Within the EMU, only Greece has a smaller correlation with the other countries as 0.5; the Greek correlation is even negative. For Greece, giving up the power over monetary policy was not optimal in the years of investigation. Among the candidate countries, only Bulgaria has correlation above 0.5; Hungary and the Slovak Republic exhibit negative correlations.

Then again, portfolio similarity is only a contribution to business cycle convergence. Other components of the business cycles, like income development, should be supported to achieve consumption correlation or trade linkages should be intensified. For the mentioned countries, especially those with negative correlation towards the EMU countries, mere portfolio similarity is not enough to pursue in order to achieve convergence of business cycles.

9. Summary

The motivation of the dissertation arises from the perspective of a member of the European Union. In an optimal currency area, business cycles are perfectly correlated. If business cycles are not highly correlated, different signs emanating from different countries might lead to inflation containment policies that are not optimal for all countries.

The main ambition of the dissertation is to contribute to the solution of the question as to whether private portfolio composition contributes to business cycle convergence. The possibility of a portfolio contribution to business cycle convergence has not been discussed in the literature so far. At first sight, the interdependence might not be intuitive. The logical chain of the interdependence is built up in seven hypotheses:

1. The consumption-wealth linkage exists.
2. The IAPM is a plausible investment strategy. It is likely that investors behave according to it; therefore, the optimal portfolio weights derived by the IAPM can act as a benchmark to measure home bias.
3. Portfolios in the sample became more similar.
4. A lower home bias is an influencing parameter for a higher similarity of portfolios.
5. A higher similarity of portfolios results in more similar returns out of this investment.
6. Similar investment contributes to consumption cycle convergence.
7. A convergence of consumption cycles contributes to business cycle convergence.

The hypotheses have been proved in the dissertation by different methods. A sample of 18 European countries was used for an empirical analysis of the hypotheses in a time range from 2001 till 2006. The following table summarizes in which sections the conclusion was drawn that the respective hypothesis is applicable. A more thorough summary can be found in the next sections.

Table 24: Summary of Hypotheses

Hypothesis No.	Short description	section
1	consumption-wealth linkage exists	2.3.2
2	IAPM is a plausible benchmark	4.7
3	portfolio similarity increases	5.2
4	lower home bias contributes to higher portfolio similarity	5.3
5	higher portfolio similarity leads to higher similarity of returns	5.3
6	similar investment contributes to consumption convergence	7.2.5.2
7	consumption convergence leads to GDP cycle convergence	7.2.5.2

9.1 Hypothesis 1

The consumption-wealth linkage investigates the influence of marginal changes in wealth on consumption. The main interest for the dissertation lies in financial wealth. Higher financial wealth provides a capital stock for (later) consumption and a source for income out of financial wealth. A literature review reveals that the impact of wealth on consumption is much smaller as the impact of income although which the latter is economically not negligible. A marginal increase of wealth leads to about two to four percent higher consumption. The higher aggregated impact of financial wealth is, the more wealth is dispersed in a country. A concentration of wealth means less consumption out of it because of decreasing utility functions.

Own empirical analysis finds out that the Eastern European countries show substantial private financial wealth growth rates, whereas wealth stays roughly the same in EMU countries. Stocks and bonds became more important on average in the countries of the sample. The proportion of bonds and shares in a pri vate wealth portfolio amounts to roughly 42 % in 2006.

9.2 Hypothesis 2

To a certain proportion, financial wealth consists of stock market wealth or bonds. It can be observed that the proportion grew in recent years and it is expected that it will rise further. A reason for this expectation is because e.g. parts of retirement plans are increasingly invested in bonds and shares. Although the importance of these kinds of products rises, the development is not reflected in more sophisticated investment strategies.

The theoretical backgrounds of portfolio theory presented in the dissertation entail in the investment strategy offered by the Capital Asset Pricing Models (CAPM). The basic ideas of this model are that first of all, not only return expectations should be included in investment decisions but risk expectations as well. Risk can be minimized by not "betting on just one horse" but diversifying investment, e.g. over different branches and maturities. One step further goes the International Asset Pricing Model (IAPM) that recommends diversifying not only nationally but internationally. Country risks and implicitly concentration risks on branches or certain companies are reduced. Optimally all investors hold a portfolio that reflects the world market weights of a respective country. The risk aversion of an investor defines the proportion of a riskless asset in the portfolio, but still the "risky" part is diversified. It can be concluded that for this strategy the world economic development is the driving factor of risk. Theory, confirmed by empirical studies presented in the literature review, demonstrates that not only risk is reduced by following the IAPM, but return is higher than a single country strategy. The empirical study conducted in the dissertation confirmed the superiority of the IAPM on a broad country base and with a relatively new time series.

If the IAPM is a plausible investment strategy, it is a plausible starting point to measure home bias as well. Optimally, an investor holds only as much domestic assets in a portfolio as can be founded by the domestic world market weight. Home bias is the deviation of the actual weight from the optimal weight and is quite pronounced in many countries. So far many studies concentrated on a small number of countries or on institutional investors. Newer data from the IMF and Eurostat are available to give an indication for private portfolio holdings. Optimal weights are calculated by stock market data of the World Federation of Exchanges, representing many stock markets including the major ones. The data , approximates optimal (world market) weights. The empirical analysis concludes that home bias is indeed declining for most countries. The exceptions are Eastern European countries that are still reluctant in investing abroad because their financial markets have just been opened.

9.3 Hypothesis 3

A reduced home bias does not automatically mean that portfolios are diversified well because the benchmark is not only the domestic market but the world market. This leads to the aspect that a decreasing home bias does not necessarily imply a higher portfolio similarity of two countries although these topics are closely related to each other. Why does portfolio similarity contribute to business cycle convergence and why is home bias not enough? If portfolios are very similar, their performances are very alike and similar returns and losses are generated. If the marginal propensity to consume resembles, the impact of portfolio wealth on consumption has the same characteristics. This general idea applies whether portfolio holders follow the IAPM or not. Home bias, on the other hand, often goes hand in hand with portfolio similarity as the results of the empirical analysis indicate. However, it does not necessarily mean that portfolios are similar.

Similarity is measured with a specialisation index that has been applied before to measure industrial structures. The specialisation index is calculated pair wise for 153 country-pairs. The index considers the similarity of the portfolios of two countries by taking differences between the portfolio weight of a certain country into country A and B. Empirically, it was assumed for the EMU countries that the Eurozone is considered as one country with regard to the closely integrated financial markets. The results being averaged over all country-pairs clearly show that portfolios become more similar in the time of investigation: the specialisation index declined from 1.36 in 2001 to 1.08 in 2007. The results differ between country-pairs within the EMU (called EMU2) and country-pairs which consist (partly) of countries outside the EMU (EMU1 or EMU0). Whereas the EMU2 pairs have a relatively high similarity at the beginning, EMU countries tend to broaden their investment outside the EMU and do not necessarily follow the same investment strategies. On the other hand, the EMU1 group invests more and more within the Eurozone and its index declines highly.

9.4 Hypothesis 4

Hypothesis 4 could have been endued with the question: why care about home bias if portfolio similarity is enough to explain its effect on consumption? The answer is the close relationship between these two aspects. As analysed above, a low home bias does not necessarily lead to portfolio similarity. Though not necessarily, empirically there are indications that the development of both aspects follows the same path. As simple as it sounds, if home bias decreases, investment must go “somewhere abroad”. This “somewhere” is probably not coincidentally chosen. Topics such as international diversification gain more interest especially in the aftermath of the financial crisis – even in popular media. An investor is probably sensitised for portfolio allocation and thinks more carefully about diversification aspects.

9.5 Hypothesis 5

The basic idea of thesis five is that similar portfolios generate similar returns. If the marginal propensity to consume out of wealth is the same on a macroeconomic level, similar impacts on consumption can be expected. A dispersion of portfolio returns would indicate different effects on consumption out of financial wealth. Returns are calculated according to the data of the Datastream total return index. A drawback of this approach is that indices are used to approximate portfolio returns. This presumes that the aggregated portfolios of investors of country A in country B reflect the index composition of country B, otherwise returns do differ from the calculated one. As the portfolio composition within countries is not available, approximation is the best data available. Due to the high number of investors in a country the error is probably a minor one. The empirical analysis which opposes the averaged specialisation index of each country-pair to its difference in returns brings out that portfolios with a lower index have more similar returns indeed. The returns of the EMU2 pairs tend to be quite similar. Another trend is that portfolios become more similar over the years. It cannot be answered definitely whether the source of similarity derives mainly from an increased portfolio similarity or a general convergence of stock markets. Probably both developments make their contributions.

9.6 Hypothesis 6

The central points of the dissertation are hypotheses six and seven, the linkage of portfolios to consumption and business cycle convergence. This is an insight that is new to the literature. Consumption and GDP are deflated and de-trended by a Hodrick-Prescott filter to distinguish the difference between the trend component and the cycle component of the business or consumption cycle. The resulting time series are correlated in a moving time-window of five years to cancel extraordinary developments. A first positive indication for both hypotheses is conducted by opposing the specialisation index and consumption correlation or business cycle correlation respectively.

For further research, an econometric model is used to underpin the hypotheses in a more formal way. The 153 country-pairs are taken separately to uphold as much information as possible and to demonstrate the general linkage of portfolio and consumption. The chosen model is a fixed effects model, because the fixed effects model is a panel data model designed for a rather small time period (here: 2001 till 2006) and a clearly bigger number of units (here: country-pairs). Another reason for the choice of fixed estimation is that it allows for different constants, that is different initiating levels of consumption or GDP correlation of the different country-pairs. On the other hand, fixed effect estimation implies that the slopes of the correlation coefficients are the same; that means all country-pairs react identically towards a change of the regressors. The appropriateness of the fixed effects estimation is validated by the Hausman tests. In some estimations, a random effect model is implemented because it is more efficient and the Hausman test shows its consistency. Both, disposable income and financial wealth, are included on top of the portfolio similarity to get a more complete picture on consumption. To integrate financial wealth, the differences between two county-pairs are taken: The more similar financial wealth and disposable income per head are in two countries, the more similar should be effect on consumption. The usual data diagnostics are conducted and the problematic data attributes, serial correlation and heteroscedastity is accounted for by correcting standard errors.

The results of the econometric model turned out as expected for the whole sample and the EMU1 country-pairs: A lower specialisation index (that means, a higher similarity of portfolios) means increased consumption correlation; lower differences in disposable income and financial wealth shows a positive effect on consumption correlation as well. For the EMU1 pairs it is expected that especially income similarity will contribute to consumption convergence in the future. Interestingly, the countries within the EMU income and financial wealth did not prove to be significant. A reason might be because these countries are quite homogenous. Portfolio similarity, on the other hand, was highly significant in the EMU2 pairs. To conclude, portfolio similarity is important to all country groups in the sample.

9.7 Hypothesis 7

The final part of the chain is to show that consumption synchronisation is the channel for business cycle synchronisation. The method used for this estimation is a two-stage least-square approach (2SLS), using the results of the consumption estimation above as an instrumental variable for consumption. Two-stage least-squares is not used as an instrumental variable approach as it is generally used. Instrumental variables are necessary if one of the regressors is correlated with the error term, which is not applicable here. Here the approach is used to filter the effect on GDP via consumption, which is in turn influenced by portfolio similarity, financial wealth and income. The correlation of the endogenous variables with the error term is not a necessary precondition to use an instrumental variable approach though a sufficient precondition. The 2SLS approach requires that the instrumented variable, consumption correlation, is not correlated with its instruments, namely, the three variables portfolio similarity, financial wealth and income. Statistical tests indicate that this precondition of uncorrelatedness is not fulfilled. For these reasons, the instrumental variables are instrumented by their own lags to a maximum of two lags to achieve satisfactory statistical characteristics. For the country-pairs that are within the EMU the adapted equation with lags does not bring statistically significant results. It cannot be excluded that within the EMU the variables do not contribute to business cycle convergence in the time of investigation, although this transmission channel is economically intuitive. Reasons for the impact on EMU2 country-pairs might be the already predominating similar level of the variables and the high level of business cycle correlation. For the other country-pairs and the overall sample the general coherence of portfolio similarity and business cycle convergence is confirmed. This insight is important as leverage points for political actions and focuses especially for the countries outside the EMU that consider joining the monetary union. For country-pairs whose cycles are on a lower level of correlation a higher impact of the investigated variables is expected.

Hypothesis number seven closes and proves the chain to the main statement of the dissertation and novel insight: Similar portfolios contribute via a convergence of consumption cycles to a convergence of business cycles.

9.8 Outlook

The topic of portfolio similarity deserves a closer look in some respects either because of the lack of data or because of the focus of the dissertation wherein some topics have not been covered by the dissertation. Some suggestions for further research are as follows:

The role of dispersion of financial wealth in combination with the financial system needs to be analyzed in more details. So far data is missing to judge on the distribution of stock market wealth. The dispersion of wealth might be a driving factor for its impact on consumption.

An open question that is closely related to the topic of wealth distribution is the question of the financial system. If the financial system influences ECB monetary policy after some years of EMU experience went by has not been answered yet.

For the Eastern European countries comprehensive and comparative studies on the consumption-wealth linkage are missing. In a growing EMU it is important to understand how new members react to changes in wealth.

The role of portfolio similarity in the event of shocks needs to be answered. Will portfolios act as a cushion if e.g. output shocks occur? Is portfolio similarity a key for risk smoothing?

The latter topic is probably related to the question, if financial wealth and portfolio similarity lead to smaller amplitudes in business cycles. Smaller amplitudes are desirable for politicians because political pressure in a recession might be less and would save money that did not need to be repaid in growth periods.

The model could be enlarged by introducing behavioural aspects into the equation to be able to forecast investment behaviour more accurately instead of using a rational benchmark.

Finally, political implications to support the responsible handling of financial topics, especially international diversification need to be elaborated.

It is desirable to analyse with a longer timeframe whether the general relationship between portfolio similarity, consumption and GDP correlation is still valid in the future, especially after the financial crisis that portfolio strategies might change and political measurements to steer investment flows might be a consequence for portfolio allocation.

In this context it is reiterated that it is a general issue of econometrics that firstly, the economical reality is reduced on statistical time series; secondly, the past is expected to forecast the future. The first issue can be partly addressed by enlarging models with potential candidate variables. Although it will never happen in practice that all influencing factors are included (otherwise it would not be a model), the gap is made smaller. The second issue is more severe: Several crises illustrated that the past does not just contain information about the future.

As most econometric work the dissertation is to be understood as an explanation of the past and a good indication (though not soothsaying) for the developments in the future. This does not mean that the results are not justifiable: it is more important for the interpretation of the results that the insights gained by the dissertation are not only econometrically founded but economically rational and explainable as well. The econometric background in this sense confirms plausible thoughts of interdependences between financial wealth aspects, income and consumption and business cycle correlation.

References

Adjaouté, K., Danthine, J., and Isakov, D. (2005). Portfolio Diversification in Europe. In Huizinga, H. and Jonung, L. (Eds.), The Internationalisation of Asset Ownership in Europe (pp. 140-172). New York: Cambridge University Press.

Ando, A. and Modigliani, F. (1963). The "Life Cycle" Hypothesis of Saving: Aggregate Implications and Tests. The American Economic Review, 103, 55-84.

Arnold, I.J. and De Vries, C.G. (1999). Endogenous Financial Structure and the Transmission of ECB Policy. In von Hagen J. and Waller C. J. (Eds.), Regional Aspects of Monetary Policy in Europe (pp. 193-218). Boston: Kluwer.

Artis, M., Krolzig, H., and Toro, J. (2004). The European Business Cycle. Oxford Economic Papers, 56, 1-44.

Artis, M.J. (2003). Is There a European Business Cycle? CESifo Working Paper Series, 1053. San Domenico di Fiesole.

Backus, D.K., Kehoe, P.J., and Kydland, F.E. (1992). International Real Business Cycles. The Journal of Political Economy, 100, 745-775.

Baele, L., Pungulescu, C., and Ter Horst, J. (2007). Model Uncertainty, Financial Market Integration and the Home Bias Puzzle. Journal of International Money and Finance, 26, 606-630.

Banerjee, A.V. (1992). A Simple Model of Herd Behaviour. The Quarterly Journal of Economics, 107, 797-817.

Barberis, N. and Thaler, R.H. (2003). A Survey of Behavioral Finance. In Constantinides, G., Harris, M., and Stulz, R. (Eds.), Handbook of the Economics of Finance (pp. 1053-1128). Amsterdam: North-Holland.

Barrell, R. and Davis, P.E. (2004). Consumption, Financial and Real Wealth in the G-5. NIESR Discussion Papers, 232. London.

Barrell, R., Byrne, J.P., and Dury, K. (2003). The Implications of Diversity in Consumption Behaviour for the Choice of Monetary Policy Rules in Europe. Economic Modelling, 20, 275-299.

Bassanetti, A. and Zollino, F. (2008). The Effects of Housing and Financial Wealth on Personal Consumption: Aggregate Evidence for Italian Households. Bank of Italy Research Paper, A12. Rome.

Baum, C.F., Schaffer, M.E., and Stillmann, S. (2007). IVREG2: Stata Module for Extended Instrumental Variables/2SLS and GMM Estimation. URL: http://ideas.repec.org/c/boc/bocode/s425401.html. Date of retrieval: 2009-03-17.

Baum, C.F. (2006). An Introduction to Modern Econometrics Using Stata. College Station, Texas: Stata Press.

Baxter, M. and Jermann, U.J. (1997). The International Diversification Puzzle is Worse Than You Think. The American Economic Review, 87, 170-180.

Belke, A. and Heine, J.M. (2006). Specialisation Patterns and the Synchronicity of Regional Employment Cycles in Europe. International Economics and Economic Policy, 3, 91-104.

Belke, A. and Heine, J.M. (2007). On the Endogeneity of an Exogenous OCA-Criterion: Specialisation and the Correlation of Regional Business Cycles in Europe. Empirica, 34, 15-44.

Belke, A., Eppendorfer, C., and Heine, J.M. (2002). Finanzmarktstrukturen und geldpolitischer Transmissionsprozess in der EWU. Wirtschaftsdienst, 82, 435-444.

Beneish, M.D. and Yohn, T.L. (2008). Information Friction and Investor Home Bias: A Perspective on the Effect of Global IFRS Adoption on the Extent of Equity Home Bias. Journal of Accounting and Public Policy, 27, 433-443.

Black, F., Jensen, M.C., and Scholes, M.S. (1972). The Capital Asset Pricing Model: Some Empirical Tests. In Jensen, M. C. (Ed.), Studies in the Theory of Capital Markets (p. 79-121). New York: Praeger.

Bleaney, M. and Dimico, A. (2010). Geography Matters: Reconsidering the Effect of Geography on Development. Journal of African Economies (Advance Access, forthcoming). Date of publication: 2010-05-18.

Bluethgen, R., Hackethal, A., Jansen, C., and Meyer, S. (2008). The Cost of Home Bias: Empirical Evidence and Implications for Stock Market Participation. Working Paper, Oestrich-Winkel.

Bosch, T. and Schoenmaker, D. (2008). Is the Home Bias in Equities and Bonds Declining in Europe? Investment Management and Financial Innovations, 5, 90-102.

Bostic, R., Gabriel, S., and Painter, G. (2009). Housing Wealth, Financial Wealth, and Consumption: New Evidence from Micro Data. Regional Science and Urban Economics, 39, 79-89.

Brooks, R. and Del Negro, M. (2004). The Rise in Comovement Across National Stock Markets: Market Integration or IT Bubble? Journal of Empirical Finance, 11, 659-680.

Bundesministerium für Ernährung, Landwirtschaft und Verbraucherschutz (2009). Thesenpapier zur Qualität der Finanzberatung und Qualifikation der Finanzvermittler. URL: http://www.bmelv.de/cae/servlet/contentblob/656302/

publicationFile/51632/Thesenpapier-Finanzberatung.pdf. Date of retrieval: 2010-03-20.

Bundesverband deutscher Banken (2004). Das Sparverhalten in Europa ändert sich nur langsam. URL: http://www.bankenverband.de/print.asp?artid=1235andchannel=12121010. Date of retrieval: 2009-05-27.

Bühler, A. (1995). Performance-Messung: Eine empirische Untersuchung unter Berücksichtigung von Modellen mit variablen Parametern. Schweizerische Zeitschrift für Volkswirtschaft und Statistik, 131, 673-700.

Calvo, G.A. and Mendoza, E.G. (2000). Rational Contagion and the Globalization of Securities Markets. Journal of International Economics, 51, 79-113.

Chan, K., Covrig, V., and Ng, L.K. (2005). What Determines the Domestic Bias and Foreign Bias?: Evidence from Mutual Fund Equity Allocations Worldwide. Journal of Finance, 60, 1495-1534.

Čihák, M., Harjes, T., and Stavrev, E. (2009). Euro Area Monetary Policy in Uncharted Waters. IMF Working Papers, 09/185. Washington D.C.

Clark, T.E. and van Wincoop, E. (2001). Borders and Business Cycles. Journal of International Economics, 55, 59-85.

Cleveland, W.S. (1979). Robust Locally Weighted Regression and Smoothing Scatterplots. Journal of the American Statistical Association, 74, 829-836.

Cooper, I., and Kaplanis, E. (1994). Home Bias in Equity Portfolios, Inflation Hedging, and International Capital Market Equilibrium. The Review of Financial Studies, 7, 45-60.

Coval, J.D. and Moskowitz, T.J. (1999). Home Bias at Home: Local Equity Preference in Domestic Portfolios. The Journal of Finance, 54, 2045-2073.

Darvas, Z. and Szapáry, G. (2008). Business Cycle Synchronization in the Enlarged EU. Open Economies Review, 19, 1-19.

De Castro, G.L. (2007). The Wealth Effect on Consumption in the Portuguese Economy. Bank of Portugal Economic Bulletin, 13, 37-55.

De Santis, G. and Gérard, B. (1997). International Asset Pricing and Portfolio Diversification with Time-Varying Risk. The Journal of Finance, 52, 1181-1912.

De Santis, G. and Gérard, B. (2006). Financial Integration, International Portfolio Choice and the European Monetary Union. ECB Working Paper Series, 626. Frankfurt a.M.

Decamps, J. and Lovo, S. (2006). A Note on Risk Aversion and Herd Behavior in Financial Markets. Geneva Risk and Insurance, 2006, 35-42.

Disney, R., Henley, A., and Jevons, D. (2003). House Price Shocks, Negative Equity and Household Consumption in the UK. Mimeo, Nottingham.

Dreger, C. and Reimers, H. (2006). Consumption and Disposable Income in the EU Countries: The Role of Wealth Effects. Empirica, 33, 245–254.

Drukker, D.M. (2003). Testing for Serial Correlation in Linear Panel-Data Models. The Stata Journal, 3, 168–177.
Duval, R., Elmeskov, J., and Vogel, L. (2007). Structural Policies and Economic Resilience to Shocks. OECD Economics Department Working Papers, 567. Paris.
Elbourne, A. and de Haan, J. (2006). Financial Structure and Monetary Policy Transmission in Transition Countries. Journal of Comparative Economics, 34, 1-23.
Elton, E.J., Gruber, M.J., Brown, S.J., and Goetzmann, W.N. (2007). Modern Portfolio Theory and Investment Analysis. Hoboken, New Jersey: John Wiley and Sons.
Erber, G. and Hagemann, H. (2010). Monetary Policy Challenges of the ECB Facing a Divergent Inflationary Process in the EMU Area. In Fontana, G., McCombie, J., and Sawyer, M. C. (Eds.), Macroeconomics, Finance and Money: Essays in Honour of Philip Arestis (pp. 54-74). London: Palgrave Macmillan.
European Financial Certification Organisation (2010). Website of the Organisation. URL: http://www.eficert.org/. Date of retrieval: 2010-03-20.
European Financial Planning Organisation (2010). Website of the Organisation. URL: http://www.efpa-europe.org/. Date of retrieval: 2010-03-20.
Eurostat (2009). Actual Individual Consumption. URL: http://ep.eurostat.ec.europa.eu/statistics_explained/index.php/Actual_individual_consumption_%28AIC%29. Date of retrieval: 2009-12-28.
Eurosystem Household Finance and Consumption Network (2009). Survey Data on Household Finance and Consumption: Research Summary and Policy Use. ECB Occasional Paper Series, 100. Frankfurt a.M..
Fama, E.F. and French, K.R. (1992). The Cross-Section of Expected Stock Returns. The Journal of Finance, 47, 427-465.
Fama, E.F. and French, K.R. (2004). The Capital Asset Pricing Model: Theory and Evidence. Journal of Economic Perspectives, 18, 25-46.
Fama, E.F. and MacBeth, J.D. (1973). Risk, Return, and Equilibrium: Empirical Tests. The Journal of Political Economy, 81, 607-636.
Fama, E.F. (1991). Efficient Capital Markets: II. The Journal of Finance, 46, 1575-1617.
Felderer, B. and Homburg, S. (2005). Makroökonomik und neue Makroökonomik. Berlin: Springer.
Fernandes, J.L.B., Peña, J.I., and Tabak, B.M. (2009). Behavior Finance and Estimation Risk in Stochastic Portfolio Optimization. Working Paper Series, 184. Brasília.

Fidora, M., Fratzscher, M., and Thimann, C. (2007). Home Bias in Global Bond and Equity Markets: The Role of Exchange Rate Volatility. Journal of International Money and Finance, 26, 631-655.

Financial Planning Standards Board (2010). Website of the Organisation. URL: http://www.fpsb.org/. Date of retrieval: 2010-03-20.

Foad, H.S. (2008). Familiarity Breeds Investment: Immigration and Equity Home Bias. URL: http://ssrn.com/abstract=1092305. Date of retrieval: 2009-04-12.

Forbes, K.J. and Rigobon, R. (2002). No Contagion, Only Interdependence: Measuring Stock Market Comovements. The Journal of Finance, 57, 2223-2261.

Frankel, J.A. and Rose, A.K. (1998). The Endogeneity of the Optimum Currency Area Criteria. The Economic Journal, 108, 1009-1025.

Fratzscher, M. (2002). Financial Market Integration in Europe: On the Effects of EMU on Stock Markets. International Journal of Finance and Economics, 7, 165-193.

French, K.R. and Poterba, J.M. (1991). Investor Diversification and International Equity Markets. Behavioral Finance, 81, 222-226.

Garcia-Herroro, Alicia and Wooldrige, Philip (2007): Global and regional financial integration: progress in emerging markets. BIS Quarterly Review, September 2007, 57-70.

Gorman, L.R. and Jorgensen, B.N. (2002). Domestic versus International Portfolio Selection: A Statistical Examination of the Home Bias. Multinational Finance Journal, 6, 131-166.

Graham, J.R., Harvey, C.R., and Huang, H. (2009). Investor Competence, Trading Frequency, and Home Bias. Management Science Archive, 55, 1094-1106.

Greene, W.H. (2003). Econometric Analysis. Upper Saddle River, New Jersey: Pearson Education.

Gros, D. and Hefeker, C. (2004). Asymmetric Transmission of Monetary Policy: What Should the ECB Do if One Size Does Not Fit All? In Sinn, H., Widgrén, M., and Köthenbürger, M. (Eds.), European Monetary Integration (pp. 45-63). Cambridge, Massachusetts: MIT Press.

Hamburg, B., Hoffmann, M., and Keller, J. (2008). Consumption, Wealth and Business Cycles in Germany. Empirical Economics, 34, 451-476.

Heathcote, J. and Perri, F. (2004). Financial Globalization and Real Regionalization. Journal of Economic Theory, 119, 207-243.

Heinemann, F. (1998). Die Theorie der optimalen Währungsräume und die politische Reformfähigkeit: Ein vernachlässigtes Kriterium. ZEW Discussion Papers, 98-02. Mannheim.

Hey, J.D. and Morone, A. (2004). Do Markets Drive Out Lemmings – or Vice Versa? Economica, 71, 637-659.

Hill, R.C., Griffiths, W.E., and Lim, G.C. (2008). Principles of Econometrics. Hoboken, New Jersey: John Wiley and Sons.

Hodrick, R.J. and Prescott, E.C. (1997). Postwar U.S. Business Cycles: An Empirical Investigation. Journal of Money, Credit and Banking, 29, 1-16.

Horsch, A. and Paul, S. (2009). Wirtschaftswissenschaften: Braucht es einen Neuanfang? Zeitschrift für das gesamte Kreditwesen, 21, 1060-1061.

Hughes Hallet, A. and Piscitelli, L. (2002). Does One Size Fit All?: A Currency Union With Asymmetric Transmissions and a Stability Pact. International Review of Applied Economics, 16, 71-96.

Imbs, J. (1998). Co-Fluctuations. Cahiers de Recherches Economiques du Département d'Econométrie et d'Economie politique (DEEP), 9819. Lausanne.

Imbs, J. (1999). Co-Fluctuations. CEPR Discussion Paper, 2267. London.

Imbs, J. (2004). Trade, Finance, Specialisation, and Synchronization. The Review of Economics and Statistics, 86, 723-734.

International Monetary Fund (2002). Coordinated Portfolio Investment Survey Guide. Washington D.C.: International Monetary Fund.

Kalemli-Ozcan, S., Sørensen, B.E., and Yosha, O. (2005). Asymmetric Shocks and Risk Sharing in a Monetary Union: Updated Evidence and Policy Implications for Europe. In Huizinga, H. and Jonung, L. (Eds.), The Internationalisation of Asset Ownership in Europe (pp. 173-204). New York: Cambridge University Press.

Kalra, R., Stoichev, M., and Sundaram, S. (2004). Diminishing Gains from International Diversification. Financial Services Review, 13, 199-213.

Kenen, P.B. (1969). The Theory of Optimum Currency Areas: An Eclectic View. In Mundel, R. A. and Swoboda, A. K. (Eds.), Monetary Problems of the International Economy (pp. 41-60). Chicago: University of Chicago Press.

Kilka, M. and Weber, M. (2000). Home Bias in International Stock Return Expectations. The Journal of Psychology and Financial Markets, 1, 176-192.

Kim, S.J., Moshirian, F., and Wu, E. (2005). Dynamic Stock Market Integration Driven by the European Monetary Union: An Empirical Analysis. Journal of Banking and Finance, 29, 2475-2502.

Kishor, K.N. (2007). Does Consumption Respond More to Housing Wealth Than to Financial Market Wealth? If So, Why? The Journal of Real Estate Finance and Economics, 35, 427-448.

Lane, P. (2006). Global Bond Portfolios and EMU. International Journal of Central Banking, 2, 2, 1-23.

Lapp, S. (2001). Internationale Diversifikation in den Portfolios deutscher Kapitalanleger: Theorie und Empirie. Berlin: Springer.

Lettau, M. and Ludvigson, S.C. (2004). Understanding Trend and Cycle in Asset Values: Reevaluating the Wealth Effect on Consumption. American Economic Review, 94, 276-299.

Levine, R. (2002). Bank-Based or Market-Based Financial Systems: Which Is Better? Journal of Financial Intermediation, 11, 398-428.

Lewis, K.K. (1999). Trying to Explain Home Bias in Equities and Consumption. Journal of Economic Literature, 37, 571-608.

Lintner, J. (1965). The Valuation of Risk Assets and the Selection of Risky Investments in Stock Portfolios and Capital Budgets. The Review of Economics and Statistics, 47, 13-37.

Ludvigson, S.C., Steindel, C., and Lettau, M. (2002). Monetary Policy Transmission through the Consumption-Wealth Channel. Economic Policy Review, 117-133.

Ludwig, A. and Sløk, T. (2002). The Impact of Changes in Stock Prices and House Prices on Consumption in OECD Countries. IMF Working Paper, 01/2002. Washington D.C.

Magi, A. (2005). Financial Decision-making and Portfolio Choice Under Behavioral Preferences: Implications for the Equity Home Bias Puzzle. URL: http://ssrn.com/abstract=725521. Date of retrieval: 2010-03-04.

Markowitz, H. (1959). Portfolio Selection: Efficient Diversification of Investments. Oxford: Basil Blackwell.

McKinnon, R.I. (1963). Optimum Currency Areas. American Economic Review, 53, 717-725.

Mishra, A.V. (2007). International Investors' Home Bias in Portfolio Equity Investment. 14th Global Finance Conference, Melbourne, 2007-04-01.

Mojon, B. (2000). Financial Structure and the Interest Rate Channel of ECB Monetary Policy. ECB Working Paper Series, 40. Frankfurt a.M.

Mossin, J. (1966). Equilibrium in a Capital Asset Market. Econometrica, 34, 768-783.

Mundell, R.A. (1961). A Theory of Optimal Currency Areas. American Economic Review, 51, 657-665.

Mélitz, J. and Zumer, F. (2000). Interregional and International Risk Sharing and Lessons for EMU. EUI Working Paper RSC, 2000/2. Florence.

von Nitzsch, R. and Stotz, O. (2006). Zu welchen Renditeeinbußen führt der Home Bias? Finanz Betrieb, 8, 106-113.

Pakko, M.R. (1998). Characterizing Cross-Country Consumption Correlations. The Review of Economics and Statistics, 80, 169-174.

Pesaran, H.M. (2007). A Simple Panel Unit Root Test in the Presence of Cross Section Dependence. Journal of Applied Econometrics, 22, 265-312.

Pierdzioch, C. (2004). Financial Market Integration and Business Cycle Volatility in a Monetary Union. Scottish Journal of Political Economy, 51, 422-442.

Poterba, J.M. (2000). Stock Market Wealth and Consumption. The Journal of Economic Perspectives, 14, 99-118.

Pounder, L. (2009). Consumption Response to Expected Future Income. FRB International Finance Discussion Paper, 971. Washington D.C..

Pástor, L. (2000). Portfolio Selection and Asset Pricing Models. The Journal of Finance, 55, 179-223.

Rajan, R.G. and Zingales, L. (2001). Financial Systems, Industrial Structure, and Growth. Oxford Review of Economic Policy, 17, 467-482.

Ravn, M.O. and Uhlig, H. (2002). On Adjusting the Hodrick-Prescott Filter for the Frequency of Observations. The Review of Economics and Statistics, 84, 371-376.

Ricciardi, V. and Simon, H.K. (2000). What is Behavioral Finance? Business, Education and Technology Journal, 2, 1-9.

Roll, R. (1977). A Critique of the Asset Pricing Theory's Tests: Part I: On Past and Potential Testability of the Theory. Journal of Financial Economics, 4, 129-176.

Rowland, P.F. and Tesar, L.L. (2004). Multinationals and the Gains from International Diversification. Review of Economic Dynamics, 7, 789-826.

Schaffer, M.E. (2007). XTIVREG2: Stata Module to Perform Extended IV/2SLS, GMM and AC/HAC, LIML and K-Class Regression for Panel Data Models. URL: http://ideas.repec.org/c/boc/bocode/s456501.html. Date of retrieval: 2009-03-17.

Schiavo, S. (2008). Financial Integration, GDP Correlation and the Endogeneity of Optimum Currency Areas. Empirica, 75, 168-189.

Schröder, M. (2003). Benefits of Diversification and Integration for International Equity and Bond Portfolios. In Cecchini, P. (Ed.), The Incomplete European Market for Financial Services (pp. 179-185). Heidelberg: Physica.

Schroers, M.(2008, May 2). Finanzmarktkrise macht Deutsche risikoscheuer. Financial Times Deutschland, 21.

Sercu, P. and Vanpée, R. (2007). Home Bias in International Equity Portfolios: a Review. URL: http://papers.ssrn.com/sol3/papers.cfm?abstract_id=1025806. Date of retrieval: 2012-04-29.

Sharpe, W.F. and Cooper, G.M. (1972). Risk-Return Classes of New York Stock Exchange Common Stocks: 1931-1967. Financial Analysts Journal, 28, 46-81.

Sharpe, W.F. (1964). Capital Asset Prices: A Theory of Market Equilibrium Under Conditions of Risk. The Journal of Finance, 19, 425-442.

Slacalek, J. (2006). What Drives Personal Consumption?: The Role of Housing and Financial Wealth. DIW Discussion Paper, 647. Berlin.

Solnik, B.H. (1974a). An Equilibrium Model of the International Capital Market. Journal of Economic Theory, 8, 500-524.

Solnik, B.H. (1974b). Why Not Diversify Internationally Rather Than Domestically? Financial Analysts Journal, 30, 48-54.

Sousa, R.M. (2009). Wealth Effects on Consumption: Evidence from the Euro Area. ECB Working Paper, 1050. Frankfurt a.M.

Spremann, K. (2006). Portfoliomanagement. München: Oldenbourg.

StataCorp. (2007). Stata Statistical Software, Release 10: Longitudinal/Panel Data. College Station, Texas: Stata Press.

Steiner, M. and Bruns, C. (2007). Wertpapiermanagement: Professionelle Wertpapieranalyse und Portfoliostrukturierung. Stuttgart: Schäffer-Poeschel.

Stock, J.H. and Yogo, M. (2005). Testing for Weak Instruments in Linear IV Regression. In Andrews, D. and Stock, J. (Eds.), Identification and Inference for Econometric Models: Essays in Honor of Thomas Rothenberg (pp. 80-108). New York: Cambridge University Press.

Svaleryd, H. and Vlachos, J. (2005). Financial Markets, the Pattern of Industrial Specialization and Comparative Advantage: Evidence from OECD Countries. European Economic Review, 49, 113-144.

Sørensen, B.E., Wu, Y., and Zhu, Y. (2007). Home Bias and International Risk Sharing: Twin Puzzles Separated at Birth. Journal of International Money and Finance, 26, 587-605.

Sørensen, P.B. and Whitta-Jacobsen H.J. (2005). Introducing Advanced Macroeconomics: Growth and Business Cycles. London: McGraw-Hill.

Tesar, L.L. and Werner, I.M. (1995). Home Bias and High Turnover. Journal of International Money and Finance, 14, 467-492.

Tobin, J. (1958). Liquidity Preferences as Behaviour Towards Risk: The Review of Economic Studies, 25, 65-86.

Uni Credit Group (2007). Global Trends in the Dynamic of Household Wealth and Debt. URL: http://www.ba-ca.com/informationspdfs/HOUSEHOLD_FIN_S_04_07.pdf. Date of retrieval: 2007-06-19.

Van Nieuwerburgh, S. and Veldkamp, L. (2009). Information Immobility and the Home Bias Puzzle. Journal of Finance, 64, 1187-1215.

World Exchange Federation (2012). Website of the Organisation. URL: http://www.world-exchanges.org/about-wfe. Date of retrieval: 2012-04-29.

Wooldridge, J.M. (2002). Econometric Analysis of Cross Section and Panel Data. Cambridge, Massachusetts: The MIT Press.

Zydra, M.(2008, August 14). Alles auf die Deutschland-Karte: Bundesbürger sparen vor allem national – was sehr riskant ist. Süddeutsche Zeitung, 27.

Data Appendices

Data Appendix 1: Home Country Investment

Percentage of home country investment

	Austria	Belgium	Bulgaria	Denmark	Estonia	Finland	France	Germany	Greece
2001	76.32	78.33	92.98	83.32	95.75	82.82	90.47	87.12	96.61
2002	64.38	66.65	93.51	78.07	88.81	72.24	84.38	79.88	90.37
2003	46.32	50.39	90.99	64.60	78.94	56.60	75.17	70.20	79.04
2004	34.22	40.96	89.89	53.84	74.31	43.40	69.25	61.01	69.15
2005	48.57	52.01	93.22	62.46	83.86	56.29	74.96	68.32	70.49
2006	35.95	41.00	93.74	52.57	73.19	40.17	68.52	59.48	62.75
2007	33.83	27.85	n.a.	56.60	63.18	25.03	58.11	40.53	42.31
Average 2001-2007	*48.51*	*51.03*	*92.39*	*64.49*	*79.72*	*53.79*	*74.41*	*66.65*	*72.96*
Average 2001-2006	*50.96*	*54.89*	*92.39*	*65.81*	*82.48*	*58.59*	*77.12*	*71.00*	*78.07*

Percentage of home country investment

	Hungary	Italy	Netherlands	Norway	Portugal	Romania	Slovak Republic	Spain	Sweden
2001	99.01	84.70	83.50	75.53	88.17	99.97	93.85	90.23	85.63
2002	98.77	79.80	75.99	60.97	79.79	99.91	90.69	81.35	81.24
2003	98.69	68.96	63.38	43.32	66.35	99.94	76.40	69.78	71.42
2004	97.71	63.80	54.54	31.00	58.78	97.89	59.75	63.82	65.61
2005	97.65	68.82	62.41	44.80	66.56	98.47	73.69	69.80	71.55
2006	94.57	63.15	55.67	23.55	59.83	99.10	73.78	65.39	64.51
2007	92.34	56.91	46.30	4.56	47.98	99.30	n.a.	60.18	50.83
Average 2001-2007	*96.96*	*69.45*	*63.11*	*40.53*	*66.78*	*99.23*	*78.03*	*71.51*	*70.11*
Average 2001-2006	*97.73*	*71.54*	*65.92*	*46.53*	*69.91*	*99.22*	*78.03*	*73.39*	*73.33*

Data Appendix 2: Proportions of Foreign Investment

2001

Note: All numbers are in %.

investment in: / investment from:	Austria	Belgium	Bulgaria	Denmark	Estonia	Finland	France	Germany	Greece	Hungary	Italy	Nether-lands	Norway	Portugal	Romania	Slovak Republic	Spain	Sweden
EMU countries:	**90.49**	**94.99**	**1.78**	**6.02**	**3.01**	**92.88**	**95.82**	**95.16**	**97.98**	**0.33**	**93.29**	**91.29**	**8.77**	**94.74**	**0.02**	**4.48**	**96.38**	**5.22**
Austria	*76.32*	*0.19*	*0.02*	*0.08*	*0.33*	*0.23*	*0.13*	*0.49*	*0.02*	*0.01*	*0.10*	*0.41*	*0.23*	*0.10*	*0.00*	*0.26*	*0.03*	*0.05*
Belgium	*0.51*	*78.33*	*0.00*	*0.22*	*0.00*	*0.41*	*0.36*	*0.23*	*0.01*	*0.01*	*0.14*	*0.62*	*0.27*	*0.37*	*0.00*	*0.06*	*0.22*	*0.09*
Cyprus	*0.01*	*0.00*	*0.00*	*0.00*	*0.00*	*0.00*	*0.00*	*0.01*	*0.12*	*0.00*	*0.00*	*0.00*	*0.00*	*0.00*	*0.00*	*0.12*	*0.00*	*0.00*
Finland	*0.25*	*0.20*	*0.02*	*0.40*	*0.59*	*82.82*	*0.14*	*0.30*	*0.02*	*0.00*	*0.11*	*0.20*	*0.37*	*0.07*	*0.00*	*0.02*	*0.10*	*0.65*
France	*1.35*	*2.32*	*0.20*	*1.01*	*0.01*	*2.34*	*90.47*	*1.21*	*0.26*	*0.03*	*1.22*	*1.54*	*1.10*	*0.97*	*0.00*	*0.01*	*1.11*	*0.78*
Germany	*6.42*	*2.50*	*1.14*	*2.39*	*1.60*	*2.54*	*1.16*	*87.12*	*0.10*	*0.08*	*1.65*	*2.32*	*2.37*	*1.55*	*0.00*	*1.06*	*1.85*	*0.97*
Greece	*0.46*	*0.32*	*0.00*	*0.05*	*0.00*	*0.05*	*0.14*	*0.24*	*96.61*	*0.00*	*0.08*	*0.18*	*0.17*	*0.05*	*0.00*	*0.02*	*0.03*	*0.01*
Ireland	*0.39*	*0.32*	*0.00*	*0.04*	*0.00*	*0.34*	*0.16*	*0.33*	*0.02*	*0.02*	*0.45*	*0.10*	*0.15*	*0.34*	*0.00*	*0.00*	*0.11*	*0.07*
Italy	*1.07*	*3.22*	*0.29*	*0.72*	*0.14*	*1.25*	*0.99*	*1.32*	*0.20*	*0.01*	*84.70*	*1.50*	*1.86*	*0.56*	*0.00*	*0.21*	*1.36*	*0.45*
Luxembourg	*1.31*	*4.44*	*0.00*	*0.12*	*0.19*	*0.50*	*0.41*	*1.68*	*0.32*	*0.00*	*2.94*	*0.28*	*0.44*	*0.83*	*0.01*	*2.14*	*0.39*	*1.55*
Malta	*0.01*	*0.00*	*0.00*	*0.00*	*0.00*	*0.00*	*0.00*	*0.00*	*0.00*	*0.00*	*0.00*	*0.00*	*0.00*	*0.00*	*0.00*	*0.00*	*0.00*	*0.00*
Netherlands	*1.75*	*1.81*	*0.06*	*0.64*	*0.15*	*1.50*	*1.13*	*1.41*	*0.17*	*0.16*	*1.47*	*83.50*	*0.76*	*0.94*	*0.00*	*0.43*	*0.80*	*0.35*
Portugal	*0.13*	*0.22*	*0.00*	*0.02*	*0.00*	*0.09*	*0.15*	*0.18*	*0.06*	*0.01*	*0.09*	*0.08*	*0.15*	*88.17*	*0.00*	*0.04*	*0.16*	*0.02*
Slovenia	*0.07*	*0.00*	*0.00*	*0.00*	*0.00*	*0.00*	*0.00*	*0.01*	*0.00*	*0.00*	*0.00*	*0.00*	*0.00*	*0.00*	*0.00*	*0.00*	*0.00*	*0.00*
Spain	*0.46*	*1.13*	*0.06*	*0.32*	*0.00*	*0.81*	*0.57*	*0.64*	*0.06*	*0.01*	*0.32*	*0.57*	*0.89*	*0.76*	*0.00*	*0.10*	*90.23*	*0.22*
EU-countries (non EMU)	**2.43**	**1.25**	**93.08**	**86.93**	**96.51**	**3.30**	**1.08**	**1.61**	**0.58**	**99.16**	**1.15**	**1.73**	**4.52**	**0.77**	**99.97**	**94.65**	**0.97**	**87.81**
Other Europe	**0.94**	**0.40**	**0.04**	**0.88**	**0.03**	**0.47**	**0.22**	**0.54**	**0.07**	**0.04**	**0.36**	**0.50**	**76.09**	**0.65**	**0.00**	**0.06**	**0.20**	**0.78**
Asia and Arabia	**0.57**	**0.29**	**0.02**	**0.90**	**0.04**	**0.28**	**0.30**	**0.28**	**0.03**	**0.02**	**0.54**	**0.99**	**2.92**	**0.05**	**0.00**	**0.03**	**0.22**	**0.89**
Africas	**0.08**	**0.02**	**0.00**	**0.02**	**0.00**	**0.00**	**0.02**	**0.02**	**0.01**	**0.00**	**0.01**	**0.02**	**0.05**	**0.04**	**0.00**	**0.00**	**0.01**	**0.01**
Americas	**4.80**	**2.85**	**5.04**	**4.62**	**0.18**	**2.37**	**2.29**	**2.21**	**0.64**	**0.35**	**3.46**	**5.25**	**7.10**	**2.84**	**0.00**	**0.65**	**1.62**	**5.21**
Australia and Oceania	**0.17**	**0.10**	**0.00**	**0.04**	**0.00**	**0.04**	**0.06**	**0.05**	**0.01**	**0.00**	**0.08**	**0.13**	**0.35**	**0.02**	**0.00**	**0.02**	**0.00**	**0.08**
Other	**0.51**	**0.10**	**0.04**	**0.59**	**0.24**	**0.65**	**0.21**	**0.11**	**0.68**	**0.10**	**1.11**	**0.09**	**0.20**	**0.89**	**0.00**	**0.09**	**0.59**	**0.00**

2002 *Note: All numbers are in %.*

investment in: / investment from:	Austria	Belgium	Bulgaria	Denmark	Estonia	Finland	France	Germany	Greece	Hungary	Italy	Nether-lands	Norway	Portugal	Romania	Slovak Republic	Spain	Sweden
EMU countries:	**86.75**	**92.30**	**1.56**	**9.12**	**8.53**	**89.25**	**94.23**	**92.99**	**94.46**	**0.63**	**92.29**	**88.76**	**14.25**	**91.71**	**0.04**	**6.41**	**93.35**	**7.62**
Austria	*64.38*	*0.40*	*0.10*	*0.26*	*0.68*	*0.58*	*0.25*	*0.86*	*0.11*	*0.04*	*0.14*	*0.36*	*0.40*	*0.21*	*0.00*	*0.52*	*0.12*	*0.12*
Belgium	*0.81*	*66.65*	*0.00*	*0.43*	*0.05*	*0.71*	*0.64*	*0.33*	*0.03*	*0.01*	*0.24*	*0.95*	*0.41*	*0.41*	*0.00*	*0.04*	*0.40*	*0.16*
Cyprus	*0.02*	*0.00*	*0.00*	*0.00*	*0.01*	*0.00*	*0.00*	*0.01*	*0.27*	*0.00*	*0.00*	*0.00*	*0.00*	*0.01*	*0.00*	*0.58*	*0.00*	*0.00*
Finland	*0.38*	*0.28*	*0.02*	*0.31*	*1.08*	*72.24*	*0.25*	*0.37*	*0.03*	*0.00*	*0.12*	*0.27*	*0.49*	*0.14*	*0.00*	*0.02*	*0.14*	*0.75*
France	*2.18*	*3.80*	*0.34*	*1.36*	*0.40*	*4.23*	*84.38*	*1.80*	*0.70*	*0.16*	*1.83*	*2.25*	*1.92*	*2.07*	*0.00*	*0.08*	*1.87*	*1.13*
Germany	*10.08*	*3.73*	*0.50*	*4.12*	*4.12*	*3.95*	*2.07*	*79.88*	*0.37*	*0.11*	*1.91*	*4.47*	*5.37*	*2.83*	*0.00*	*1.80*	*2.88*	*1.43*
Greece	*0.87*	*0.68*	*0.12*	*0.05*	*0.00*	*0.19*	*0.27*	*0.39*	*90.37*	*0.00*	*0.17*	*0.33*	*0.24*	*0.00*	*0.00*	*0.05*	*0.08*	*0.06*
Ireland	*0.68*	*0.66*	*0.00*	*0.17*	*0.31*	*0.64*	*0.36*	*0.55*	*0.12*	*0.05*	*0.73*	*0.25*	*0.34*	*0.83*	*0.00*	*0.02*	*0.26*	*0.11*
Italy	*2.04*	*4.37*	*0.06*	*0.88*	*0.37*	*2.03*	*2.00*	*2.20*	*0.75*	*0.01*	*79.80*	*2.22*	*1.99*	*0.84*	*0.01*	*0.37*	*2.53*	*0.47*
Luxembourg	*1.60*	*6.42*	*0.00*	*0.24*	*0.17*	*0.91*	*0.65*	*2.78*	*1.07*	*0.02*	*4.97*	*0.35*	*0.47*	*1.53*	*0.02*	*1.96*	*0.85*	*2.47*
Malta	*0.01*	*0.00*	*0.00*	*0.00*	*0.00*	*0.00*	*0.00*	*0.00*	*0.00*	*0.00*	*0.00*	*0.00*	*0.00*	*0.00*	*0.00*	*0.00*	*0.00*	*0.00*
Netherlands	*2.64*	*3.11*	*0.21*	*0.72*	*1.32*	*2.43*	*1.95*	*2.34*	*0.40*	*0.23*	*1.84*	*75.99*	*1.47*	*2.02*	*0.01*	*0.77*	*2.66*	*0.60*
Portugal	*0.22*	*0.46*	*0.01*	*0.05*	*0.01*	*0.14*	*0.30*	*0.35*	*0.15*	*0.00*	*0.13*	*0.11*	*0.19*	*79.79*	*0.00*	*0.05*	*0.21*	*0.02*
Slovenia	*0.10*	*0.00*	*0.05*	*0.00*	*0.01*	*0.00*	*0.00*	*0.02*	*0.00*	*0.00*	*0.01*	*0.00*	*0.00*	*0.00*	*0.00*	*0.00*	*0.00*	*0.00*
Spain	*0.76*	*1.72*	*0.14*	*0.53*	*0.01*	*1.21*	*1.11*	*1.10*	*0.09*	*0.01*	*0.40*	*1.20*	*0.95*	*1.05*	*0.00*	*0.16*	*81.35*	*0.30*
EU-countries (non EMU)	**2.43**	**4.29**	**2.05**	**94.03**	**81.86**	**90.96**	**5.95**	**1.57**	**2.38**	**1.37**	**98.95**	**1.39**	**2.65**	**8.56**	**1.60**	**99.94**	**91.38**	**2.12**
Other Europe	**1.36**	**0.66**	**0.25**	**0.98**	**0.05**	**0.67**	**0.25**	**0.70**	**0.21**	**0.08**	**0.67**	**0.73**	**61.70**	**1.36**	**0.00**	**0.10**	**0.30**	**0.82**
Asia and Arabia	**0.68**	**0.39**	**0.01**	**1.11**	**0.11**	**0.32**	**0.37**	**0.54**	**0.08**	**0.08**	**0.48**	**0.78**	**2.89**	**0.05**	**0.01**	**0.02**	**0.15**	**1.17**
Africas	**0.09**	**0.03**	**0.00**	**0.05**	**0.01**	**0.00**	**0.03**	**0.04**	**0.01**	**0.00**	**0.02**	**0.03**	**0.05**	**0.06**	**0.00**	**0.00**	**0.02**	**0.01**
Americas	**6.18**	**4.22**	**3.93**	**5.83**	**0.31**	**2.94**	**3.18**	**3.09**	**2.18**	**0.17**	**3.62**	**6.78**	**10.67**	**4.71**	**0.01**	**1.80**	**3.65**	**6.16**
Australia and Oceania	**0.17**	**0.19**	**0.19**	**0.00**	**0.10**	**0.00**	**0.04**	**0.09**	**0.07**	**0.06**	**0.03**	**0.12**	**0.17**	**0.72**	**0.04**	**0.00**	**0.00**	**0.05**
Other	**0.46**	**0.17**	**0.22**	**0.95**	**0.03**	**0.83**	**0.28**	**0.18**	**1.63**	**0.05**	**1.41**	**0.09**	**1.17**	**0.48**	**0.00**	**0.28**	**0.36**	**0.03**

2003

Note: All numbers are in %.

investment in: / investment from:	Austria	Belgium	Bulgaria	Denmark	Estonia	Finland	France	Germany	Greece	Hungary	Italy	Nether-lands	Norway	Portugal	Romania	Slovak Republic	Spain	Sweden
EMU countries:	**81.50**	**90.00**	**3.35**	**14.73**	**14.65**	**83.02**	**91.14**	**89.98**	**87.79**	**0.58**	**88.95**	**80.63**	**23.11**	**88.04**	**0.05**	**14.16**	**89.04**	**11.65**
Austria	*46.32*	*0.81*	*0.16*	*0.39*	*0.78*	*1.09*	*0.39*	*1.23*	*1.06*	*0.03*	*0.25*	*0.48*	*0.85*	*0.25*	*0.00*	*2.37*	*0.17*	*0.08*
Belgium	*0.92*	*50.39*	*0.09*	*0.44*	*1.39*	*1.08*	*0.96*	*0.47*	*0.14*	*0.01*	*0.37*	*1.02*	*0.46*	*0.85*	*0.00*	*0.05*	*0.55*	*0.15*
Cyprus	*0.05*	*0.01*	*0.00*	*0.00*	*0.04*	*0.00*	*0.01*	*0.02*	*0.45*	*0.00*	*0.00*	*0.01*	*0.00*	*0.01*	*0.00*	*0.00*	*0.00*	*0.01*
Finland	*0.66*	*0.45*	*0.09*	*0.76*	*2.27*	*56.60*	*0.34*	*0.53*	*0.07*	*0.00*	*0.16*	*0.30*	*0.67*	*0.18*	*0.00*	*0.14*	*0.17*	*1.14*
France	*3.58*	*6.51*	*0.23*	*1.99*	*1.01*	*5.33*	*75.17*	*3.02*	*1.95*	*0.06*	*2.90*	*3.44*	*3.32*	*4.23*	*0.00*	*0.83*	*3.68*	*1.53*
Germany	*15.34*	*5.14*	*0.82*	*6.29*	*5.13*	*5.58*	*3.41*	*70.20*	*1.41*	*0.09*	*3.76*	*6.66*	*8.21*	*4.97*	*0.00*	*2.92*	*4.58*	*2.16*
Greece	*1.66*	*1.44*	*0.15*	*0.19*	*0.04*	*0.38*	*0.47*	*0.61*	*79.04*	*0.00*	*0.42*	*0.36*	*0.46*	*0.17*	*0.00*	*0.05*	*0.17*	*0.11*
Ireland	*1.26*	*0.92*	*0.10*	*0.65*	*0.03*	*1.71*	*0.65*	*1.04*	*0.12*	*0.07*	*1.33*	*0.57*	*0.50*	*2.51*	*0.00*	*0.02*	*0.63*	*0.22*
Italy	*3.06*	*7.28*	*0.42*	*1.15*	*0.53*	*2.81*	*3.29*	*2.71*	*0.81*	*0.02*	*68.96*	*2.36*	*2.76*	*1.90*	*0.01*	*1.81*	*4.09*	*0.62*
Luxembourg	*2.67*	*9.15*	*0.53*	*0.41*	*0.49*	*1.86*	*0.92*	*4.23*	*1.88*	*0.12*	*7.44*	*0.65*	*0.99*	*1.90*	*0.03*	*3.97*	*1.41*	*4.03*
Malta	*0.01*	*0.00*	*0.00*	*0.00*	*0.00*	*0.00*	*0.00*	*0.00*	*0.00*	*0.00*	*0.00*	*0.00*	*0.00*	*0.00*	*0.00*	*0.00*	*0.00*	*0.00*
Netherlands	*4.26*	*4.91*	*0.47*	*1.47*	*2.82*	*3.76*	*3.09*	*3.53*	*0.67*	*0.19*	*2.47*	*63.38*	*2.19*	*2.90*	*0.00*	*1.85*	*3.43*	*1.11*
Portugal	*0.35*	*0.78*	*0.02*	*0.06*	*0.04*	*0.43*	*0.48*	*0.42*	*0.12*	*0.00*	*0.27*	*0.15*	*0.28*	*66.35*	*0.00*	*0.06*	*0.38*	*0.04*
Slovenia	*0.13*	*0.00*	*0.08*	*0.00*	*0.06*	*0.00*	*0.01*	*0.03*	*0.00*	*0.00*	*0.01*	*0.01*	*0.01*	*0.00*	*0.00*	*0.02*	*0.00*	*0.00*
Spain	*1.23*	*2.20*	*0.20*	*0.94*	*0.00*	*2.40*	*1.96*	*1.94*	*0.07*	*0.01*	*0.62*	*1.24*	*2.40*	*1.83*	*0.00*	*0.06*	*69.78*	*0.44*
EU-countries (non EMU)	**2.43**	**6.13**	**2.93**	**91.61**	**70.03**	**83.14**	**10.06**	**2.69**	**3.03**	**3.30**	**98.88**	**2.04**	**4.06**	**10.87**	**2.46**	**99.94**	**83.11**	**3.01**
Other Europe	**2.14**	**0.92**	**0.42**	**1.52**	**0.32**	**1.33**	**0.48**	**1.39**	**0.46**	**0.06**	**0.87**	**1.09**	**44.59**	**1.89**	**0.00**	**0.16**	**0.39**	**1.44**
Asia and Arabia	**0.96**	**0.43**	**0.08**	**1.98**	**0.22**	**0.85**	**0.74**	**0.87**	**0.19**	**0.15**	**0.73**	**1.57**	**4.59**	**0.06**	**0.01**	**0.04**	**0.29**	**1.73**
Africas	**0.13**	**0.03**	**0.00**	**0.08**	**0.00**	**0.00**	**0.04**	**0.07**	**0.33**	**0.00**	**0.03**	**0.06**	**0.10**	**0.09**	**0.00**	**0.00**	**0.03**	**0.01**
Americas	**8.31**	**5.15**	**4.05**	**10.46**	**1.24**	**4.28**	**4.43**	**4.28**	**3.31**	**0.27**	**5.66**	**11.27**	**15.03**	**6.60**	**0.01**	**1.99**	**5.13**	**9.25**
Australia and Oceania	**0.17**	**0.31**	**0.21**	**0.00**	**0.21**	**0.03**	**0.16**	**0.16**	**0.13**	**0.07**	**0.03**	**0.13**	**0.38**	**0.78**	**0.07**	**0.00**	**0.01**	**0.14**
Other	**0.52**	**0.33**	**0.49**	**0.98**	**0.41**	**0.31**	**0.33**	**0.25**	**4.54**	**0.02**	**1.59**	**0.93**	**0.93**	**0.78**	**0.00**	**0.53**	**1.97**	**0.04**

2004 *Note: All numbers are in %.*

investment in: / investment from:	Austria	Belgium	Bulgaria	Denmark	Estonia	Finland	France	Germany	Greece	Hungary	Italy	Nether-lands	Norway	Portugal	Romania	Slovak Republic	Spain	Sweden
EMU countries:	**77.60**	**89.36**	**6.55**	**19.80**	**15.01**	**77.38**	**88.44**	**87.80**	**80.10**	**1.21**	**87.47**	**77.10**	**29.29**	**85.76**	**2.09**	**22.34**	**86.67**	**15.03**
Austria	*34.22*	*0.98*	*0.20*	*0.26*	*0.61*	*1.32*	*0.44*	*1.64*	*0.87*	*0.14*	*0.30*	*0.62*	*0.83*	*0.12*	*0.03*	*3.43*	*0.23*	*0.11*
Belgium	*1.11*	*40.96*	*0.23*	*0.54*	*0.75*	*1.21*	*1.19*	*0.53*	*0.04*	*0.02*	*0.44*	*1.31*	*0.53*	*1.03*	*0.00*	*0.08*	*0.72*	*0.26*
Cyprus	*0.26*	*0.02*	*0.00*	*0.00*	*0.03*	*0.00*	*0.01*	*0.04*	*0.40*	*0.00*	*0.01*	*0.01*	*0.01*	*0.00*	*0.00*	*0.00*	*0.00*	*0.00*
Finland	*0.71*	*0.63*	*0.04*	*0.80*	*2.06*	*43.40*	*0.38*	*0.62*	*0.06*	*0.00*	*0.20*	*0.32*	*0.74*	*0.18*	*0.00*	*1.23*	*0.25*	*1.45*
France	*4.65*	*8.72*	*0.62*	*3.08*	*1.83*	*7.34*	*69.25*	*4.01*	*1.44*	*0.08*	*3.43*	*4.46*	*4.69*	*4.99*	*0.02*	*1.63*	*4.57*	*1.94*
Germany	*17.72*	*5.87*	*0.72*	*8.79*	*3.87*	*7.54*	*3.54*	*61.01*	*3.58*	*0.25*	*4.70*	*8.05*	*10.53*	*6.29*	*1.99*	*5.18*	*4.48*	*3.06*
Greece	*1.96*	*1.99*	*0.08*	*0.18*	*0.06*	*0.62*	*0.65*	*0.81*	*69.15*	*0.00*	*0.55*	*0.72*	*0.78*	*0.31*	*0.00*	*0.08*	*0.22*	*0.17*
Ireland	*2.15*	*1.48*	*0.00*	*0.81*	*0.64*	*2.01*	*1.04*	*1.84*	*0.17*	*0.12*	*1.66*	*0.72*	*0.90*	*4.96*	*0.00*	*1.24*	*1.09*	*0.45*
Italy	*4.08*	*8.90*	*2.32*	*1.42*	*0.50*	*2.60*	*4.06*	*3.94*	*0.37*	*0.03*	*63.80*	*3.14*	*2.98*	*1.79*	*0.01*	*0.99*	*4.79*	*0.69*
Luxembourg	*3.29*	*10.07*	*0.32*	*1.07*	*0.93*	*2.98*	*1.20*	*5.79*	*2.77*	*0.42*	*8.51*	*1.10*	*1.64*	*2.23*	*0.03*	*4.23*	*2.53*	*4.77*
Malta	*0.01*	*0.00*	*0.00*	*0.00*	*0.00*	*0.00*	*0.00*	*0.00*	*0.00*	*0.00*	*0.01*	*0.00*	*0.00*	*0.00*	*0.00*	*0.00*	*0.00*	*0.00*
Netherlands	*5.14*	*6.13*	*0.57*	*1.62*	*3.59*	*4.29*	*3.63*	*3.99*	*1.00*	*0.14*	*2.69*	*54.54*	*2.73*	*2.68*	*0.00*	*4.08*	*3.65*	*1.31*
Portugal	*0.46*	*0.98*	*0.00*	*0.02*	*0.03*	*0.40*	*0.60*	*0.50*	*0.12*	*0.00*	*0.34*	*0.18*	*0.23*	*58.78*	*0.00*	*0.07*	*0.32*	*0.03*
Slovenia	*0.13*	*0.01*	*0.08*	*0.00*	*0.05*	*0.00*	*0.00*	*0.02*	*0.01*	*0.00*	*0.01*	*0.01*	*0.01*	*0.00*	*0.00*	*0.02*	*0.00*	*0.00*
Spain	*1.72*	*2.63*	*1.36*	*1.19*	*0.07*	*3.68*	*2.45*	*3.09*	*0.12*	*0.01*	*0.82*	*1.93*	*2.68*	*2.39*	*0.00*	*0.07*	*63.82*	*0.79*
EU-countries (non EMU)	**2.43**	**7.77**	**3.75**	**90.56**	**61.87**	**81.23**	**13.51**	**3.67**	**4.02**	**6.71**	**97.93**	**2.34**	**4.48**	**11.34**	**2.79**	**97.89**	**69.64**	**3.88**
Other Europe	**2.87**	**1.00**	**1.24**	**1.85**	**1.06**	**1.78**	**0.64**	**1.69**	**1.06**	**0.07**	**0.86**	**1.13**	**32.33**	**2.44**	**0.02**	**0.42**	**0.42**	**1.57**
Asia and Arabia	**1.20**	**0.41**	**0.03**	**3.03**	**0.36**	**1.27**	**1.11**	**1.16**	**0.22**	**0.17**	**0.81**	**2.38**	**5.26**	**0.04**	**0.00**	**0.14**	**0.33**	**2.11**
Africas	**0.15**	**0.03**	**0.00**	**0.19**	**0.00**	**0.00**	**0.04**	**0.09**	**0.18**	**0.25**	**0.04**	**0.11**	**0.34**	**0.09**	**0.00**	**0.01**	**0.03**	**0.01**
Americas	**9.38**	**4.86**	**1.34**	**12.34**	**1.97**	**5.07**	**5.32**	**4.66**	**3.67**	**0.32**	**6.13**	**13.18**	**19.91**	**8.14**	**0.00**	**5.21**	**5.88**	**10.09**
Australia and Oceania	**0.17**	**0.43**	**0.27**	**0.00**	**0.25**	**0.15**	**0.23**	**0.39**	**0.21**	**0.08**	**0.04**	**0.17**	**0.45**	**0.92**	**0.13**	**0.00**	**0.01**	**0.33**
Other	**0.60**	**0.33**	**0.29**	**0.68**	**0.21**	**0.75**	**0.39**	**0.36**	**7.98**	**0.01**	**2.18**	**1.17**	**0.61**	**0.62**	**0.00**	**2.22**	**2.47**	**0.10**

2005

Note: All numbers are in %.

investment in: / investment from:	Austria	Belgium	Bulgaria	Denmark	Estonia	Finland	France	Germany	Greece	Hungary	Italy	Nether-lands	Norway	Portugal	Romania	Slovak Republic	Spain	Sweden
EMU countries:	**81.82**	**91.36**	**3.74**	**14.80**	**8.92**	**81.70**	**90.20**	**90.18**	**81.16**	**1.29**	**89.92**	**81.16**	**21.83**	**88.89**	**1.50**	**15.86**	**89.50**	**11.79**
Austria	*48.57*	*0.74*	*0.13*	*0.17*	*1.00*	*0.91*	*0.38*	*1.23*	*0.69*	*0.19*	*0.32*	*0.51*	*0.52*	*0.15*	*0.54*	*3.69*	*0.20*	*0.12*
Belgium	*0.78*	*52.01*	*1.26*	*0.43*	*0.82*	*0.66*	*0.87*	*0.37*	*0.04*	*0.05*	*0.36*	*0.92*	*0.33*	*0.53*	*0.00*	*0.20*	*0.59*	*0.19*
Cyprus	*0.38*	*0.02*	*0.00*	*0.00*	*0.03*	*0.00*	*0.00*	*0.03*	*0.33*	*0.01*	*0.00*	*0.01*	*0.00*	*0.02*	*0.00*	*0.00*	*0.00*	*0.00*
Finland	*0.53*	*0.52*	*0.07*	*0.58*	*1.01*	*56.29*	*0.28*	*0.43*	*0.03*	*0.00*	*0.16*	*0.25*	*0.72*	*0.10*	*0.00*	*0.98*	*0.15*	*1.20*
France	*3.67*	*7.35*	*0.19*	*2.15*	*0.86*	*4.94*	*74.96*	*3.10*	*1.51*	*0.04*	*2.95*	*3.77*	*3.17*	*4.45*	*0.03*	*0.70*	*4.61*	*1.47*
Germany	*12.56*	*4.58*	*0.87*	*6.19*	*1.99*	*5.36*	*2.67*	*68.32*	*3.37*	*0.29*	*4.54*	*6.04*	*7.71*	*4.41*	*0.89*	*3.63*	*3.95*	*2.31*
Greece	*1.39*	*1.51*	*0.01*	*0.21*	*0.01*	*0.62*	*0.49*	*0.74*	*70.49*	*0.00*	*0.54*	*0.59*	*0.63*	*0.33*	*0.00*	*0.04*	*0.18*	*0.14*
Ireland	*2.03*	*1.16*	*0.01*	*0.97*	*0.17*	*2.22*	*1.03*	*1.55*	*0.44*	*0.13*	*1.55*	*0.72*	*0.83*	*4.84*	*0.00*	*0.95*	*0.96*	*0.77*
Italy	*3.05*	*6.78*	*0.37*	*0.94*	*0.61*	*2.04*	*3.06*	*3.41*	*0.57*	*0.01*	*68.82*	*2.91*	*2.73*	*1.63*	*0.01*	*0.70*	*3.80*	*0.65*
Luxembourg	*3.05*	*9.03*	*0.24*	*0.82*	*0.87*	*2.84*	*1.17*	*4.95*	*2.46*	*0.46*	*7.30*	*1.07*	*1.35*	*1.80*	*0.02*	*2.60*	*2.35*	*3.42*
Malta	*0.01*	*0.00*	*0.00*	*0.00*	*0.00*	*0.00*	*0.00*	*0.00*	*0.00*	*0.00*	*0.01*	*0.00*	*0.00*	*0.00*	*0.00*	*0.00*	*0.00*	*0.00*
Netherlands	*3.71*	*4.87*	*0.47*	*1.22*	*1.43*	*3.08*	*2.60*	*2.76*	*0.88*	*0.09*	*2.37*	*62.41*	*1.82*	*2.27*	*0.00*	*2.25*	*2.65*	*0.79*
Portugal	*0.38*	*0.75*	*0.10*	*0.04*	*0.04*	*0.17*	*0.46*	*0.42*	*0.10*	*0.00*	*0.21*	*0.22*	*0.30*	*66.56*	*0.00*	*0.04*	*0.26*	*0.03*
Slovenia	*0.07*	*0.00*	*0.02*	*0.00*	*0.06*	*0.00*	*0.00*	*0.01*	*0.00*	*0.02*	*0.00*	*0.00*	*0.00*	*0.00*	*0.00*	*0.04*	*0.00*	*0.00*
Spain	*1.64*	*2.05*	*0.00*	*1.05*	*0.03*	*2.59*	*2.22*	*2.87*	*0.25*	*0.00*	*0.77*	*1.73*	*1.73*	*1.81*	*0.00*	*0.05*	*69.80*	*0.69*
EU-countries (non EMU)	**2.43**	**6.44**	**2.99**	**93.73**	**68.76**	**88.19**	**10.29**	**3.01**	**3.37**	**8.45**	**97.86**	**1.75**	**3.59**	**9.14**	**2.51**	**98.48**	**77.93**	**3.11**
Other Europe	**2.52**	**0.83**	**0.57**	**1.84**	**0.75**	**1.36**	**0.64**	**1.29**	**0.97**	**0.08**	**0.72**	**1.02**	**46.10**	**1.66**	**0.02**	**0.59**	**0.37**	**1.70**
Asia and Arabia	**1.34**	**0.36**	**0.34**	**3.35**	**0.65**	**1.77**	**1.15**	**0.90**	**0.21**	**0.07**	**0.78**	**2.16**	**5.41**	**0.06**	**0.00**	**0.19**	**0.35**	**2.12**
Africas	**0.11**	**0.03**	**0.00**	**0.19**	**0.00**	**0.00**	**0.03**	**0.04**	**0.06**	**0.16**	**0.04**	**0.13**	**0.08**	**0.06**	**0.00**	**0.01**	**0.02**	**0.01**
Americas	**7.00**	**3.98**	**1.38**	**10.38**	**1.30**	**4.30**	**4.46**	**3.73**	**3.56**	**0.50**	**5.04**	**11.12**	**15.45**	**6.36**	**0.00**	**4.00**	**3.77**	**8.14**
Australia and Oceania	**0.17**	**0.31**	**0.21**	**0.00**	**0.20**	**0.06**	**0.18**	**0.23**	**0.19**	**0.03**	**0.01**	**0.13**	**0.44**	**0.93**	**0.09**	**0.00**	**0.06**	**0.22**
Other	**0.46**	**0.25**	**0.22**	**0.48**	**0.12**	**0.41**	**0.28**	**0.29**	**5.57**	**0.05**	**1.62**	**0.38**	**1.06**	**0.37**	**0.00**	**1.36**	**2.66**	**0.10**

2006

Note: All numbers are in %.

investment in: / investment from:	Austria	Belgium	Bulgaria	Denmark	Estonia	Finland	France	Germany	Greece	Hungary	Italy	Nether-lands	Norway	Portugal	Romania	Slovak Republic	Spain	Sweden
EMU countries:	**77.00**	**86.96**	**3.61**	**18.18**	**15.41**	**74.51**	**87.48**	**86.80**	**74.45**	**3.63**	**89.07**	**77.69**	**32.33**	**84.96**	**0.69**	**17.38**	**86.77**	**14.36**
Austria	*35.48*	*0.86*	*0.19*	*0.28*	*0.72*	*1.22*	*0.53*	*1.68*	*0.66*	*0.53*	*0.49*	*0.64*	*0.80*	*0.28*	*0.41*	*4.05*	*0.25*	*0.14*
Belgium	*0.84*	*40.56*	*0.61*	*0.39*	*1.28*	*0.87*	*1.05*	*0.53*	*0.06*	*0.15*	*0.37*	*0.98*	*0.26*	*0.57*	*0.00*	*0.06*	*0.57*	*0.17*
Cyprus	*0.72*	*0.04*	*0.00*	*0.01*	*0.14*	*0.00*	*0.02*	*0.03*	*0.64*	*0.00*	*0.01*	*0.01*	*0.03*	*0.02*	*0.00*	*0.17*	*0.00*	*0.00*
Finland	*0.61*	*0.44*	*0.01*	*0.90*	*1.63*	*40.11*	*0.32*	*0.51*	*0.04*	*0.00*	*0.17*	*0.32*	*0.94*	*0.06*	*0.00*	*1.01*	*0.16*	*1.82*
France	*4.46*	*8.97*	*0.26*	*2.43*	*2.23*	*6.59*	*68.21*	*3.60*	*1.55*	*0.18*	*4.18*	*3.76*	*4.78*	*4.63*	*0.02*	*0.72*	*4.62*	*1.61*
Germany	*14.77*	*5.22*	*0.53*	*7.33*	*3.46*	*7.32*	*3.13*	*59.15*	*3.83*	*0.64*	*4.80*	*6.75*	*11.60*	*4.65*	*0.24*	*3.21*	*3.65*	*2.58*
Greece	*1.68*	*1.52*	*0.45*	*0.34*	*0.06*	*0.83*	*0.69*	*0.80*	*61.58*	*0.00*	*0.58*	*0.69*	*0.78*	*0.71*	*0.00*	*0.05*	*0.21*	*0.16*
Ireland	*2.96*	*2.10*	*0.12*	*1.28*	*0.55*	*3.48*	*1.54*	*2.37*	*0.86*	*0.20*	*2.16*	*1.06*	*1.52*	*3.14*	*0.00*	*1.41*	*1.46*	*1.08*
Italy	*3.72*	*5.97*	*0.32*	*1.01*	*0.49*	*2.29*	*3.99*	*3.51*	*0.70*	*0.02*	*61.16*	*3.42*	*3.77*	*2.52*	*0.01*	*1.07*	*3.85*	*0.68*
Luxembourg	*4.36*	*11.91*	*0.58*	*1.29*	*1.93*	*4.49*	*1.62*	*6.33*	*2.85*	*1.61*	*11.06*	*2.15*	*1.46*	*2.56*	*0.01*	*1.54*	*3.39*	*4.32*
Malta	*0.02*	*0.00*	*0.00*	*0.00*	*0.00*	*0.00*	*0.00*	*0.00*	*0.00*	*0.00*	*0.01*	*0.00*	*0.00*	*0.00*	*0.00*	*0.00*	*0.00*	*0.00*
Netherlands	*4.67*	*5.63*	*0.51*	*1.50*	*2.70*	*3.68*	*2.92*	*3.24*	*1.18*	*0.27*	*2.67*	*55.50*	*2.33*	*2.79*	*0.00*	*3.96*	*3.05*	*0.97*
Portugal	*0.38*	*0.76*	*0.00*	*0.07*	*0.01*	*0.27*	*0.55*	*0.49*	*0.09*	*0.00*	*0.27*	*0.20*	*0.52*	*59.66*	*0.00*	*0.03*	*0.42*	*0.04*
Slovenia	*0.09*	*0.06*	*0.02*	*0.00*	*0.06*	*0.00*	*0.00*	*0.01*	*0.00*	*0.00*	*0.00*	*0.00*	*0.01*	*0.00*	*0.00*	*0.03*	*0.00*	*0.00*
Spain	*2.23*	*2.91*	*0.00*	*1.36*	*0.13*	*3.37*	*2.92*	*4.54*	*0.42*	*0.01*	*1.13*	*2.21*	*3.52*	*3.37*	*0.00*	*0.08*	*65.13*	*0.79*
EU-countries (non EMU)	**2.43**	**8.25**	**4.02**	**92.98**	**61.25**	**79.65**	**13.76**	**3.78**	**4.67**	**12.44**	**94.93**	**1.84**	**4.75**	**12.97**	**3.72**	**99.18**	**75.93**	**3.79**
Other Europe	**3.37**	**1.38**	**0.57**	**2.83**	**1.27**	**1.95**	**0.92**	**1.80**	**1.66**	**0.19**	**0.76**	**1.23**	**24.04**	**1.77**	**0.00**	**0.79**	**0.47**	**2.35**
Asia and Arabia	**2.05**	**0.67**	**0.16**	**4.36**	**1.42**	**2.58**	**1.48**	**0.97**	**0.33**	**0.17**	**0.77**	**2.59**	**5.73**	**0.19**	**0.00**	**0.37**	**0.48**	**2.76**
Africas	**0.13**	**0.03**	**0.00**	**0.24**	**0.00**	**0.00**	**0.04**	**0.06**	**0.07**	**0.01**	**0.04**	**0.14**	**0.20**	**0.09**	**0.00**	**0.01**	**0.05**	**0.03**
Americas	**8.26**	**6.28**	**1.53**	**12.23**	**1.99**	**6.47**	**5.70**	**5.05**	**4.44**	**1.01**	**5.41**	**12.52**	**20.70**	**8.59**	**0.00**	**4.08**	**4.43**	**9.41**
Australia and Oceania	**0.17**	**0.47**	**0.23**	**0.04**	**0.35**	**0.12**	**0.31**	**0.27**	**0.32**	**0.03**	**0.06**	**0.14**	**0.58**	**1.37**	**0.00**	**0.00**	**0.01**	**0.22**
Other	**0.47**	**0.43**	**1.11**	**0.55**	**0.14**	**0.42**	**0.31**	**0.33**	**6.58**	**0.01**	**1.99**	**0.49**	**2.66**	**0.68**	**0.13**	**1.43**	**3.80**	**0.12**

2007

Note: All numbers are in %.

investment in: / investment from:	Austria	Belgium	Bulgaria	Denmark	Estonia	Finland	France	Germany	Greece	Hungary	Italy	Nether-lands	Norway	Portugal	Romania	Slovak Republic	Spain	Sweden
EMU countries:	**64.58**	**67.55**	**5.59**	**20.81**	**23.01**	**54.93**	**75.33**	**68.66**	**56.74**	**7.32**	**84.41**	**67.02**	**35.38**	**72.44**	**0.86**	**23.00**	**78.65**	**18.65**
Austria	*17.56*	*1.14*	*0.34*	*0.34*	*2.35*	*1.37*	*0.84*	*2.11*	*1.09*	*1.16*	*0.62*	*0.80*	*1.14*	*0.55*	*0.41*	*4.79*	*0.33*	*0.24*
Belgium	*1.12*	*19.57*	*0.73*	*0.54*	*1.02*	*1.32*	*0.99*	*0.83*	*0.08*	*0.17*	*0.50*	*1.08*	*1.09*	*0.78*	*0.00*	*0.15*	*0.72*	*0.21*
Cyprus	*1.01*	*0.03*	*0.00*	*0.03*	*0.35*	*0.01*	*0.03*	*0.05*	*1.26*	*0.01*	*0.01*	*0.02*	*0.11*	*0.04*	*0.02*	*0.36*	*0.00*	*0.01*
Finland	*0.74*	*0.68*	*0.00*	*1.43*	*3.73*	*20.72*	*0.43*	*0.73*	*0.08*	*0.00*	*0.17*	*0.38*	*1.64*	*0.08*	*0.00*	*1.64*	*0.23*	*2.25*
France	*5.60*	*10.83*	*0.28*	*3.31*	*3.91*	*8.15*	*56.28*	*5.84*	*2.42*	*0.21*	*5.14*	*5.12*	*7.51*	*5.74*	*0.02*	*2.09*	*6.27*	*2.27*
Germany	*19.08*	*6.39*	*1.50*	*8.22*	*5.02*	*8.27*	*5.97*	*38.16*	*5.30*	*0.87*	*5.24*	*7.00*	*13.39*	*5.90*	*0.29*	*4.41*	*4.60*	*3.43*
Greece	*2.43*	*1.99*	*0.56*	*0.34*	*0.04*	*1.05*	*0.92*	*0.91*	*39.31*	*0.01*	*0.85*	*0.97*	*0.98*	*1.30*	*0.03*	*0.10*	*0.23*	*0.24*
Ireland	*3.97*	*3.86*	*0.43*	*2.50*	*0.57*	*4.27*	*2.67*	*3.29*	*1.18*	*0.57*	*2.66*	*1.78*	*2.51*	*5.75*	*0.00*	*3.05*	*1.78*	*1.74*
Italy	*5.19*	*6.12*	*0.31*	*1.40*	*0.15*	*2.91*	*4.58*	*4.99*	*0.77*	*0.04*	*54.94*	*3.94*	*4.26*	*3.65*	*0.01*	*1.49*	*3.96*	*1.00*
Luxembourg	*5.95*	*16.71*	*1.40*	*2.22*	*3.99*	*6.43*	*2.53*	*11.22*	*4.57*	*3.82*	*14.22*	*3.10*	*2.36*	*4.54*	*0.06*	*4.13*	*3.91*	*7.12*
Malta	*0.02*	*0.00*	*0.00*	*0.01*	*0.05*	*0.08*	*0.00*	*0.00*	*0.00*	*0.00*	*0.02*	*0.00*	*0.00*	*0.00*	*0.00*	*0.00*	*0.00*	*0.02*
Netherlands	*0.00*	*0.00*	*0.00*	*0.00*	*0.00*	*0.00*	*0.00*	*0.00*	*0.00*	*0.00*	*0.00*	*42.48*	*0.00*	*0.00*	*0.00*	*0.00*	*0.00*	*0.00*
Portugal	*1.49*	*0.17*	*0.02*	*0.25*	*1.81*	*0.34*	*0.07*	*0.37*	*0.69*	*0.46*	*0.02*	*0.17*	*0.10*	*44.06*	*0.00*	*0.78*	*0.02*	*0.10*
Slovenia	*0.28*	*0.02*	*0.00*	*0.01*	*0.02*	*0.02*	*0.01*	*0.06*	*0.00*	*0.00*	*0.00*	*0.02*	*0.01*	*0.00*	*0.00*	*0.00*	*0.01*	*0.00*
Spain	*0.14*	*0.03*	*0.00*	*0.22*	*0.01*	*0.00*	*0.03*	*0.10*	*0.00*	*0.00*	*0.03*	*0.16*	*0.27*	*0.05*	*0.00*	*0.01*	*56.57*	*0.03*
EU-countries(non EMU)	**2.43**	**3.25**	**1.23**	**91.16**	**34.21**	**64.37**	**2.85**	**0.30**	**1.19**	**0.75**	**90.32**	**0.13**	**0.62**	**3.42**	**0.34**	**98.97**	**60.18**	**0.14**
Other Europe	**2.92**	**2.39**	**0.38**	**6.19**	**0.95**	**11.04**	**0.92**	**1.66**	**1.13**	**0.14**	**0.71**	**0.97**	**-1.73**	**1.99**	**0.00**	**0.64**	**0.37**	**0.21**
Asia and Arabia	**6.49**	**6.45**	**0.78**	**10.55**	**2.44**	**8.55**	**6.70**	**9.09**	**3.02**	**0.18**	**2.43**	**7.11**	**16.95**	**6.37**	**0.02**	**0.81**	**1.37**	**7.43**
Africas	**0.94**	**0.15**	**0.33**	**0.92**	**2.88**	**1.16**	**0.07**	**0.20**	**0.54**	**0.13**	**0.10**	**0.32**	**0.36**	**0.13**	**0.00**	**0.23**	**0.11**	**0.68**
Americas	**20.72**	**21.35**	**1.60**	**25.40**	**6.09**	**20.49**	**14.81**	**18.49**	**27.71**	**1.84**	**11.95**	**22.53**	**42.03**	**18.07**	**0.13**	**14.93**	**13.26**	**18.95**
Australia and Oceania	**0.17**	**1.10**	**0.88**	**0.16**	**0.87**	**0.26**	**0.49**	**1.45**	**0.69**	**0.20**	**0.06**	**0.26**	**1.02**	**1.57**	**0.36**	**0.00**	**0.08**	**0.47**
Other	**0.00**	**0.00**	**0.00**	**1.05**	**0.00**	**0.49**	**0.42**	**0.02**	**9.92**	**0.00**	**0.00**	**0.41**	**2.01**	**0.30**	**0.03**	**0.11**	**5.63**	**0.00**

Data Appendix 3: Specialisation Index (SPEC) per Country and Year

SPEC 2001	AUT	BEL	BUL	DEN	EST	FIN	FRA	GER	GRE	HUN	ITA	NET	NOR	POR	ROM	SLO	ESP	SWE
AUT		1.69	1.89	1.74	1.93	1.72	1.78	1.63	1.93	1.97	1.72	1.69	1.71	1.80	1.99	1.90	1.80	1.78
BEL			1.92	1.79	1.94	1.71	1.77	1.72	1.94	1.98	1.67	1.72	1.74	1.81	2.00	1.89	1.79	1.82
BUL				1.87	1.96	1.91	1.93	1.92	1.97	1.99	1.91	1.86	1.86	1.93	2.00	1.96	1.94	1.86
DEN					1.93	1.74	1.83	1.79	1.94	1.98	1.80	1.73	1.69	1.85	1.99	1.93	1.84	1.73
EST						1.92	1.95	1.93	1.97	1.99	1.93	1.93	1.93	1.94	2.00	1.95	1.94	1.94
FIN							1.78	1.74	1.94	1.98	1.76	1.73	1.72	1.82	1.99	1.92	1.80	1.78
FRA								1.80	1.94	1.98	1.79	1.79	1.81	1.83	2.00	1.93	1.82	1.86
GER									1.94	1.98	1.74	1.75	1.75	1.82	2.00	1.90	1.81	1.82
GRE										1.98	1.93	1.94	1.94	1.93	1.99	1.95	1.94	1.95
HUN											1.97	1.98	1.98	1.97	2.00	1.98	1.98	1.98
ITA												1.76	1.77	1.81	1.99	1.88	1.80	1.81
NET													1.69	1.83	2.00	1.93	1.81	1.77
NOR														1.83	2.00	1.92	1.80	1.72
POR															1.99	1.91	1.82	1.87
ROM																2.00	1.99	2.00
SLO																	1.93	1.91
ESP																		1.88
SWE																		

SPEC

2002	AUT	BEL	BUL	DEN	EST	FIN	FRA	GER	GRE	HUN	ITA	NET	NOR	POR	ROM	SLO	ESP	SWE
AUT		1.52	1.87	1.61	1.81	1.55	1.65	1.43	1.81	1.96	1.64	1.54	1.52	1.65	1.99	1.83	1.63	1.71
BEL			1.90	1.68	1.84	1.55	1.62	1.56	1.82	1.98	1.54	1.56	1.61	1.67	2.00	1.84	1.63	1.73
BUL				1.88	1.96	1.90	1.92	1.91	1.91	1.98	1.90	1.88	1.87	1.93	1.99	1.93	1.93	1.89
DEN					1.82	1.64	1.75	1.68	1.85	1.97	1.74	1.62	1.54	1.77	1.99	1.87	1.75	1.67
EST						1.79	1.88	1.82	1.93	1.98	1.87	1.83	1.80	1.87	2.00	1.91	1.87	1.89
FIN							1.63	1.60	1.83	1.97	1.68	1.58	1.55	1.70	1.99	1.85	1.66	1.68
FRA								1.67	1.84	1.98	1.69	1.67	1.68	1.72	2.00	1.87	1.69	1.80
GER									1.82	1.97	1.63	1.60	1.59	1.68	2.00	1.83	1.66	1.74
GRE										1.96	1.82	1.84	1.83	1.84	1.98	1.88	1.84	1.85
HUN											1.96	1.98	1.97	1.97	2.00	1.98	1.98	1.98
ITA												1.69	1.69	1.71	1.98	1.83	1.70	1.75
NET													1.52	1.72	2.00	1.87	1.66	1.70
NOR														1.72	1.99	1.86	1.68	1.62
POR															1.99	1.85	1.68	1.81
ROM																2.00	1.99	2.00
SLO																	1.86	1.86
ESP																		1.80
SWE																		

SPEC **2003**	AUT	BEL	BUL	DEN	EST	FIN	FRA	GER	GRE	HUN	ITA	NET	NOR	POR	ROM	SLO	ESP	SWE
AUT		1.52	1.87	1.61	1.81	1.55	1.65	1.43	1.81	1.96	1.64	1.54	1.52	1.65	1.99	1.83	1.63	1.71
BEL			1.90	1.68	1.84	1.55	1.62	1.56	1.82	1.98	1.54	1.56	1.61	1.67	2.00	1.84	1.63	1.73
BUL				1.88	1.96	1.90	1.92	1.91	1.91	1.98	1.90	1.88	1.87	1.93	1.99	1.93	1.93	1.89
DEN					1.82	1.64	1.75	1.68	1.85	1.97	1.74	1.62	1.54	1.77	1.99	1.87	1.75	1.67
EST						1.79	1.88	1.82	1.93	1.98	1.87	1.83	1.80	1.87	2.00	1.91	1.87	1.89
FIN							1.63	1.60	1.83	1.97	1.68	1.58	1.55	1.70	1.99	1.85	1.66	1.68
FRA								1.67	1.84	1.98	1.69	1.67	1.68	1.72	2.00	1.87	1.69	1.80
GER									1.82	1.97	1.63	1.60	1.59	1.68	2.00	1.83	1.66	1.74
GRE										1.96	1.82	1.84	1.83	1.84	1.98	1.88	1.84	1.85
HUN											1.96	1.98	1.97	1.97	2.00	1.98	1.98	1.98
ITA												1.69	1.69	1.71	1.98	1.83	1.70	1.75
NET													1.52	1.72	2.00	1.87	1.66	1.70
NOR														1.72	1.99	1.86	1.68	1.62
POR															1.99	1.85	1.68	1.81
ROM																2.00	1.99	2.00
SLO																	1.86	1.86
ESP																		1.80
SWE																		

SPEC 2004	AUT	BEL	BUL	DEN	EST	FIN	FRA	GER	GRE	HUN	ITA	NET	NOR	POR	ROM	SLO	ESP	SWE
AUT		1.16	1.81	1.27	1.57	1.13	1.32	0.95	1.48	1.93	1.33	1.15	1.12	1.33	1.95	1.40	1.28	1.46
BEL			1.83	0.00	1.62	1.18	1.26	1.18	1.53	1.96	1.16	1.27	1.31	1.38	1.95	1.48	1.31	1.53
BUL				1.84	1.87	1.83	1.83	1.82	1.81	1.97	1.82	1.82	1.83	1.84	1.97	1.86	1.81	1.88
DEN					1.65	1.28	1.51	1.38	1.57	1.95	1.49	1.22	1.11	1.52	1.95	1.60	1.49	1.33
EST						1.58	1.65	1.62	1.65	1.95	1.66	1.63	1.63	1.67	1.95	1.63	1.63	1.69
FIN							1.30	1.20	1.49	1.96	1.38	1.24	1.13	1.37	1.95	1.48	1.31	1.36
FRA								1.36	1.58	1.96	1.43	1.35	1.37	1.46	1.95	1.59	1.35	1.60
GER									1.54	1.95	1.30	1.27	1.21	1.40	1.95	1.45	1.33	1.51
GRE										1.88	1.55	1.56	1.51	1.59	1.87	1.58	1.54	1.58
HUN											1.94	1.95	1.95	1.96	1.99	1.81	1.94	1.96
ITA												1.42	1.41	1.47	1.94	1.51	1.38	1.54
NET													1.08	1.44	1.55	1.55	1.37	1.43
NOR														1.43	1.95	1.56	1.37	1.34
POR															1.95	1.58	1.39	1.65
ROM																1.94	1.93	1.96
SLO																	1.54	1.62
ESP																		1.58
SWE																		

SPEC 2005	AUT	BEL	BUL	DEN	EST	FIN	FRA	GER	GRE	HUN	ITA	NET	NOR	POR	ROM	SLO	ESP	SWE
AUT		1.33	1.87	1.44	1.72	1.30	1.46	1.19	1.53	1.93	1.42	1.32	1.31	1.46	1.96	1.51	1.42	1.55
BEL			1.88	1.57	1.78	1.37	1.40	1.35	1.59	1.95	1.30	1.40	1.46	1.49	1.97	1.63	1.42	1.62
BUL				1.89	1.88	1.89	1.89	1.90	1.85	1.97	1.89	1.88	1.89	1.90	1.97	1.89	1.87	1.90
DEN					1.79	1.43	1.60	1.52	1.63	1.95	1.57	1.38	1.27	1.62	1.97	1.68	1.59	1.45
EST						1.75	1.79	1.77	1.75	1.95	1.79	1.78	1.78	1.81	1.96	1.75	1.78	1.80
FIN							1.45	1.37	1.57	1.95	1.46	1.40	1.34	1.47	1.97	1.61	1.42	1.45
FRA								1.48	1.65	1.96	1.53	1.47	1.50	1.54	1.97	1.70	1.46	1.66
GER									1.59	1.95	1.40	1.42	1.38	1.52	1.97	1.62	1.44	1.61
GRE										1.90	1.61	1.62	1.58	1.62	1.91	1.65	1.59	1.64
HUN											1.94	1.95	1.95	1.96	1.99	1.92	1.93	1.96
ITA												1.48	1.49	1.54	1.96	1.63	1.48	1.63
NET													1.25	1.54	1.97	1.67	1.47	1.44
NOR														1.55	1.96	1.64	1.49	1.44
POR															1.97	1.69	1.48	1.71
ROM																1.96	1.95	1.98
SLO																	1.65	1.69
ESP																		1.65
SWE																		

SPEC 2006	AUT	BEL	BUL	DEN	EST	FIN	FRA	GER	GRE	HUN	ITA	NET	NOR	POR	ROM	SLO	ESP	SWE
AUT		1.13	1.88	1.32	1.55	1.07	1.33	0.98	1.44	1.87	1.33	1.27	1.09	1.29	1.98	1.49	1.36	1.46
BEL			1.89	1.45	1.62	1.16	1.24	1.18	1.51	1.89	1.17	1.35	1.26	1.36	1.98	1.61	1.38	1.52
BUL				1.89	1.88	1.89	1.89	1.89	1.83	1.93	1.89	1.89	1.88	1.89	1.99	1.91	1.86	1.90
DEN					1.66	1.23	1.51	1.40	1.53	1.90	1.53	1.29	1.10	1.53	1.98	1.66	1.54	1.38
EST						1.58	1.66	1.63	1.64	1.88	1.67	1.68	1.64	1.64	1.98	1.66	1.64	1.69
FIN							1.30	1.16	1.47	1.89	1.36	1.30	1.10	1.31	1.98	1.59	1.39	1.40
FRA								1.36	1.56	1.90	1.44	1.42	1.32	1.41	1.98	1.65	1.41	1.60
GER									1.51	1.89	1.32	1.34	1.15	1.36	1.98	1.59	1.40	1.53
GRE										1.84	1.56	1.54	1.44	1.52	1.93	1.65	1.52	1.56
HUN											1.90	1.90	1.88	1.90	1.98	1.88	1.87	1.90
ITA												1.47	1.40	1.44	1.98	1.65	1.42	1.60
NET													1.15	1.47	1.98	1.69	1.48	1.46
NOR														1.38	1.97	1.61	1.40	1.39
POR															1.98	1.66	1.42	1.63
ROM																1.98	1.95	1.99
SLO																	1.64	1.70
ESP																		1.59
SWE																		

SPEC 2007	AUT	BEL	BUL	DEN	EST	FIN	FRA	GER	GRE	HUN	ITA	NET	NOR	POR	ROM	SLO	ESP	SWE
AUT		1.01	.c	1.36	1.44	0.98	1.16	0.81	1.24	1.82	1.25	1.19	0.99	1.16	1.99	.c	1.30	1.35
BEL			.c	1.39	1.52	0.96	1.03	0.85	1.30	1.85	1.04	1.21	1.05	1.15	1.99	.c	1.28	1.34
BUL				.c	.c	.c	.c	.c	.c	.c	.c	.c	.c	.c	.c	.c	.c	.c
DEN					1.62	1.21	1.43	1.32	1.39	1.89	1.50	1.30	1.13	1.49	1.98	.c	1.50	1.27
EST						1.43	1.58	1.50	1.47	1.84	1.58	1.60	1.52	1.54	1.99	.c	1.55	1.58
FIN							1.10	0.92	1.24	1.85	1.24	1.16	0.85	1.14	1.98	.c	1.29	1.19
FRA								1.12	1.37	1.87	1.29	1.25	1.10	1.22	1.98	.c	1.30	1.47
GER									1.29	1.84	1.11	1.14	0.85	1.14	1.99	.c	1.28	1.27
GRE										1.76	1.37	1.36	1.23	1.33	1.89	.c	1.39	1.36
HUN											1.86	1.86	1.85	1.86	1.99	.c	1.82	1.87
ITA												1.36	1.29	1.32	1.99	.c	1.35	1.44
NET													0.95	1.32	1.98	.c	1.38	1.29
NOR														1.19	1.97	.c	1.29	1.17
POR															1.98	.c	1.31	1.49
ROM																.c	1.93	1.99
SLO																	.c	.c
ESP																		1.49
SWE																		

Data Appendix 4: Fitted Values of Portfolio Return vs. SPEC

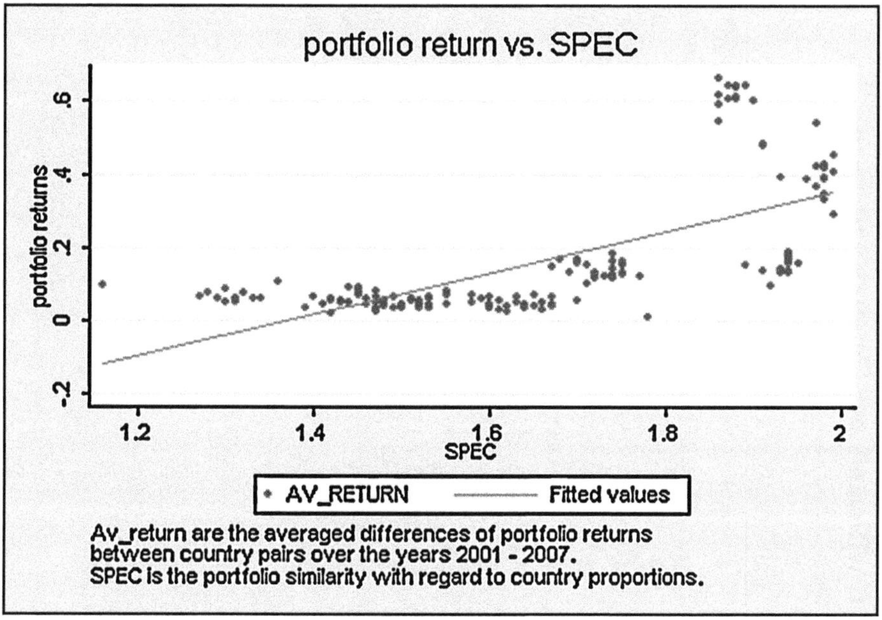

Database: Eurostat; IMF; own calculations

Data Appendix 5: Consumption Correlation Coefficients per Country and Year

Consumption correlation coefficients (moving average)

1999	AUT	BEL	BUL	DEN	EST	FIN	FRA	GER	GRE	HUN	ITA	NET	NOR	POR	ROM	SLO	ESP	SWE
AUT		0,95	-0,20	-0,38	-0,89	0,97	0,95	0,89	.a	-0,41	0,78	0,99	0,00	0,93	.a	-0,73	0,95	0,60
BEL			-0,47	-0,36	-0,76	0,88	0,94	0,78	.a	-0,39	0,73	0,91	-0,05	0,79	.a	-0,48	0,86	0,53
BUL				-0,27	0,09	-0,02	-0,37	0,03	.a	0,48	0,10	-0,15	0,55	0,09	.a	-0,43	-0,04	0,08
DEN					0,15	-0,44	-0,33	-0,53	.a	-0,62	-0,56	-0,33	-0,59	-0,29	.a	0,28	-0,52	-0,07
EST						-0,83	-0,91	-0,92	.a	0,65	-0,47	-0,94	0,32	-0,85	.a	0,86	-0,91	-0,36
FIN							0,86	0,86	.a	-0,27	0,88	0,96	0,20	0,97	.a	-0,78	0,93	0,72
FRA								0,90	.a	-0,52	0,57	0,95	-0,25	0,79	.a	-0,63	0,94	0,35
GER									.a	-0,31	0,58	0,92	-0,08	0,81	.a	-0,84	0,98	0,28
GRE										.a	.a	.a	.a	.a	.a	.a	.a	.a
HUN											0,14	-0,47	0,82	-0,35	.a	0,32	-0,31	-0,09
ITA												0,72	0,61	0,83	.a	-0,54	0,69	0,85
NET													-0,07	0,94	.a	-0,79	0,96	0,56
NOR														0,16	.a	-0,05	-0,01	0,49
POR															.a	-0,86	0,88	0,77
ROM																.a	.a	.a
SLO																	-0,82	-0,44
ESP																		0,41
SWE																		

Consumption correlation coefficients (moving average)

2000	AUT	BEL	BUL	DEN	EST	FIN	FRA	GER	GRE	HUN	ITA	NET	NOR	POR	ROM	SLO	ESP	SWE
AUT		0,91	0,07	-0,36	-0,85	0,93	0,90	0,83	.a	-0,22	0,93	0,97	0,00	0,92	.a	-0,65	0,94	0,70
BEL			-0,25	-0,47	-0,60	0,76	0,92	0,67	.a	-0,05	0,81	0,86	0,13	0,72	.a	-0,32	0,79	0,62
BUL				-0,26	-0,54	0,04	0,02	0,41	.a	0,26	-0,07	0,25	0,35	0,36	.a	-0,78	0,24	0,11
DEN					0,41	-0,02	-0,69	-0,62	.a	-0,76	0,01	-0,50	-0,74	-0,24	.a	0,30	-0,45	0,01
EST						-0,81	-0,76	-0,94	.a	0,14	-0,73	-0,91	-0,05	-0,89	.a	0,94	-0,94	-0,50
FIN							0,71	0,71	.a	-0,55	0,98	0,86	-0,33	0,89	.a	-0,65	0,88	0,68
FRA								0,88	.a	0,11	0,70	0,91	0,23	0,72	.a	-0,52	0,90	0,43
GER									.a	0,01	0,62	0,88	0,12	0,75	.a	-0,80	0,96	0,29
GRE										.a	.a	.a	.a	.a	.a	.a	.a	.a
HUN											-0,53	-0,05	0,94	-0,20	.a	0,08	-0,20	-0,15
ITA												0,84	-0,28	0,88	.a	-0,55	0,82	0,76
NET													0,18	0,94	.a	-0,75	0,94	0,69
NOR														0,08	.a	-0,11	-0,05	0,18
POR															.a	-0,82	0,85	0,83
ROM																.a	.a	.a
SLO																	-0,76	-0,47
ESP																		0,46
SWE																		

Consumption correlation coefficients (moving average)

2001	AUT	BEL	BUL	DEN	EST	FIN	FRA	GER	GRE	HUN	ITA	NET	NOR	POR	ROM	SLO	ESP	SWE
AUT		0,93	-0,52	0,54	-0,86	0,95	0,87	0,71	.a	-0,71	0,97	0,98	-0,21	0,87	0,20	-0,10	0,92	0,60
BEL			-0,73	0,30	-0,64	0,78	0,96	0,66	.a	-0,41	0,83	0,93	0,04	0,73	-0,13	0,23	0,81	0,55
BUL				0,43	0,14	-0,22	-0,71	-0,54	.a	-0,09	-0,34	-0,43	0,02	-0,08	0,70	-0,33	-0,29	-0,28
DEN					-0,72	0,76	0,26	0,17	.a	-0,75	0,67	0,63	-0,05	0,86	0,85	-0,28	0,68	0,35
EST						-0,96	-0,65	-0,75	.a	0,95	-0,91	-0,85	0,52	-0,84	-0,56	0,45	-0,93	-0,36
FIN							0,73	0,66	.a	-0,87	0,98	0,95	-0,31	0,95	0,50	-0,29	0,95	0,55
FRA								0,79	.a	-0,38	0,74	0,88	0,01	0,64	-0,20	0,30	0,85	0,28
GER									.a	-0,59	0,62	0,65	-0,53	0,41	-0,04	-0,15	0,79	-0,06
GRE										.a	.a	.a	.a	.a	.a	.a	.a	.a
HUN											-0,82	-0,68	0,65	-0,76	-0,74	0,69	-0,77	-0,37
ITA												0,96	-0,30	0,93	0,41	-0,28	0,90	0,67
NET													-0,08	0,92	0,25	0,00	0,94	0,58
NOR														-0,04	-0,34	0,87	-0,23	0,02
POR															0,56	-0,14	0,87	0,63
ROM																-0,66	0,34	0,24
SLO																	-0,09	-0,20
ESP																		0,30
SWE																		

Consumption correlation coefficients (moving average)

2002	AUT	BEL	BUL	DEN	EST	FIN	FRA	GER	GRE	HUN	ITA	NET	NOR	POR	ROM	SLO	ESP	SWE
AUT		0,99	-0,51	0,68	-0,81	0,99	0,90	0,73	0,91	-0,92	0,99	0,95	-0,05	0,95	0,95	-0,12	0,93	0,59
BEL			-0,40	0,70	-0,75	0,97	0,92	0,69	0,95	-0,86	0,99	0,97	0,09	0,98	0,97	0,01	0,92	0,59
BUL				-0,42	0,81	-0,57	-0,15	-0,31	-0,22	0,76	-0,49	-0,21	0,84	-0,30	-0,44	0,88	-0,45	-0,45
DEN					-0,76	0,77	0,50	0,22	0,65	-0,60	0,63	0,57	-0,02	0,77	0,82	0,05	0,76	0,44
EST						-0,88	-0,60	-0,62	-0,55	0,94	-0,76	-0,60	0,52	-0,68	-0,76	0,46	-0,87	-0,36
FIN							0,86	0,70	0,87	-0,94	0,97	0,90	-0,12	0,93	0,96	-0,16	0,96	0,56
FRA								0,85	0,85	-0,75	0,89	0,97	0,22	0,87	0,81	0,21	0,90	0,28
GER									0,50	-0,78	0,70	0,73	-0,18	0,55	0,51	-0,12	0,79	-0,04
GRE										-0,68	0,93	0,95	0,32	0,98	0,95	0,17	0,78	0,71
HUN											-0,90	-0,77	0,43	-0,76	-0,81	0,45	-0,89	-0,45
ITA												0,95	-0,01	0,94	0,95	-0,12	0,89	0,65
NET													0,25	0,95	0,90	0,17	0,87	0,51
NOR														0,22	0,09	0,94	-0,09	0,04
POR															0,98	0,15	0,88	0,63
ROM																0,00	0,88	0,70
SLO																	-0,03	-0,25
ESP																		0,30
SWE																		

Consumption correlation coefficients (moving average)

2003	AUT	BEL	BUL	DEN	EST	FIN	FRA	GER	GRE	HUN	ITA	NET	NOR	POR	ROM	SLO	ESP	SWE
AUT		0,65	-0,43	0,62	-0,81	0,59	0,72	0,60	0,75	-0,67	0,77	0,76	-0,15	0,86	0,73	-0,21	0,98	-0,60
BEL			0,15	0,25	-0,49	0,95	0,93	0,87	0,69	-0,78	0,96	0,89	0,00	0,73	0,03	0,42	0,73	-0,90
BUL				-0,44	0,76	-0,05	0,22	0,02	0,22	0,42	-0,06	0,23	0,81	-0,03	-0,51	0,93	-0,38	-0,28
DEN					-0,70	0,27	0,16	-0,11	0,53	-0,22	0,24	0,24	-0,03	0,73	0,79	-0,17	0,70	0,06
EST						-0,62	-0,37	-0,42	-0,33	0,79	-0,62	-0,37	0,61	-0,59	-0,57	0,50	-0,84	0,26
FIN							0,78	0,83	0,48	-0,89	0,93	0,72	-0,28	0,60	-0,05	0,24	0,70	-0,77
FRA								0,88	0,82	-0,65	0,93	0,99	0,18	0,77	0,16	0,42	0,74	-0,97
GER									0,46	-0,84	0,94	0,81	-0,22	0,46	-0,10	0,17	0,60	-0,94
GRE										-0,27	0,65	0,89	0,50	0,95	0,56	0,43	0,78	-0,68
HUN											-0,88	-0,57	0,62	-0,44	-0,06	0,20	-0,71	0,65
ITA												0,89	-0,17	0,71	0,14	0,18	0,81	-0,91
NET													0,26	0,83	0,27	0,42	0,77	-0,94
NOR														0,26	0,06	0,76	-0,14	-0,13
POR															0,65	0,25	0,91	-0,61
ROM																-0,40	0,67	0,03
SLO																	-0,10	-0,42
ESP																		-0,61
SWE																		

Consumption correlation coefficients (moving average)

2004	AUT	BEL	BUL	DEN	EST	FIN	FRA	GER	GRE	HUN	ITA	NET	NOR	POR	ROM	SLO	ESP	SWE
AUT		0,21	0,36	0,91	0,68	0,57	0,52	0,35	0,87	-0,75	0,82	-0,32	-0,07	0,75	0,98	-0,80	0,94	0,68
BEL			0,65	0,00	0,43	0,73	0,61	0,17	0,51	-0,32	0,57	0,09	0,39	0,55	0,14	0,15	0,32	0,02
BUL				0,33	0,86	0,61	0,86	0,73	0,77	-0,46	0,72	-0,06	0,49	0,35	0,24	-0,13	0,20	-0,12
DEN					0,56	0,72	0,49	0,17	0,81	-0,72	0,82	-0,26	-0,06	0,85	0,89	-0,64	0,97	0,70
EST						0,74	0,70	0,88	0,92	-0,80	0,92	-0,45	0,09	0,37	0,54	-0,61	0,47	0,34
FIN							0,40	0,59	0,74	-0,87	0,90	-0,58	-0,20	0,41	0,41	-0,52	0,54	0,61
FRA								0,38	0,79	-0,25	0,63	0,31	0,74	0,70	0,50	-0,05	0,45	-0,19
GER									0,62	-0,72	0,70	-0,64	-0,14	-0,12	0,17	-0,55	0,06	0,25
GRE										-0,77	0,95	-0,27	0,19	0,70	0,79	-0,62	0,76	0,43
HUN											-0,91	0,81	0,46	-0,29	-0,59	0,87	-0,62	-0,82
ITA												-0,50	-0,05	0,57	0,69	-0,69	0,71	0,59
NET													0,84	0,28	0,78	0,78	-0,17	-0,79
NOR														0,43	0,01	0,58	-0,04	-0,75
POR															0,81	-0,23	0,87	0,25
ROM																-0,72	0,96	0,60
SLO																	-0,65	-0,87
ESP																		0,67
SWE																		

Consumption correlation coefficients (moving average)

2005	AUT	BEL	BUL	DEN	EST	FIN	FRA	GER	GRE	HUN	ITA	NET	NOR	POR	ROM	SLO	ESP	SWE
AUT		0,27	0,55	0,86	0,46	0,45	0,42	0,27	0,88	-0,68	0,45	-0,06	0,41	0,87	0,72	-0,50	0,75	0,42
BEL			0,56	0,66	0,88	0,92	0,91	-0,01	0,57	-0,65	0,96	0,15	0,56	0,58	0,77	0,59	0,78	0,97
BUL				0,53	0,86	0,74	0,68	0,78	0,87	-0,86	0,73	-0,37	0,50	0,40	0,54	-0,12	0,48	0,49
DEN					0,65	0,77	0,66	0,04	0,84	-0,79	0,74	0,02	0,42	0,96	0,87	-0,10	0,94	0,80
EST						0,88	0,95	0,37	0,80	-0,78	0,97	0,04	0,73	0,58	0,80	0,34	0,74	0,82
FIN							0,80	0,28	0,74	-0,89	0,92	-0,22	0,37	0,60	0,71	0,25	0,75	0,91
FRA								0,09	0,70	-0,61	0,97	0,32	0,84	0,65	0,89	0,50	0,82	0,86
GER									0,52	-0,58	0,16	-0,72	0,01	-0,12	-0,07	-0,49	-0,12	-0,11
GRE										-0,90	0,74	-0,18	0,55	0,78	0,79	-0,26	0,78	0,61
HUN											-0,75	0,48	-0,25	-0,61	-0,61	0,20	-0,66	-0,68
ITA												0,13	0,69	0,66	0,86	0,44	0,84	0,93
NET													0,62	0,27	0,40	0,57	0,30	0,51
NOR														0,56	0,80	0,40	0,65	0,51
POR															0,92	-0,06	0,96	0,73
ROM																0,24	0,98	0,84
SLO																	0,18	0,48
ESP																		0,88
SWE																		

Consumption correlation coefficients (moving average)

2006	AUT	BEL	BUL	DEN	EST	FIN	FRA	GER	GRE	HUN	ITA	NET	NOR	POR	ROM	SLO	ESP	SWE
AUT		-0,13	0,59	0,76	0,56	-0,04	0,41	0,77	0,86	-0,54	0,39	-0,47	0,45	0,64	0,51	-0,66	0,59	0,25
BEL			0,59	0,31	0,54	0,87	0,75	0,11	0,36	-0,52	0,75	0,17	0,55	0,41	0,66	0,49	0,36	0,63
BUL				0,60	0,59	0,78	0,60	0,80	0,89	-0,93	0,63	-0,11	0,48	0,67	0,63	0,00	0,38	0,38
DEN					0,95	0,21	0,80	0,71	0,85	-0,67	0,85	-0,72	0,52	0,48	0,68	-0,65	0,93	0,81
EST						0,36	0,92	0,57	0,77	-0,65	0,96	-0,61	0,59	0,47	0,76	-0,45	0,95	0,94
FIN							0,49	0,39	0,46	-0,74	0,54	0,19	0,30	0,35	0,44	0,48	0,09	0,36
FRA								0,34	0,69	-0,54	0,97	-0,26	0,81	0,65	0,92	-0,10	0,88	0,89
GER									0,86	-0,90	0,46	-0,60	0,08	0,32	0,27	-0,54	0,41	0,32
GRE										-0,85	0,71	-0,41	0,57	0,72	0,71	-0,40	0,67	0,52
HUN											-0,65	0,41	-0,23	-0,39	-0,44	0,21	-0,42	-0,49
ITA												-0,42	0,66	0,51	0,82	-0,19	0,88	0,95
NET													0,19	0,23	0,01	0,90	-0,61	-0,56
NOR														0,92	0,97	0,13	0,64	0,49
POR															0,88	0,09	0,48	0,25
ROM																0,03	0,76	0,66
SLO																	-0,54	-0,31
ESP																		0,89
SWE																		

Data Appendix 6: GDP Correlation Coefficients per Country and Year

GDP correlation coefficients (moving average)

1999	AUT	BEL	BUL	DEN	EST	FIN	FRA	GER	GRE	HUN	ITA	NET	NOR	POR	ROM	SLO	ESP	SWE
AUT		0,97	0,19	0,84	-0,70	0,73	0,91	0,94	-0,13	-0,66	-0,25	0,82	0,28	0,97	.b	-0,80	0,76	0,68
BEL			0,14	0,83	-0,58	0,62	0,82	0,84	-0,04	-0,58	-0,28	0,76	0,32	0,93	.b	-0,71	0,63	0,82
BUL				-0,33	-0,72	-0,29	0,01	0,25	0,00	-0,71	-0,85	-0,30	-0,78	0,02	.b	-0,41	-0,07	-0,19
DEN					-0,28	0,82	0,84	0,77	0,06	-0,16	0,30	0,97	0,75	0,93	.b	-0,64	0,82	0,74
EST						-0,45	-0,69	-0,83	0,32	0,91	0,59	-0,39	0,38	-0,60	.b	0,77	-0,58	-0,03
FIN							0,94	0,81	-0,44	-0,35	0,28	0,92	0,48	0,81	.b	-0,53	0,88	0,30
FRA								0,96	-0,36	-0,60	-0,02	0,91	0,33	0,93	.b	-0,73	0,90	0,44
GER									-0,22	-0,69	-0,18	0,84	0,20	0,93	.b	-0,88	0,89	0,41
GRE										0,53	0,26	-0,08	0,37	-0,03	.b	-0,22	-0,07	0,26
HUN											0,79	-0,23	0,52	-0,48	.b	0,51	-0,33	-0,11
ITA												0,33	0,79	-0,01	.b	0,14	0,27	-0,06
NET													0,68	0,93	.b	-0,69	0,93	0,56
NOR														0,48	.b	-0,20	0,49	0,56
POR															.b	-0,82	0,87	0,68
ROM																.b	.b	.b
SLO																	-0,83	-0,34
ESP																		0,28
SWE																		

GDP correlation coefficients (moving average)

2000	AUT	BEL	BUL	DEN	EST	FIN	FRA	GER	GRE	HUN	ITA	NET	NOR	POR	ROM	SLO	ESP	SWE
AUT		0,97	0,06	0,88	-0,10	0,50	0,77	0,85	0,80	-0,19	0,14	0,79	0,58	0,96	-0,80	-0,74	0,64	0,87
BEL			0,12	0,84	0,04	0,43	0,65	0,69	0,74	-0,28	-0,02	0,68	0,47	0,87	-0,65	-0,59	0,46	0,95
BUL				-0,07	-0,20	-0,09	-0,39	-0,07	0,52	-0,90	-0,71	-0,27	-0,75	-0,14	-0,03	-0,26	-0,14	-0,03
DEN					0,24	0,84	0,89	0,78	0,56	-0,22	0,46	0,95	0,68	0,92	-0,60	-0,56	0,78	0,76
EST						0,45	0,03	-0,39	-0,52	-0,20	0,22	0,14	0,10	-0,10	0,62	0,65	-0,18	0,23
FIN							0,78	0,55	0,21	-0,25	0,68	0,87	0,54	0,62	-0,28	-0,31	0,78	0,34
FRA								0,88	0,44	0,18	0,73	0,98	0,89	0,92	-0,71	-0,62	0,91	0,55
GER									0,77	0,04	0,44	0,85	0,67	0,93	-0,95	-0,91	0,90	0,50
GRE										-0,44	-0,22	0,46	0,10	0,70	-0,84	-0,91	0,53	0,53
HUN											0,51	0,01	0,57	0,00	-0,07	0,15	0,02	-0,18
ITA												0,69	0,80	0,41	-0,22	-0,12	0,69	-0,04
NET													0,81	0,91	-0,65	-0,59	0,90	0,58
NOR														0,75	-0,52	-0,32	0,67	0,49
POR															-0,84	-0,75	0,81	0,77
ROM																0,96	-0,76	-0,45
SLO																	-0,76	-0,33
ESP																		0,26
SWE																		

GDP correlation coefficients (moving average)

2001	AUT	BEL	BUL	DEN	EST	FIN	FRA	GER	GRE	HUN	ITA	NET	NOR	POR	ROM	SLO	ESP	SWE
AUT		1,00	0,54	0,92	0,09	0,80	0,79	0,88	0,18	-0,62	0,29	0,79	0,56	0,93	-0,60	-0,34	0,49	0,78
BEL			0,52	0,89	0,08	0,75	0,76	0,85	0,19	-0,59	0,25	0,75	0,54	0,92	-0,61	-0,31	0,42	0,81
BUL				0,43	-0,49	0,41	0,21	0,60	0,67	-0,90	-0,23	0,22	-0,28	0,45	-0,96	-0,96	0,30	0,16
DEN					0,12	0,96	0,96	0,97	-0,11	-0,52	0,63	0,95	0,73	0,98	-0,40	-0,24	0,75	0,56
EST						0,00	0,20	-0,02	-0,10	0,07	0,25	0,38	0,35	0,00	0,47	0,43	0,25	0,46
FIN							0,97	0,97	-0,25	-0,45	0,75	0,93	0,73	0,95	-0,32	-0,23	0,84	0,32
FRA								0,91	-0,37	-0,30	0,81	0,97	0,87	0,93	-0,14	-0,02	0,81	0,43
GER									0,00	-0,65	0,56	0,90	0,59	0,95	-0,53	-0,43	0,80	0,43
GRE										-0,74	-0,77	-0,24	-0,69	-0,13	-0,75	-0,77	-0,20	0,30
HUN											0,15	-0,41	0,18	-0,47	0,86	0,90	-0,47	-0,37
ITA												0,76	0,85	0,58	0,38	0,34	0,77	-0,05
NET													0,80	0,88	-0,15	-0,08	0,86	0,49
NOR														0,73	0,28	0,48	0,53	0,40
POR															-0,44	-0,23	0,65	0,56
ROM																0,89	-0,10	-0,35
SLO																	-0,26	-0,02
ESP																		0,06
SWE																		

GDP correlation coefficients (moving average)

2002	AUT	BEL	BUL	DEN	EST	FIN	FRA	GER	GRE	HUN	ITA	NET	NOR	POR	ROM	SLO	ESP	SWE
AUT		0,84	0,45	0,92	0,58	0,83	0,90	0,90	-0,35	-0,60	0,49	0,92	0,86	0,95	-0,91	0,05	0,64	0,75
BEL			0,62	0,86	0,14	0,71	0,59	0,64	0,09	-0,55	0,49	0,63	0,53	0,77	-0,81	-0,21	0,39	0,83
BUL				0,68	0,02	0,65	0,40	0,55	0,33	-0,85	0,62	0,53	0,14	0,46	-0,66	-0,85	0,70	0,28
DEN					0,31	0,96	0,89	0,93	-0,30	-0,64	0,77	0,91	0,79	0,96	-0,84	-0,19	0,78	0,56
EST						0,25	0,56	0,55	-0,35	-0,52	-0,17	0,63	0,54	0,44	-0,63	0,20	0,44	0,44
FIN							0,92	0,95	-0,45	-0,56	0,89	0,91	0,81	0,94	-0,71	-0,17	0,86	0,32
FRA								0,99	-0,65	-0,50	0,68	0,98	0,95	0,97	-0,74	0,11	0,83	0,38
GER									-0,53	-0,63	0,71	0,99	0,89	0,96	-0,81	-0,05	0,89	0,41
GRE										-0,24	-0,39	-0,51	-0,77	-0,52	0,02	-0,66	-0,40	0,20
HUN											-0,31	-0,67	-0,26	-0,50	0,86	0,68	-0,73	-0,48
ITA												0,64	0,57	0,71	-0,35	-0,26	0,75	-0,05
NET													0,89	0,95	-0,84	-0,05	0,88	0,45
NOR														0,93	-0,61	0,39	0,64	0,39
POR															-0,79	0,07	0,75	0,53
ROM																0,29	-0,67	-0,79
SLO																	-0,37	0,01
ESP																		0,08
SWE																		

GDP correlation coefficients (moving average)

2003	AUT	BEL	BUL	DEN	EST	FIN	FRA	GER	GRE	HUN	ITA	NET	NOR	POR	ROM	SLO	ESP	SWE
AUT		0,84	0,45	0,92	0,58	0,83	0,90	0,90	-0,35	-0,60	0,49	0,92	0,86	0,95	-0,91	0,05	0,64	0,75
BEL			0,62	0,86	0,14	0,71	0,59	0,64	0,09	-0,55	0,49	0,63	0,53	0,77	-0,81	-0,21	0,39	0,83
BUL				0,68	0,02	0,65	0,40	0,55	0,33	-0,85	0,62	0,53	0,14	0,46	-0,66	-0,85	0,70	0,28
DEN					0,31	0,96	0,89	0,93	-0,30	-0,64	0,77	0,91	0,79	0,96	-0,84	-0,19	0,78	0,56
EST						0,25	0,56	0,55	-0,35	-0,52	-0,17	0,63	0,54	0,44	-0,63	0,20	0,44	0,44
FIN							0,92	0,95	-0,45	-0,56	0,89	0,91	0,81	0,94	-0,71	-0,17	0,86	0,32
FRA								0,99	-0,65	-0,50	0,68	0,98	0,95	0,97	-0,74	0,11	0,83	0,38
GER									-0,53	-0,63	0,71	0,99	0,89	0,96	-0,81	-0,05	0,89	0,41
GRE										-0,24	-0,39	-0,51	-0,77	-0,52	0,02	-0,66	-0,40	0,20
HUN											-0,31	-0,67	-0,26	-0,50	0,86	0,68	-0,73	-0,48
ITA												0,64	0,57	0,71	-0,35	-0,26	0,75	-0,05
NET													0,89	0,95	-0,84	-0,05	0,88	0,45
NOR														0,93	-0,61	0,39	0,64	0,39
POR															-0,79	0,07	0,75	0,53
ROM																0,29	-0,67	-0,79
SLO																	-0,37	0,01
ESP																		0,08
SWE																		

GDP correlation coefficients (moving average)

2004	AUT	BEL	BUL	DEN	EST	FIN	FRA	GER	GRE	HUN	ITA	NET	NOR	POR	ROM	SLO	ESP	SWE
AUT		0,60	0,29	0,88	0,73	0,69	0,82	0,09	-0,35	-0,37	0,37	0,94	0,79	0,65	0,65	-0,52	0,84	0,60
BEL			0,51	0,78	0,30	0,76	0,34	0,10	0,26	-0,41	0,71	0,36	0,19	0,43	0,34	-0,53	0,52	0,73
BUL				0,15	0,52	0,44	0,30	0,65	0,43	-0,63	0,45	0,15	-0,26	-0,09	-0,16	-0,25	0,26	0,73
DEN					0,59	0,58	0,49	-0,27	-0,06	-0,44	0,31	0,69	0,62	0,52	0,81	-0,74	0,88	0,67
EST						0,19	0,46	0,03	0,09	-0,81	-0,12	0,61	0,32	-0,01	0,65	-0,72	0,88	0,79
FIN							0,79	0,54	-0,34	0,05	0,92	0,68	0,55	0,84	0,02	-0,01	0,28	0,35
FRA								0,55	-0,68	0,04	0,56	0,94	0,81	0,81	0,15	0,05	0,41	0,22
GER									-0,23	0,14	0,63	0,23	0,00	0,30	-0,67	0,52	-0,30	0,03
GRE										-0,65	-0,19	-0,64	-0,82	-0,75	0,03	-0,50	0,06	0,52
HUN											0,20	-0,10	0,21	0,43	-0,54	0,86	-0,72	-0,91
ITA												0,36	0,25	0,71	-0,30	0,21	-0,05	0,20
NET													0,91	0,76	0,48	-0,22	0,66	0,32
NOR														0,84	0,48	-0,07	0,49	-0,01
POR															0,10	0,19	0,19	-0,07
ROM																-0,86	0,90	0,53
SLO																	-0,88	-0,83
ESP																		0,78
SWE																		

GDP correlation coefficients (moving average)

2005	AUT	BEL	BUL	DEN	EST	FIN	FRA	GER	GRE	HUN	ITA	NET	NOR	POR	ROM	SLO	ESP	SWE
AUT		0,84	0,69	0,89	0,94	0,86	0,92	0,55	0,00	-0,79	0,67	0,98	0,62	0,89	0,93	0,12	0,99	0,92
BEL			0,81	0,75	0,76	0,99	0,86	0,72	0,46	-0,59	0,96	0,80	0,19	0,93	0,81	0,38	0,85	0,94
BUL				0,42	0,80	0,86	0,83	0,95	0,58	-0,74	0,86	0,69	-0,11	0,67	0,54	0,47	0,70	0,90
DEN					0,68	0,69	0,66	0,19	0,00	-0,67	0,56	0,79	0,74	0,77	0,80	-0,22	0,84	0,74
EST						0,83	0,97	0,73	0,01	-0,80	0,63	0,97	0,46	0,81	0,86	0,31	0,95	0,92
FIN							0,93	0,80	0,41	-0,61	0,94	0,85	0,17	0,94	0,83	0,49	0,88	0,97
FRA								0,80	0,12	-0,67	0,76	0,91	0,34	0,91	0,91	0,49	0,96	0,95
GER									0,52	-0,52	0,79	0,60	-0,27	0,62	0,49	0,72	0,60	0,80
GRE										-0,23	0,68	-0,08	-0,65	0,14	-0,15	0,23	-0,02	0,35
HUN											-0,51	-0,72	-0,40	-0,48	-0,51	0,18	-0,71	-0,78
ITA												0,63	-0,09	0,82	0,62	0,48	0,69	0,88
NET													0,59	0,89	0,95	0,26	0,99	0,90
NOR														0,39	0,62	-0,45	0,58	0,27
POR															0,95	0,45	0,93	0,89
ROM																0,33	0,97	0,83
SLO																	0,26	0,36
ESP																		0,92
SWE																		

GDP correlation coefficients (moving average)

2006	AUT	BEL	BUL	DEN	EST	FIN	FRA	GER	GRE	HUN	ITA	NET	NOR	POR	ROM	SLO	ESP	SWE
AUT		0,65	0,64	0,79	0,81	0,78	0,92	0,63	-0,07	-0,77	0,49	0,96	0,38	0,83	0,90	0,09	0,69	0,76
BEL			0,51	0,67	0,91	0,74	0,86	0,68	0,64	-0,47	0,95	0,50	-0,42	0,71	0,57	-0,17	0,89	0,97
BUL				0,16	0,39	0,89	0,69	0,96	0,22	-0,67	0,61	0,68	-0,06	0,65	0,49	0,52	0,21	0,53
DEN					0,92	0,37	0,73	0,20	0,15	-0,66	0,44	0,61	0,20	0,50	0,64	-0,52	0,91	0,80
EST						0,62	0,88	0,49	0,41	-0,66	0,75	0,64	-0,09	0,67	0,67	-0,36	0,98	0,97
FIN							0,90	0,96	0,20	-0,53	0,75	0,81	-0,05	0,92	0,77	0,48	0,49	0,72
FRA								0,78	0,21	-0,63	0,76	0,87	0,04	0,92	0,88	0,12	0,80	0,89
GER									0,34	-0,53	0,77	0,66	-0,21	0,77	0,56	0,51	0,35	0,65
GRE										-0,18	0,77	-0,26	-0,92	-0,01	-0,26	-0,40	0,44	0,57
HUN											-0,41	-0,66	-0,20	-0,37	-0,42	0,16	-0,50	-0,64
ITA												0,37	-0,61	0,63	0,40	-0,04	0,72	0,89
NET													0,50	0,87	0,94	0,34	0,51	0,59
NOR														0,14	0,44	0,21	-0,16	-0,28
POR															0,94	0,42	0,60	0,69
ROM																0,30	0,60	0,61
SLO																	-0,47	-0,26
ESP																		0,93
SWE																		

Data Appendix 7: Regression with Border

First stage regression (on CPT) Fixed effects estimation	**Overall** x	**EMU1** x	**EMU2** x
SPEC (t-value)	-0.6272344*** -3.83	-0.3396852* -1.79	-2.543656*** -6.30
RELFW (t-value)	-1.208567*** -5.06	-1.235773*** -4.01	-
RELINC (t-value)	-1.534342** -2.10	-2.919631*** -3.42	-
BORDER (t-value)	-0.4101895*** -4.96	-0.3075805*** -3.70	-
R-squared F-Statistics	0.1190 13.61	0.1964 13.72	0.2985 13.23

Second stage regression (on GDP, separate estimation) Random effects estimation	**Overall** x	**EMU1** x	**EMU2** x
CPT (t-value)	0.3543124*** 13.09	0.3607235*** 9.79	0.1396011*** 3.84
Border (t-value)	-	-	-
R-squared $\chi2$	0.2245 178.48	0.1897 96.66	0.0104 16.27

*, **, *** *indicates significance at the 10, 5 and 1 % levels, respectively*

HOHENHEIMER VOLKSWIRTSCHAFTLICHE SCHRIFTEN

Band 1 Walter Deffaa: Anonymisierte Befragungen mit zufallsverschlüsselten Antworten. Die Randomized-Response-Technik (RRT). Methodische Grundlagen, Modelle und Anwendungen. 1982.

Band 2 Thomas Michael Baum: Staatsverschuldung und Stabilisierungspolitik in der Demokratie. Zur neoinstitutionalistischen Kritik der keynesianischen Fiskalpolitik. 1982.

Band 3 Klaus Schröter: Die wettbewerbspolitische Behandlung der leitungsgebundenen Energiewirtschaft. Dargestellt am Beispiel der Fernwärmewirtschaft der Bundesrepublik Deutschland. 1986.

Band 4 Hugo Mann: Theorie und Politik der Steuerreform in der Demokratie. 1987.

Band 5 Max Christoph Wewel: Intervallarithmetische Dependenzanalyse in der Ökonometrie. Ein konjekturaler Ansatz. 1987.

Band 6 Heinrich Pascher: Die U.S.-amerikanische Deregulation Policy im Luftverkehrs- und Bankenbereich. 1987.

Band 7 Harald Lob: Die Entwicklung der französischen Wettbewerbspolitik bis zur Verordnung Nr. 86-1243 vom 01. Dezember 1986. Eine exemplarische Untersuchung der Erfassung der Behinderungsstrategie auf der Grundlage des Konzepts eines wirksamen Wettbewerbs. 1988.

Band 8 Ulrich Kirschner: Die Erfassung der Nachfragemacht von Handelsunternehmen. Eine Analyse der ökonomischen Beurteilungskriterien und der wettbewerbsrechtlichen Instrumente im Bereich der Verhaltenskontrolle.1988.

Band 9 Friedhelm Herb: Marktwirtschaftliche Innovationspolitik. 1988.

Band 10 Claus Schnabel: Zur ökonomischen Analyse der Gewerkschaften in der Bundesrepublik Deutschland. Theoretische und empirische Untersuchungen von Mitgliederentwicklung, Verhalten und Einfluß auf wirtschaftliche Größen. 1989.

Band 11 Jan B. Rittaler: Industrial Concentration and the Chicago School of Antitrust Analysis. A Critical Evaluation on the Basis of Effective Competition. 1989.

Band 12 Thomas Märtz: Interessengruppen und Gruppeninteressen in der Demokratie. Zur Theorie des Rent-Seeking. 1990.

Band 13 Andreas Maurer: Statistische Verfahren zur Ermittlung von oligopolistischen Strukturen. 1990.

Band 14 Peter Mendler: Zur ökonomischen und politisch-institutionellen Analyse öffentlicher Kredithilfen. 1992.

Band 15 Heinrich J. Engelke: Die Interpretation der Rundfunkfreiheit des Grundgesetzes: Eine Analyse aus ökonomischer Sicht. 1992.

Band 16 Thomas Fischer: Staat, Recht und Verfassung im Denken von Walter Eucken. Zu den staats- und rechtstheoretischen Grundlagen einer wirtschaftsordnungspolitischen Konzeption. 1993.

Band 17 Stefan Elßer: Innovationswettbewerb. Determinanten und Unternehmensverhalten. 1993.

Band 18 Reinhard Scharff: Regionalpolitik und regionale Entwicklungspotentiale. Eine kritische Analyse. 1993.

Band 19 Karin Beckmann: Probleme der Regionalpolitik im Zuge der Vollendung des Europäischen Binnenmarktes. Eine ökonomische Analyse. 1995.

Band 20 Bernd Nolte: Engpaßfaktoren der Innovation und Innovationsinfrastruktur. Eine theoretische und empirische Analyse für ländliche Wirtschaftsräume in Baden-Württemberg. 1996.

Band 21 Klaus-Rainer Brintzinger: Die Nationalökonomie an den Universitäten Freiburg, Heidelberg und Tübingen 1918 - 1945. Eine institutionenhistorische, vergleichende Studie der wirtschaftswissenschaftlichen Fakultäten und Abteilungen südwestdeutscher Universitäten. 1996.

Band 22 Steffen Binder: Die Idee der Konsumentensouveränität in der Wettbewerbstheorie. Teleokratische vs. nomokratische Auffassung. 1996.

Band 23 Alexander Burger: Deregulierungspotentiale in der Gesetzlichen Rentenversicherung. Reformnotwendigkeiten versus Reformmöglichkeiten. 1996.

Band 24 Burkhard Scherer: Regionale Entwicklungspolitik. Konzeption einer dezentralisierten und integrierten Regionalpolitik. 1997.

Band 25 Frauke Wolf: Lorenzkurvendisparität. Neuere Entwicklungen, Erweiterungen und Anwendungen. 1997.

Band 26 Hans Pitlik: Politische Ökonomie des Föderalismus. Föderative Kompetenzverteilung im Lichte der konstitutionellen Ökonomik. 1997.

Band 27 Stephan Seiter: Der Beitrag Nicholas Kaldors zur Neuen Wachstumstheorie. Eine vergleichende Studie vor dem Hintergrund der Debatte über den Verdoorn-Zusammenhang. 1997.

Band 28 André Schmidt: Ordnungspolitische Perspektiven der europäischen Integration im Spannungsfeld von Wettbewerbs- und Industriepolitik. 1998.

Band 29 Bernd Blessin: Innovations- und Umweltmanagement in kleinen und mittleren Unternehmen. Eine theoretische und empirische Analyse. 1998.

Band 30 Oliver Letzgus: Die Ökonomie internationalen Umweltschutzes. 1999.

Band 31 Claudia Hafner: Systemwettbewerb versus Harmonisierung in Europa. Am Beispiel des Arbeitsmarktes. 1999.

Band 32 Jürgen Kulle: Ökonomie der Musikindustrie. Eine Analyse der körperlichen und unkörperlichen Musikverwertung mit Hilfe von Tonträgern und Netzen. 1998.

Band 33 Michael Ganske: Intertemporale Aspekte von Staatsverschuldung und Außenhandel. 1999.

Band 34 Margit Ströbele: Die Deregulierungswirkungen der europäischen Integration. Das Beispiel der Sondermärkte. 1999.

Band 35 Marion Benesch: Devisenmarktinterventionen in Theorie und Praxis. Eine umfassende Analyse ihrer Zielsetzungen, Wirkungsweisen und wirtschaftspolitischen Bedeutung. 1999.

Band 36 Torsten Gruber: Unterschiedliche geldpolitische Transmissionsmechanismen und Stabilitätskulturen als mögliche Ursachen geldpolitischer Spannungen in der Europäischen Währungsunion. 2000.

Band 37 Bertram Melzig-Thiel: Arbeit in der Informationsgesellschaft. Chancen und Risiken neuer Informations- und Kommunikationstechnologien für die Beschäftigung. 2000.

Band 38 Annette Fritz: Die Entsorgungswirtschaft im Spannungsfeld zwischen Abfallpolitik und Kartellrecht. Eine industrieökonomische Branchenstudie. 2001.

Band 39 Harald Strotmann: Arbeitsplatzdynamik in der baden-württembergischen Industrie. Eine Analyse mit amtlichen Betriebspaneldaten. 2002.

Band 40 Dietrich Benner: Qualitätsungewißheit bei Gütern mit Vertrauenseigenschaften. Entwicklung und Anwendung eines entscheidungstheoretisch fundierten Analyserahmens. 2002.

Band 41 Jürgen M. Schechler: Sozialkapital und Netzwerkökonomik. 2002.

Band 42 Kay-Uwe May: Haushaltskonsolidierung durch Ausgabekürzungen. Restriktionen und Strategien. 2002.

Band 43 Peter Kühnl: Der Wechselkurs als Zwischenziel der Geldpolitik im Aufholprozess. Die monetärkeynesianische Entwicklungsstrategie der Berliner Schule vor dem Hintergrund der makroökonomischen Entwicklung ausgewählter Länder Mittel- und Osteuropas. 2003.

Band 44 Steffen Wirth: Nichtparametrische Analyse von Bildungsertragsraten. Neuere Entwicklungen und Anwendungen. 2003.

Band 45 Bernhard Holwegler: Innovation, Diffusion und Beschäftigung. Die ökonomische Theorie der Technologiediffusion und ihr Beitrag zur Erklärung technologischer Arbeitslosigkeit. 2003.

Band 46 Guntram R. M. Hepperle: Zukunftsorientierte Industriepolitik. Möglichkeiten und Grenzen. 2004.

Band 47 Udo Vullhorst: Stabilisierungspolitik bei supranationaler Geldpolitik und nationaler Fiskalpolitik. Eine spieltheoretische Betrachung. 2004.

Band 48 Matthias Rösch: Die Bedeutung von Investivlöhnen und Gewinnbeteiligungen für Einkommensverteilung und Beschäftigung. 2004.

Band 49 Michael Bubik: Erfolgskriterien für Unternehmenszusammenschlüsse. Eine theoretische und exemplarische Analyse. 2005.

Band 50 Jörg Weltin: Internationale Unternehmensbesteuerung. Allokation der Besteuerungsrechte unter veränderten Rahmenbedingungen. 2005.

Band 51 Susanne Reichart: Zum Konvergenzprozess der mittel- und osteuropäischen EU-Beitrittsländer. 2005.

Band 52 Daniel Hartmann: Geldpolitik und Beschäftigung. Die geldpolitische Strategie der Federal Reserve: Vorbild oder Auslaufmodell? 2005.

Band 53 Marc Peter Radke: Explaining Financial Crises. A Cyclical Approach. 2005.

Band 54 Katja Hölsch: Umverteilungseffekte in Europa. Eine Analyse für ausgewählte Länder. 2006.

Band 55 Ulrike Lehr: Contingent Valuation Daten und Bayes'sche Verfahren. Ein Vorschlag zur Verbesserung von Umweltbewertung und Nutzentransfer. 2006.

Band 56 Jutta Maute: Hyperinflation, Currency Board, and Bust. The Case of Argentina. 2006.

Band 57 Michael Knittel: Geldpolitik und Stabilität des Bankensystems. Das Liquiditätsproblem aus Sicht der Theoriegeschichte und der gegenwärtigen Finanzmarktentwicklung. 2007.

Band 58 Oliver Frör: Rationality Concepts in Environmental Valuation. 2007.

Band 59 Jochen Gert Arend Wiegmann: Produktivitätsentwicklung in Deutschland. 2008.

Band 60 Nicola Meier: China – The New Developmental State? An Empirical Analysis of the Automotive Industry. 2009.

Band 61 Carsten H. Wander: Logistik und Wettbewerb. Zur Rolle logistischer (Re-)Organisation in einer wettbewerbsbasierten Marktwirtschaft. 2009.

Band 62 Sven Wydra: Produktions- und Beschäftigungseffekte neuer Technologien. Am Beispiel der Biotechnologie. 2010.

Band 63 Andreas Schaal: Die Relevanz von Venture Capital für Innovation und Beschäftigung. Theoretische Klärung und empirische Analyse. 2010

Band 64 Sybille Sobczak: Geldpolitik und Vermögensmärkte. Volkswirtschaftliche Bedeutung von und geldpolitische Reaktion auf Asset Price Bubbles. 2010

Band 65 Constanze Dobler: The Impact of Formal and Informal Institutions on Economic Growth. A Case Study on the MENA Region. 2011.

Band 66 Tobias Börger: Social Desirability and Environmental Valuation. 2012.

Band 67 Julian Christ: Innovative Places in Europe. Research Clustering, Co-Patenting Networks and the Growth of Regions. 2012.

Band 68 Christian Böber: China in Transition. Poverty, Income Decomposition and Labor Allocation of Agricultural Households in Hebei Province. 2012.

Band 69 Jennifer Schneider: European Business Cycle Convergence. Portfolio Similarity and a Declining Home Bias of Private Investors. 2013.

www.peterlang.de

www.ingramcontent.com/pod-product-compliance
Ingram Content Group UK Ltd.
Pitfield, Milton Keynes, MK11 3LW, UK
UKHW021829100926
8556IPUK00004B/244

9 783631 639740